ALSC

The Powers of The Past
The Education of Desire
"Why Do Ruling Classes Fear History?" and Other Questions
Thomas Paine: Firebrand of Revolution
Are We Good Citizens?
Thomas Paine and the Promise of America
The Fight for the Four Freedoms
Take Hold of Our History: Make America Radical Again

EDITOR

History, Classes, and Nation-States: Selected Writings of V.G. Kiernan
The Face of the Crowd: Selected Essays of George Rudé
Poets, Politics, and the People: Selected Essays of V.G. Kiernan
E.P. Thompson: Critical Perspectives (with Keith McClelland)
The American Radical (with Mari Jo Buhle and Paul Buhle)
Imperialism and Its Contradictions: Selected Essays of V.G. Kiernan
FDR on Democracy

The British Marxist
Historians

The British Marxist Historians

Harvey J. Kaye

Winchester, UK
Washington, USA

JOHN HUNT PUBLISHING

First published by Zero Books, 2022
Zero Books is an imprint of John Hunt Publishing Ltd., No. 3 East St., Alresford,
Hampshire SO24 9EE, UK
office@jhpbooks.com
www.johnhuntpublishing.com
www.zero-books.net

For distributor details and how to order please visit the 'Ordering' section on our website.

Text copyright: Harvey J. Kaye 2021

ISBN: 978 1 78904 864 3
978 1 78904 865 0 (ebook)
Library of Congress Control Number: 2021950846

All rights reserved. Except for brief quotations in critical articles or reviews, no part of this
book may be reproduced in any manner without prior written permission from the publishers.

The rights of Harvey J. Kaye as author have been asserted in accordance with the Copyright,
Designs and Patents Act 1988.

A CIP catalogue record for this book is available from the British Library.

Design: Matthew Greenfield

UK: Printed and bound by CPI Group (UK) Ltd, Croydon, CR0 4YY
Printed in North America by CPI GPS partners

We operate a distinctive and ethical publishing philosophy in
all areas of our business, from our global network of authors to
production and worldwide distribution.

Contents

For Rhiannon, Fiona, and especially Lorna

Prelims to the 1995 Edition

The British Marxist Historians

The British Marxist Historians remains the first and most complete study of the founders of one of the most influential contemporary academic traditions in history and social theory. In this classic text, Kaye looks at Maurice Dobb and the debate on the transition to capitalism,- Rodney Hilton on feudalism and the English peasantry,- Christopher Hill on the English Revolution,- Eric Hobsbawm on workers, peasants and world history,- and E. R Thompson on the making of the English working class. Kaye compares their perspective on history with other approaches, such as that of the French *Annales* school, and concludes with a discussion of the contribution of the British Marxist historians to the formation of a democratic historical consciousness. *The British Marxist Historians* is an indispensable book for anyone interested in the intellectual history of the late twentieth century.

For a note on the author, please see the back flap.

The British Marxist Historians: *An Introductory Analysis*
HARVEY J. KAYE
THE BRITISH MARXIST HISTORIANS
Copyright © 1984,1995 /?? by Harvey J. Kaye
All rights reserved. Printed in the United States of America.

ISBN 0-312-12733-2 (cloth)
ISBN 0-312-12668-9 (paper)
Library of Congress Cataloging-in-Publication Data Kaye, Harvey J.
The British Marxist Historians: an introductory analysis / Harvey J. Kaye.
p. cm

Originally published: New York: Polity Press, 1984.
Includes bibliographical references (p.) and index.
ISBN 0-312-12733-2 (cloth)
ISBN 0-312-12668-9 (alk. paper)
1. Economic history—Historiography. 2. Historical materialism.
3. Marxian historiography—Great Britain. I. Title.
HC26.K39 1995
335.4′072041—dc20 95-16073
CIP
First published 1984 by Polity Press.
First St. Martin's Edition: October 1995 10 987654321

Preface to the 1984 Edition

I had three intentions in writing this book on the British Marxist historians – Maurice Dobb, Rodney Hilton, Christopher Hill, Eric Hobsbawm and E. P. Thompson. First, to provide an introduction to their writings for historians and social scientists who might only be familiar with one or another of them. As I hope this book makes clear, the British Marxist historians whom I discuss have not only made important individual contributions to historical studies but, together, they have made a collective contribution to both history and social theory. In fact, I view their work as a theoretical tradition which, in the context of the present dialogue between history and sociology, has much to contribute. This book was, therefore, written in opposition to the current tendency to treat these historians separately, and the derived assertion that there is a theoretical break in their work, somewhere between Dobb and Thompson. It does not seek to offer a critical assessment of the substantive historical claims which the historians have made. Second, I have written the book to acknowledge not only the contributions of these historians to historical studies and social theory but also their important contribution to the making of a democratic and socialist historical consciousness. I consider their work to be of scholarly *and* political consequence. And third, I have written to acknowledge my own indebtedness to them. My work as a teacher and writer of history/sociology – focusing on the transition to capitalism and on peasant and labour subjects – has depended in great part on ideas and hypotheses, i.e. theory, derived from their historical writings. I hope they find that I have done them justice.

Having said this, I do feel the need to apologize for two omissions. This book does not treat the writings of two other outstanding British Marxist historians: Victor Kiernan and George Rudé.

Should I ever have the opportunity to write a more extensive study of this group, I promise to seek to correct these omissions.

Typically, in the writing of a book one incurs many debts and this one has been no exception. Thus, I must first acknowledge the essential support of the National Endowment for the Humanities (NEH) for two Summer Fellowships: the first, in 1981, to participate in the NEH Summer Seminar, 'Labor and the Industrial Revolution', held at the Institute for Advanced Study, Princeton, and the second, in 1983, to write two of the chapters of this book. Also, I want to thank the University of Wisconsin – Green Bay Research Council for additional support.

Some of the points elaborated in this study originally appeared in two articles: 'History and Social Theory: Notes on the Contribution of British Marxist Historiography to Our Understanding of Class', *The Canadian Review of Sociology and Anthropology,* 20 (2) (1983); and 'Totality: Its Application to Historical and Social Analysis by Wallerstein and Genovese', *Historical Reflections/Reflexions Historiques,* 6 (2), (1979). For permission to repeat the arguments made in those pieces, I must thank the editorial boards of the two journals. For permission to quote at length from works they publish, I must thank: Merlin Press and Monthly Review for EP Thompson, *The Poverty of Theory and Other Essays,* (1978); Routledge and Kegan Paul and International Publishers for Maurice Dobb, *Studies in the Development of Capitalism,* (1946, 1963 rev. edition); and Victor Gollancz for E. P. Thompson, *The Making of the English Working Class,* (1963; 1968 rev. edition; 1980 edition with new preface).

In addition to providing the basis for this study, I want to thank Christopher Hill, Rodney Hilton and Jean Birrell, and Edward and Dorothy Thompson for their comments, criticisms and hospitality during my stay in Britain in January 1983. Especially, I want to thank Christopher Hill and Rodney Hilton for reading and commenting on several portions of the manuscript.

My colleagues in the NEH Summer Seminar made important contributions to the writing of the article from which this book grew. In particular, I want to thank the director, William Sewell Jr, the senior member of the group, Robin Brooks, and Jim Jackson. Also, I should thank the participants in the Second Summer Institute on Culture and Society, held at St Cloud, Minnesota in 1979. It was at that time that I was first asked to talk on the work which later developed into an article and then this book. Especially, I must acknowledge the comments and criticisms of Frederic Jameson and William Langen.

For providing the opportunity to develop my work into a book, I am indebted to Anthony Giddens. During the past two years Tony has given continuous encouragement and helpful and extensive intellectual and editorial criticism.

Colleagues and friends with whom I was fortunate to be able to discuss and argue about different ideas include: Cris Kay, Bill and Judy Langen, Joyce Salisbury, Michael Zilles, Ron Sexton, Ron Baba, Carol Pollis, Craig Lockard and (though we have yet to meet face-to-face) Ellen Meiksins Wood. For reading through the entire manuscript and making helpful suggestions, I must thank Tony Galt. In their own ways, my parents and parents-in-law have also contributed to the making of this book.

Finally, this book is dedicated to my daughters, Rhiannon and Fiona and, most especially, to my wife, Lorna, who grew up in the English Midlands, the daughter of a Welsh mother and a Scottish father. I dedicate this book particularly to her, not only because she has been an editor and typist of the work but also because she is the best colleague, companion and comrade of all.

Harvey J. Kaye March 1984

Foreword to the 1995 Edition
by Eric Hobsbawm

It is not easy for someone who is one of the main subjects of a book to write a foreword to it. However, there are good objective reasons why Harvey Kaye's *The British Marxist Historians* should be published in a new edition and being in the book is not an automatic disqualification for commenting on these.

The first of these is that, for reasons which still await satisfactory enquiry, the influence of Marx among British historians has been unusually strong; or alternatively, British Marxist intellectuals have been unusually attracted to history, especially those from the generation of the 1930s and 1940s, which includes most of the British Marxist historians who are Harvey Kaye's subjects in this and his other works. This influence was not confined to professional historians. It may be seen in the historical studies of British left-wing scientists, like J. D. Bernal and – the most monumental example – *Science and Civilization in China*, the work of the great Joseph Needham, whose scholarship ranged from embryology to a brief monograph on the seventeenth-century Levellers and who was rightly described by his obituarists in March 1995 as the Erasmus of the twentieth century. Such an influence is not to be found in countries with far stronger Marxist parties, like France and Italy. Indeed, it has been pointed out that the French equivalent of the Marxist influence in British historiography is the *Annales* school of the Bloch and Braudel eras, which has a different intellectual pedigree.

The second reason, as Kaye points out, is that the British Marxist historians together represent 'a theoretical tradition'. They do this, probably, because they also formed, at a crucial stage of their professional development, an actual collective entity, the

Historians' Group of the (British) Communist Party, which flourished from 1946 until 1956, when it broke under the strains of that year of crisis and disillusion among Communists – but not before demonstrating its collective commitment to a Marxist history critical of party and Soviet orthodoxy. The Marxist contribution to British (and international) historiography comes from, or through, the work of those associated with this group. This included the founding of a major historical journal, *Past & Present* (1952). The work of pre-war Marxist historians who moved away from their original political anchorage is, perhaps unfairly, neglected, as is the influence on history of pre-war Marxist preoccupations, such as, which drew several of the pre-war student communists involved in 'colonial work' in Cambridge into non-European history (C. H. Norman, H. S. Ferns, Jack Gallagher and V. G. Kiernan). Among these, only Victor Kiernan is numbered among the post-war Marxist historians. It was through the members and activities of the Group that the main international impact of British Marxist history was made – not least on Marxist historians of other countries.

The third reason is that the history of historiography has in the past twenty years become a field whose importance is increasingly recognized. How do historians actually come to write what they do? How can they, steeped in the politics and ideologies of their times and places, produce not just a set of mutually incompatible pamphlets with footnotes, or mutually incommunicable manifestos of loyalty to some national or other identity group, but a common universe of discourse within which, at least in theory and over a period of time, common debate, perhaps even common judgement, is possible on subjects as permanently explosive and divisive as the history of the French Revolution and the history of slavery in America? A study of the Marxist historians and their contribution to the general development of historiography can be instructive, because it demonstrates in what manner interaction took place between a group that was once both ideologically and politically isolated and the common universe of historical enquiry. In other words, how our historical understanding of the past progresses. It may also illustrate the complexity of the historian's contribution to the development of his subject, which may be substantial, even if his or her actual findings and interpretations do not win general assent. The British Marxist historians are a useful case-study, since their actual impact and achievement, individual and collective, is not to be denied – so much can be claimed by one of them without excessive vanity – but part of their work has not in some respects resisted time and peer assessment.

Harvey Kaye's *The British Marxist Historians* – supplemented since its first publication by his other works on members of the Group not fully dealt with here, George Rudé and Victor Kiernan – is the fullest treatment of this 'theoretical tradition' so far, and an excellent introduction to it. Beyond this one of the main protagonists of the tradition cannot reasonably go without crossing the fuzzy but real line between legitimate comment and self-advertisement (or self-defence). In any case, readers will judge the merits of the book, and its treatment of the historians and trends discussed, for themselves. That there is sufficient interest in the subject to warrant this new edition is naturally welcome news to the survivors among the historians about whom Kaye writes. However, I think it can be shown that the re-publication of this book is justified on stronger grounds than this. It is a lasting contribution to the history of twentieth-century Marxism, to a corner of British cultural history, and to the study of how history and historians work.

E.J. Hobsbawm, April 1995

Preface to the 1995 Edition

In the original preface I note the reasons for my having written *The British Marxist Historians* and I record there my appreciations and acknowledgements. This reprinting now affords me the opportunity to speak of how the work came to be and of what value I believe it still possesses, especially for students of history and social science. I begin with the story of the making of the book.

While there was never any doubt about my interest in and commitment to historical study and thought, my student and ensuing academic career actually originated not in British or American but in Latin American studies. Pursuing a Ph.D. in the mid-1970s at Louisiana State University, I was eager to write a historical-sociological dissertation on landlord–peasant relations in Spanish America. However, like many of my generation, I was frustrated by the theoretical perspectives still dominating the field and the social sciences generally. Looking for alternatives, I distinctly recall wandering one day after lunch into the tiny bookstore owned by an older couple just across from the LSU campus and browsing in its small American History section, the shelves of which were populated mostly by books on southern slavery. (Looking back, I imagine the storeowners were themselves radicals from an earlier decade).

Among the books I found there were several works of the then-Marxist scholar Eugene Genovese (see, in particular, pp. 55-58 below). They fascinated me. In fact, I bought and devoured every one of them. In Genovese's work on the slaveholders' regime – with his attention to relations of exploitation and oppression *and* the diverse conflicts they motivated – I discovered the critical Marxian theoretical approach which best helped me to comprehend the histories and struggles of the agrarian working people of Mexico and the Andean highlands (and in honour of his historical contributions I entitled my dissertation 'The Political Economy of Seigneurialism' after his first book, *The Political Economy of Slavery*). Moreover, by way of both his many references and his generous correspondence with me, Genovese led me to explore the writings of the English historians, in particular those of Maurice Dobb, Rodney Hilton, Christopher Hill, Eric Hobsbawm and E. P. Thompson (I was familiar with some of these writers from my general undergraduate studies in history, especially Hobsbawm for, like many a history major, I had read his classic, *The Age of Revolution* [1962], and also because he himself had begun to write on Latin America). And the fact that my wife, Loma, is British, allowed me to rationalize reading British studies when I was supposed to be doing other things.

Completing the Ph.D. and, after many a job-hunt, securing first a one-year position in Minnesota and then a tenure-track post here in Wisconsin, I kept on surveying the work of the British historians, making my way through each of their many titles.

In 1979, the Marxist Literary Group of the Modem Language Association was holding its second Summer Institute on Culture and Society at St Cloud State University, and among the notables scheduled to participate was the British cultural studies scholar Stuart Hall, who was to speak on the 'structuralist versus historicist' arguments then underway in Britain. Aware of my interest in the work of the British Marxist historians – whose writings represented the 'historicist' side of the debate – my friend and former colleague at St Cloud, Bill Langen, who happened to be the local organizer of the program, insisted I come and sit in on the meetings. However, at the last minute, Stuart Hall was unable to make it over from England due to a crisis at the University of Birmingham, where he was then director of the Centre for Contemporary Cultural Studies (noted in the text for the historiographical initiatives which emanated from it in the late 1970s and early 1980s).

Learning of Hall's cancellation over a late and festive dinner (and, fortunately, without asking my permission, for I likely would have declined), Bill Langen volunteered me to Frederic Jameson, the leading figure of the Literary Group, to speak in his place. I was unable to say no. And the next day I gave my first public talk on the British Marxists. Given the reaction of those in attendance, it did not go very well. Not only was I a novice, I had rushed to organize my notes and, making matters worse, I spoke immediately after the inimitable Gayatri Spivak finished introducing the ideas of 'Jacques Derrida and (post-structural) deconstructionism' to the assembled literary critics, the overwhelming majority of whom were decidedly of the *structuralist* persuasion. In fact, I don't think they understood her talk; but they understood mine and, thus, were able to take out on me both their apparent hostilities toward history and their anxiety about this new thing called 'deconstruction'. (Only my friend Bill Langen and Fred Jameson offered any follow-up praise and, perhaps, they were just being polite.)

I put aside the notes; that is, until two years later when I was selected to take part in a National Endowment for the Humanities summer seminar on Labor and the Industrial Revolution. It was not my original intention to work on the historians, but Bill Sewell Jr., the seminar director, urged me to put aside my original plans in favour of turning my notes into a paper. Two months later, when I delivered the paper to the group, his comment was that the whole thing was 'too big for a paper' for, however effectively I had shown that the historians shared an approach, a problematic and a political and cultural project, their respective labours still demanded individual treatment. So, he said, 'You should turn it into a book.'

Submitting the essay to a journal – and having been informed to expect to wait up to six months for a decision on publication – I decided to try it out as well on Cambridge University social and political theorist Anthony Giddens, asking if he, too, thought it had the makings of a book. A few weeks later, to my surprise and delight, I had a book contract in hand from his publishers. I was soon immersed in historiography, social theory and British Studies.

The response to the publication of *The British Marxist Historians* was decidedly favourable. Admittedly not all, but the great majority, of the reviews were critically appreciative and welcoming of the book. What I especially liked was the remarkably inter-disciplinary reception it received, for it indicated the existence of a much wider community of interest in the historians and their work than even I had imagined. Reviews appeared not only in history journals and publications of the intellectual and political Left, but across the humanities and social sciences, from literature to social policy. Also notable has been the response beyond Britain, the United States and the other English-speaking countries: a Japanese edition of the book appeared in 1989; a Spanish edition in 1992; and a Chinese edition is currently being prepared in Taiwan. (By the way, after the book was published, I had the opportunity finally to meet Stuart Hall, now a professor at Britain's Open University, on the occasion of a visit he made to Wisconsin. Taking him to lunch, I announced that the meal was my treat because I 'owed' him for *not* showing up in 1979.)

The story is told for more than autobiographical reasons. And I hope it speaks of more than accident, chance and serendipity.

Reflecting the very social organization of industrial capitalism, intellectual efforts and knowledge in the social sciences are too often strictly compartmentalized by discipline (anthropology, economics, political science, sociology...) and, in historical studies, by political era and nation state. Therefore, *critical* historical and social study will often depend on border-crossing and time-travelling not only for ideas and insights, but also to look for the deeper connections and determinations, perhaps especially so in a world now made one (though not whole) by a global capitalist economy. I think for students this means not only immersing oneself in a discipline of work and a body of knowledge, but also developing an intellectual curiosity which is prepared to go against the grain and to enter into other territories. Who knows what will transpire?

How do I view the work today, ten years after its original publication? My scholarly interests have shifted somewhat from historiography and social theory to historical memory and public culture, taking in, on the one hand, the problem of the political uses and abuses of the past – the subject of my book, The *Powers of the Past* (1991), and a forthcoming volume of essays, 'Why Do Ruling Classes Fear History?' *and* Other Questions(1996) – and, on the other, the problem of cultivating critical historical memory, consciousness and imagination (motivating editorial work with Mari Jo Buhle and Paul Buhle on *The American Radical* [1994] and with Elliott Gorn on a book series on American radicalism).

My intellectual and political commitments, however, remain essentially what they were. I continue to believe – contrary to the claims of conservatives and neo-conservatives, who have been politically ascendant for too many years now – that the questions and hypotheses Marx posed about the making of history and, specifically, the making of the modern world remain powerful and indispensable. Morally, intellectually, and politically, where better to commence one's analysis of past and present (and possible futures) than by asking about the relations of exploitation and oppression and the conflicts they engender?

In this respect, I continue to see the labours of the British Marxist historians as models for historical study and thought. And, of course, so very much has been accomplished by others influenced by their original investigations and scholarly example. As I discuss in a second historiographical volume, *The Education of Desire: Marxists and the Writing of History* (1992), the work of the British Marxists has been further developed – and imaginatively so – by varieties of critical historians working not only on questions of class and class struggle, but also on those of race, ethnicity and gender, and they have taken it into every field of social study and every geographical corner. Indeed, in certain areas their efforts have been superseded, as they themselves have hoped and expected.

Moreover, while the British historians were already senior figures, they were far from retired from historical scholarship when I completed the writing of this book. In the years since, Rodney Hilton, Christopher Hill, Eric Hobsbawm and, until his untimely death in 1993, Edward Thompson have continued to write and make significant contributions to historical studies. In the early 1980s, Rodney Hilton had already begun to shift his attentions from the medieval English countryside to urban life, leading to the monograph, *English and French Towns in Feudal Society: A Comparative Study* (1992). And here I should also note the collection in a single volume of the contributions to the continuing debate on 'the transition from feudalism to capitalism' which were published in the 1970s in the pages of *Past & Present*, a debate in which Hilton played a major role *(The Brenner Debate,* edited by T. H. Aston anti C. H. E. Philpin [1985]).

Christopher Hill, too, has continued to produce a steady and impressive stream of work on seventeenth-century English culture and society. In addition to four volumes of his collected essays on matters literary, religious, political, and intellectual, he has authored two major studies, *A Turbulent, Seditious, and Factious People: John Bunyan and His Church* (1988), and *The English Bible and the Seventeenth-Century Revolution* (1995).

Eric Hobsbawm not only completed *The Age of Empire, 1875-1914* (1987), thereby rounding out his study of the 'long nineteenth-century'; he has gone on, in *The Age of Extremes: A History of the World, 1914-1991* (1994), to provide a grand synthesis of the 'short twentieth century' in the wake of the collapse of the Soviet Union and its empire. Additionally, Hobsbawm has published a collection of his political writings from the 'age of Thatcherism', *Politics for a Rational Left* (1989), two sets of distinguished lectures, *Echoes of the Marseillaise: Two Centuries Look Back on the French Revolution* (1990) and *Nations and Nationalism since 1780* (1990) and a welcome new edition of his jazz criticism, *The Jazz Scene* (1993).

Finally, E. P. Thompson who in the early 1980s had taken a leave from history writing to campaign against the resurgent Cold War as co-founder and leading voice of END (European Nuclear Disarmament), returned to his study later in the decade, in ill-health but as intellectually sharp as ever, to finish the several works he had promised, before passing away at the young age of 69. First appeared *Customs in Common: Studies in Traditional Popular Culture* (1991), a collection of his celebrated eighteenth-century articles. Next came *Alien Homage: Edward Thompson and Rabindranath Tagore* (1993), a study of his father's personal and intellectual relationship with the famed Indian writer. Lastly, he accomplished his long-awaited 'Blake book', *Witness Against the Beast: William Blake and the Moral Law* (1993), and also delivered a further collection of revised historical and critical essays, *Persons and Polemics* (1994). On Thompson's death, generations of radical historians and progressives around the world mourned.

I promised in my original preface that if I had the opportunity to enlarge the book I would add chapters on two other great historians of the Group, Victor Kiernan and George Rudé. As things happened, I produced a second volume, *The Education of Desire*, with comprehensive chapters on each of them, and both Kiernan and Rudé graciously afforded me the further opportunity to edit collections of their respective essays: V. G. Kiernan, *History, Classes and Nation-States* (1988), *Poets, Politics and the People* (1989) and *Imperialism and Its Contradictions* (1995); and George Rudé, *The Face of the Crowd* (1988).

Still, as Christopher Hill has reminded me, there are chapters to be written on the work of the women of the original Historians' Group, such as Dona Torr, Margot Heinemann, Dorothy Thompson and Bridget HLU, and on the respective works of John Saville and the late A. L. Morton (on whom I already have done a short piece, included in *The Education of Desire*). Along similar lines, many an American colleague has suggested a volume on American Marxist and radical historians, such as Philip Foner, Herbert Aptheker, David Montgomery, Herbert Gutman, Eugene Genovese, Warren Susman, Al Young and Howard Zinn – and, I agree, they would make a great subject for a book project.

Finally, there are new and continuing appreciations to be registered. For a start, I want to thank Eric Hobsbawm for accepting my invitation to write the Foreword to this new edition of the book. As I said above, my very first encounter with the scholarship of the British Marxist historians was by way of his work, specifically, his classic text, *The Age of Revolution, 1789-1848* (in fact, I still have my original marked-up copy). I am truly honoured by his willingness to append his name to this work.

I also want to publicly record my further appreciation of Eric Hobsbawm, Christopher and Bridget Hill, and Edward and Dorothy Thompson for coming, during the course of the last several years, to visit my family and me in Wisconsin in order to speak before and meet with my students and colleagues at the University of Wisconsin-Green Bay. Their participation in our annual Historical Perspectives Lecture Series has greatly contributed to making the UWGB Center for History and Social Change the successful venture it is.

Additionally, I must thank Michael Flamini, Senior Editor in the Scholarly and Reference Division at St. Martin's Press, for his enthusiastic response to the idea of re-publishing this work.

Yet, most important, I want to reaffirm the dedication of the original edition – to my daughters, Rhiannon and Fiona, and, especially, my wife, Loma, who remains the best colleague, companion and comrade of all.

Harvey J. Kaye,
July 1995

Preface to the New Edition

The history of all hitherto existing society is the history of class struggles.
Karl Marx and Friedrich Engels, The Communist Manifesto, 1848

Only that historian will have the gift of fanning the spark of hope in the past who is firmly convinced that even the dead will not be safe from the enemy if he wins. And this enemy has not ceased to be victorious.
Walter Benjamin, Theses on the Philosophy of History, 1940

I think you must like history, as I liked it when I was your age, because it deals with living people and everything that concerns people, as many people as possible, all people in the world, in so far as they unite together in society and work and struggle and make a bid for a better life. All that can't fail to please you more than anything else, isn't that right?
Antonio Gramsci, in a letter from a Fascist prison to his son Delio shortly before his death in 1937

Here in the United States, we have endured more than four decades of class war from above. Forty-five years of determined campaigns by the corporate elite and their conservative and neoliberal allies to undo the progressive democratic achievements of the 1930s and the 1960s. Forty-five years of the rich enhancing their power and making themselves grossly richer at the expense of workers and their families. Forty-five years in which labor unions, working-class communities and democratic solidarities have been smashed. And yet, popular struggles not only persist, but actually have gained strength in recent years. While we have yet to win history-making democratic victories, we definitely have seen a resurgence in working-class activism and in popular interest, especially among young people, in reviving the struggle for social democracy or, if you prefer, democratic socialism. In short, despite the strength of the right, we have reason to hope and to act anew. But we also have much to learn – and that includes educating ourselves to questions of class and class struggle past and present.

I hope that this work – my very first book, originally published in the winter of 1984-85 by Polity Press and published anew in 1995 by St Martin's with a new Preface and a Foreword by Eric Hobsbawm – can still contribute to that education.

In the course of the post-war years, from the late 1940s to the 1960s, the British Marxist historians – Maurice Dobb, Rodney Hilton, Christopher Hill, Eric Hobsbawm and EP Thompson, along with colleagues and comrades such as George Rudé, Victor Kiernan and John Saville – succeeded in bringing Marxian questions directly into the historical discipline. Doing so, they transformed our understanding not only of class and class struggle, but also of how working people themselves have participated in the making of history. And empowered by their scholarly writings and arguments, generations of 'radical historians' have worked hard and productively to emulate their labors and to carry on the task of 'fanning the spark of hope in the past'.

Pursuing 'history from the bottom up', the British Marxists taught us to ask critical questions. Critical questions about not only social relations of exploitation and oppression past and present and the diverse means by which elites and ruling classes have worked to secure and maintain their wealth and power, but also how exploited and oppressed peoples – peasants, slaves, workers – have both endured that exploitation and oppression *and,* possessed of ideas and aspirations of their own, regularly sought, both individually and collectively, to resist the power of those who ruled them, at times to openly rebel against them, and occasionally to actually try to overthrow them.

Moreover, the Historians emboldened many of us to believe that our own labors might serve to critically inform and democratically shape popular historical memory, consciousness and imagination and, thereby, encourage working people to see that struggles for freedom, equality and democracy matter – powerfully so.

In the original Preface of 1984, and at greater length in that of 1995 (both of which are still included here), I explained the academic and political aspirations behind the writing of this book and the somewhat serendipitous origins of both this work and a later volume of essays I wrote on the Group, *The Education of Desire: Marxists and the Writing of History* (1992, with a Foreword by Christopher Hill). I will not repeat those things. But I do want to once again state my indebtedness to the Historians. They met with me; they afforded me recollections, ideas, and materials; *and* they came to trust me and to treat me as a friend. In that spirit, I want to record here a few experiences from those years 'working on the British Marxist historians' – experiences that shaped my own historical sensibilities and practices.

In January 1983, I travelled to London with a group of undergraduate students for a one-month study tour. Already deeply engaged in preparing the chapters of this book, I wrote ahead to Hilton, Hill, Hobsbawm and Thompson hoping I might be able to arrange to interview each of them in person. And to my good fortune, Rodney, Christopher and Edward all agreed to meet. Rodney hosted me in Birmingham for a day of lively exchanges and arguments about politics and popular struggles past and present; Christopher and I spent a fabulous afternoon in oral-historical conversation in Oxford (which critically guided my writing and saved me from committing some silly mistakes); and Edward very graciously invited me to spend a couple of days with him and his wife, historian Dorothy Thompson, at their home just outside of Worcester.

I have written elsewhere of my stay with Edward and

Dorothy [see "A Tribute to EP Thompson, Marxist Historian and Radical Democrat, 1924-1993" in my book *Why Do Ruling Classes Fear History* (1996)], but I feel compelled to recount one incident in particular. Returning to London from Worcester by train, I was lucky enough to be accompanied by Edward, who was then deeply involved in the campaign for European Nuclear Disarmament (END) and that day was on his way to the BBC studios to debate an American 'defense analyst'. Walking onto the station platform, he apologized for needing to sit in a smoking car on the train; I lied and said I could handle it, for I had no intention of giving up time with him by sitting apart in a no-smoking carriage. Settled on board he threw himself into his notes, using me as his test audience. I never really heard the details of his arguments (or at least I can't recall them now) because I wasn't so much listening as watching and studying him. He was a truly fascinating figure. Time and the countryside passed by...But all of a sudden, he stopped and began to gaze out of the window of the moving train. The momentary silence and the look in his eyes alerted me to concentrate on what he would have to say. I expected a few lines on either Thatcherism and Reaganism or the imperative to halt the arms race and prevent global nuclear annihilation. Instead, however, he spoke of the eighteenth century. Pointing away to fields and a wooded rise in the distance, he told me about the area we were journeying through – of aristocrat and gentry and of the working people who suffered them and attempted to resist their encroachments and depredations.

I further remember how, later, on the plane back to the States, when I had chance to reflect on that time with Edward, I thought about how his turning away from his notes to consider the historical landscape probably revealed a longing to return to the past and historical study – and that was no doubt part of it. In time, however, I realized that it involved far more than that. I came to believe, and I do so all the more today, that what

I witnessed in that afternoon's act of remembrance was Edward Thompson reinvigorating his historical consciousness by resurrecting earlier episodes of 'freeborn Englishmen' defending themselves and their liberties against the powers that be.

Two years later, in January 1985, soon after the original publication of this work, I returned to London with a group of undergraduates. Knowing I was coming over, Rodney, the medievalist of the Group, invited me to visit him again in Birmingham. This time, in addition to arranging a dinner party to celebrate the book's appearance that, to my great surprise and delight, included the Hills and the Thompsons, he kindly insisted on taking me for a day-out by car to visit historical sites in the English West Midlands. We stopped at a series of places and, after enjoying a good pub lunch, took a walk around Warwick town centre, which included stepping into the Collegiate Church of St Mary (Anglican). There, Rodney, then about the age I am now, directed my attention to the impressive tombs of Thomas Beauchamp, the 12th Earl of Warwick, and his wife. But before Rodney could say a single word about them, a sizable fellow approached us asking, 'May I tell you about his Lordship's exploits on horseback?' To which Rodney, seemingly instinctively, retorted: '*No*, but you can tell us, if you're up to it, about how he exploited his peasants and how they may have resisted it.' I loved it! Even in retirement, he continued to ask the questions he had asked as a young man – which led me to say to myself that I hoped I would too.

I also cannot help but relate how Eric Hobsbawm originally kept his distance from me. Replying to my request for an interview (in a letter I first found annoying, but now cherish), he wrote: 'It is hard enough to get used to the idea that one is a research topic. I think maybe the best thing is for topics to stay still and let the authors who write about them develop their ideas without being kibbitzed. I mean, if you wrote about Turner's frontier thesis, wouldn't you be glad he's not going to come in on the act himself any longer?' So, we did not meet...

Several years later, however – apparently encouraged by his dearest friends among the historians, Victor Kiernan and George Rudé (on each of whom see *The Education of Desire*) – Eric actually reached out to me and invited me to meet him my next time in London. Our ensuing lunch led to further meetings; his willingness to write the Foreword to the second edition of this book; a splendid visit to Green Bay in 1994 to spend a few days with my family and I and to speak to and meet with my colleagues and students. The visit also included a long walk in a heavily wooded park on the Door Peninsula of Wisconsin and a very private conversation on why he had not left the British Communist Party in 1956 in protest at the Soviet invasion of Hungary as most of his historian comrades had. Notably, given his original reticence to meet, we would maintain in contact until his passing in 2012.

Though they are all gone now, I want to thank them as well for pushing me beyond historiography: 'Stop writing about us...and start telling the American story anew,' each of them urged me – which is what I have tried to do ever since.

Finally, I want to thank Doug Lain and Zero Books for making *The British Marxist Historians* available once again. I hope these chapters encourage you too to attend to their words, think anew about struggles past and present, and possibly not only write history from the bottom up, but actually contribute to the making of it.

Harvey J. Kaye
March 21, 2021

Chapter 1

Introduction

I would only say that the more sociological history becomes and the more historical sociology becomes, the better for both. E. H. Carr, What is History?[1]

Over the past several years history and sociology have been involved in a symbiotic relationship, revealed by the growth and development of *social* history and *historical* sociology. This represents quite a dramatic change in the practices of each discipline and, especially, in the relationship between them. As evidence of this, we might consider the growth of journals in this area. At first, all we had in the English language were *Past & Present,* founded in 1952 by four of the historians to be discussed in this book, and *Comparative Studies in Society and History,* begun several years later. We now have, in addition to these two pioneering journals, the *Journal of Social History, Review,* the *Journal of Inter-disciplinary History, Social History,* and *Social Science History* – to name the most intentionally historical-sociological of the newer journals. Furthermore, a look at journals of both history and sociology would indicate a renewed interest in historical questions informed by sociology and social issues in historical perspective. There have also been book-length discussions of the new relationship, such as Peter Burke's *Sociology and History,* Charles Tilly's *As Sociology Meets History,* and the late Philip Abrams' *Historical Sociology.*[2] Even if it is the case that many historians would still reject the above-quoted recommendation of E. H. Carr, and that as many sociologists would still dissent from C. Wright Mills' declaration in *The Sociological Imagination* that 'all sociology worthy of the name is 'historical sociology'[3] nevertheless what were viewed as radical (if not absurd) assertions by Carr and Mills in 1960 are now seen (at least in some circles) as quite legitimate.

Yet there remains a significant problem in the relationship which has been established between the (supposedly separate) disciplines of history and sociology, due in great part, no doubt, to the assumptions which historians and sociologists continue to hold regarding each other's and their own disciplines. As Gareth Stedman Jones observes, 'there is a persistent tendency on the part of both historians and sociologists to view sociology as the source of methods and theories, and history as the source of data, case studies, or illustrations from the past (as opposed to the present), in which sociological theory is to be tested.'[4] Whether or not one subscribes (as I do) to the proposition advanced by Philip Abrams and Anthony Giddens that history and sociology are, when properly conceived, not two separate disciplines but a single one,[5] the relationship between them is too limited, and poorly conceived as well. First of all, to be blunt about it, sociological theory is of pretty uneven quality. Second, and this point has also been made before, history has been as 'theoretical' a pursuit as sociology, in spite of continuing protestations to the contrary. Thus, historians should have as much to offer to social theory as sociologists.

The neglect of the contributions which historians might make to social theory has not been characteristic of non- Marxist scholars alone. That is, until most recently,[6] Marxist studies of social thought have also failed to acknowledge the work of (even Marxist) historians in theoretical terms, in spite of the central importance of history in the thought and writings of Marx himself. Thus, in otherwise comprehensive and stimulating works, such as Perry Anderson's *Considerations on Western Marxism*,[7] no discussion is provided of Marxist historiography as theoretically consequential. (It should be noted, however, that Anderson acknowledges that Marxist historiography needs to be reconsidered in just such terms.)[8] In this book I have set out from the assumption that historians do have as much to contribute to social theory as sociologists (and, I would add, philosophers). But, of course, in the same way that not all sociologists' theories have been of the same worth, neither have all historians'.

Intended in part as a contribution to the continuing and further development of the symbiosis between history and sociology, this study presents an introduction to, and survey and examination of, the work of the British Marxist historians. By 'British Marxist historians', I refer specifically to Maurice Dobb, an economist who made important contributions to economic history; Rodney Hilton, whose contributions have, particularly, been to the fields of medieval history and peasant studies; Christopher Hill, whose work has reshaped our understanding of the English Revolution of the seventeenth-century; Eric Hobsbawm, who has worked in a variety of historical fields, but most importantly in labour, peasant and world-history studies; and E. P. Thompson, who has contributed so much to eighteenth- and early nineteenth-century English social history. As will be shown, there is no denying the outstanding individual contributions these historians have made to their respective fields of study, and collectively the contribution they have made to the study of social history. But it is my further contention that, in addition to their individual and collective contributions to historiography, the British Marxist historians together represent – in the strongest sense – a theoretical tradition. (It should be made clear that this tradition has by no means been limited to the five historians to be discussed, but they are the most outstanding scholars and represent its core.)

My argument is based, first, on the fact that the British Marxist historians have shared a common theoretical problematic. To borrow a line from the American historian Eugene Genovese who has himself been strongly influenced by their work, they have sought 'to transcend the narrowly economic notion of class and come to terms with the base-superstructure problem that has plagued Marxism since its inception'.[9] That is, Marxism has long been wedded to a conception of the social totality based on the model, or metaphor, of *base and superstructure,* wherein the base is defined as the *determining* technological and/or economic dimension(s) and the superstructure is defined as the *determined* political, juridical, cultural, and ideological dimensions. Such a conception, model, or metaphor of the social totality is often attributed to Marx himself, and for supporting evidence one is usually directed to the preface to *A Contribution to the Critique of Political Economy,* where Marx is seen to have presented his approach to historical and social analysis:

> The general conclusion at which I arrived and which, once reached, became the guiding principle of my studies can be summarized as follows. In the social production of their existence, men inevitably enter into definite relations, which are independent of their will, namely relations of production appropriate to a given stage in the development of their material forces of production. The totality of these relations of production constitutes the economic structure of society, the real foundation, on which arises a legal and political superstructure and to which correspond definite forms of social consciousness. The mode of production of material life conditions the general process of social, political and intellectual life. It is not the consciousness of men that determines their existence, but their social existence that determines their consciousness.[10]

Social analysts have construed the model as proposing economic determinism, although it is questionable whether Marx's preceding quote necessarily implies that. The British Marxist historians, having recognized this tendency, have been anxious to develop a Marxist historiography distanced from the economic determinism with which it had been (and still is) too often associated and, thus, they have sought to reconstruct Marxist analysis. As we shall see, they have not rejected all sense of determination. For, as Raymond Williams writes – and they would strongly agree: 'A Marxism with many of the concepts of determination it now has is quite radically disabled. [But] A Marxism without some concept of determination is in effect worthless.'[11]

In addition to having shared the common theoretical problematic of overcoming the economic determinism of the base-superstructure model, the British Marxist historians have also shared a common *historical* problematic. Framing their varied historical studies is the issue of the origins, development, and expansion of capitalism – understood not in the limited sense of economic change but as social change in the broadest sense. Often referred to as the transition from feudalism to capitalism, this process is not only the central issue of Maurice Dobb's *Studies in the Development of Capitalism*[12] and the debate which followed its publication.[13] It can also be seen in such diverse works as Christopher Hill's *Society and Puritanism in Pre-Revolutionary* England,[14] E. P. Thompson's *The Making of the English Working Class*[15] and Eric Hobsbawm's *Primitive Rebels*.[16]

Yet, as a theoretical tradition, the British Marxist historians have done more than share common theoretical and historical concerns. In the course of dealing with and confronting the issues involved in these problematics, they have also developed what can be viewed as a common approach to historical study, one I will term *class-struggle analysis.* (This, it will be shown, is not the same as that which is usually referred to as 'class analysis'.) Basically, the British Marxist historians have not only approached their studies with the materialist hypothesis of the preface to *A Contribution to the Critique of Political Economy* noted above, but also with Marx's historical proposition in the *Communist Manifesto* that 'the history of all hitherto existing society is the history of class struggles'.

Closely related to their class-struggle analyses of history, the British Marxist historians have also made important contributions to the development of the historical perspective known as *history from below* or, with specific reference to their writings, *history from the bottom up.* That is, as opposed to a history written from the perspective of the elites or ruling classes – which traditionally has characterized historical studies – the British Marxist historians (particularly Hilton, Hill, Hobsbawm, and Thompson) have taken seriously the historical experiences, actions and struggles of the 'lower classes', recovering the past which was *made* by them but was not *written* by them: Hilton and Hobsbawm on peasants; Hill and Thompson on the 'common people' and Hobsbawm and Thompson on the working class.

These historians have, indeed, made a further contribution to history and social theory. For, in their efforts to transcend economic determinism and explore the transition to capitalism, Dobb, Hilton, Hill, Hobsbawm and Thompson have developed Marxism as a theory of class determination,[17] the core proposition of which is that class struggle has been central to the historical process. I intend to elaborate upon what Eugene Genovese means when he says that the British Marxist historians, in working out their theory through historical practice (i.e. not by way of theory in, and for, itself), have 'contributed immeasurably more toward the development of a Marxian interpretation than have countless volumes on "dialectical and historical materialism"'.[18]

Before proceeding, I should add – so that the significance of their contribution can be more readily appreciated – that the prevalent understanding of the Marxist model of class is that offered by Barrington Moore Jr: 'According to the Marxist scheme, the workers start from a generally inert situation, capable at most of instinctive revolt. Through the experience of industrialization, which brings them together in huge factories to impose on them a common fate, they acquire a revolutionary consciousness.'[19] As we shall see, this is not the model of class of the British Marxist historians.

Another aspect of the work of these historians (which I will consider at the close of this book) is their contribution to contemporary British political culture. They have participated, by way of their writings, in the making of what exists in Britain of a democratic and socialist historical consciousness.

An Outline of the Book

This book is organized in the following manner. Chapters 2-6 take up the work of the British Marxist historians, respectively, examining the contributions each has made to his particular field(s) and period(s) of historical study, and to the development of their collective contribution to history and social theory. Thus Chapter 2 discusses the work of Maurice Dobb, most especially his book. *Studies in the Development of Capitalism,* in which he pursues a class-struggle analysis of the transition to capitalism and, thereby, charts the historical problematic and approach of the British Marxist historians. Also discussed in Chapter 2 are the debate to which Dobb's book gave rise and some recent writings on the transition which indicate the continuing relevance and importance of Dobb's arguments to historical and social studies.

Chapter 3 examines the work of Rodney Hilton in the context of peasant and, especially, medieval historical studies, focusing, in particular, on his insistence upon the centrality of class struggle to medieval historical development and the historical contribution of the English peasantry. Chapter 4 considers the numerous writings of Christopher Hill on the seventeenth-century, especially the English Revolution, in terms of his contributions to the thesis that the revolution was a bourgeois one and to the recognition of the failed 'democratic revolution' within the revolution. Moreover, it is shown that for both Hilton and Hill, class-struggle analysis has by no means been limited to politico-economic questions.

Chapter 5 discusses the temporally and spatially wide-ranging historical studies of Eric Hobsbawm, especially his contributions to labour, peasant and world-history studies and to the broadening of that which is to be considered *class experience.* Chapter 6 examines the work of E. P. Thompson: first., *The Making of the English Working Class,* then his eighteenth-century studies and, finally, his writings on historiography and social theory. In particular, the chapter considers Thompson's contributions to the question of *class formation* and *consciousness* in relation to class struggle.

Following these, Chapter 7 examines the British Marxist historians' collective contribution: their development of the perspective of history from the bottom up – in comparison to other approaches to history from below; and their development of Marxism as a theory of class determination. Finally, the chapter closes with a consideration of their contribution to the (political) problem of historical consciousness.

The remainder of this introduction will examine briefly the background to, or 'formation' of, the British Marxist historians as a historical and theoretical tradition.

The Formation of a Theoretical Tradition

To work as a Marxist historian in Britain means to work within a tradition founded by Marx, enriched by independent and complementary insights by William Morris, enlarged in recent times in specialist ways by such men and women as V. Gordon Childe, Maurice Dobb, Dona Torr and George Thomson, and to have as colleagues such scholars as Christopher Hill, Rodney Hilton, Eric Hobsbawm, V. G. Kiernan and (with others whom one might mention) the editors of this Register [John Saville and Ralph Miliband]. I could find no possible cause for dishonour in claiming a place in this tradition. E. P. Thompson[20]

Although I will argue that Dobb, Hilton, Hill, Hobsbawm and Thompson represent a theoretical tradition, three recent essays have treated these historians somewhat differently. In one such essay, Raphael Samuel discusses the 'sources of Marxist history' and considers the British Marxist historians in terms of what he sees as having been a century-long tradition of British Marxist historiography originating with Marx himself.[21] In a second essay, Eric Hobsbawm writes of the Communist Party Historians' Group which they were so active in, and central to, during the years 1946-56.[22] In a divergent context, Richard Johnson examines their work in relation to what he contends was a particular post-war (i.e. the late 1950s and 1960s) 'structure of feeling' in British historical and social studies.[23]

In his analysis, Raphael Samuel presents a basic, but quite comprehensive, history of the past century (1880-1980) of British Marxist historiography. His main project is to discuss the 'mutations' of British Marxist historical studies since Marx's time in relation to: the social and cultural backgrounds of the many historians who have made up the Marxist historical tradition in Britain during the past century; the impact over the years of various thematic concerns which emerged from different socialist and non-socialist political and intellectual movements; and the changing historical circumstances (political and economic) which respective generations of British Marxist historians have confronted. Thus, for example, Samuel writes of the influence of liberal and radical democratic historians such as the Hammonds (who will be discussed in Chapter 5 on Eric Hobsbawm) as well as of the influence of such non-Marxist socialist historians as G. D. H. Cole and R. H. Tawney (the latter will be discussed in Chapter 4 on Christopher Hill). He assesses their influences with special reference to what he terms 'people's history',[24] for it was a major source of what was to become history from the bottom up in the work of Hilton, Hill, Hobsbawm and Thompson.

Samuel also discusses the influence of Protestant Nonconformity on different generations of British Marxist historians. He points out that sometimes the influence was quite direct, that is, by way of a Methodist upbringing and/or education as, for example, in the cases of Christopher Hill and E. P. Thompson (a proposition which Thompson rejects in his own case). Sometimes it was indirect, as in the relationship between the Independent Labour Party and Methodism in the West Riding. (In this regard, we should note that Rodney Hilton's parents were active in the ILP, and he has himself commented on his upbringing in an 'irreligious, cultural tradition of Nonconformism'.) Moreover, Samuel argues, the influence of Nonconformity on British Marxist historiography can be seen in the efforts of some of the historians to uncover and present the 'radical heritage' of Puritanism, Dissent and Nonconformity. This is evidenced most clearly, as we shall see, in the work of Christopher Hill on Puritanism and the radical religious sects. Additionally, under the general heading of 'Scientific Rationalism', Samuel considers the influence of such political and intellectual currents as 'free thought', anti-clericalism, science, productivism, and progressivism.

Eric Hobsbawm states – contrary to Samuel – that, prior to the Communist Party Historians' Group, 'there was no tradition of Marxist history in Britain.[25] But whether or not Samuel presents a fully convincing argument for the existence of a continuously developing British Marxist historical tradition (and I believe he does), he shows that the formation of such a tradition was an open process, involving a variety of sometimes quite contradictory influences.

It is generally acknowledged that the years 1946-56 were most significant in the formation of a British Marxist historical tradition. For it was in that period that Dobb, Hilton, Hill, Hobsbawm, and (to a lesser extent) Thompson, along with others (most notably, Victor Kiernan, George Rudé, A. L.

Morton, John Saville and Dorothy Thompson), were active members of the Communist Party Historians' Group. In support of my argument that the British Marxist historians represent a theoretical tradition, I quote from Hobsbawm's introduction to his article on the Group, when he says that 'for reasons which are even now difficult to understand, the bulk of British Marxist theoretical effort was directed into historical work'.[26]

In his article, Hobsbawm discusses the formation and organization of the Group; its publishing efforts; its relations with the Communist Party; the response of its members to the crises of 1956-7; and the contributions which the Group and its members have made, then and since, to historical studies. Hobsbawm recalls that the Group grew out of discussions immediately after the Second World War to plan a conference on A. L. Morton's *A People's History of England*.[27] (The book had originally been published in 1938 to provide a popular Marxist text on English history. The conference was to discuss the revision of the work in light of subsequent studies.) Christopher Hill recollects that the actual initiative to form the Group came from, amongst others, Hilton, Hobsbawm, Kiernan, and himself – all of whom Hobsbawm identifies, along with John Saville and Max Morris, as having been the Group's most active and leading members in the period 1946-56. These historians had either finished their degrees and begun their research in the mid-1930s (like Hill and Kiernan) or had done so just before or just after the war (like Hilton and Hobsbawm). It should be remembered that these historians developed their intellectual and political commitments in the midst of, and in response to, the Depression, and in confrontation with fascism, both as Marxists and through their wartime military service. In addition to this young generation of historians, there were a number of older scholars, most significantly Maurice Dobb (whose most important historical study will be considered in the next chapter) and Dona Torr (whose influence will be noted shortly).

Hobsbawm observes that 'for some the Group was, if not exactly a way of life, then at least a small cause, as well as a minor way of structuring leisure. For most it was also a friendship,' adding that 'physical austerity, intellectual excitement, political passion and friendship are probably what the survivors remember best – but also a sense of equality'. By equality he means that all recognized that they were 'equally explorers of largely unknown territory. Few...'hesitated to speak in discussion, even fewer to criticize, none to accept criticism'.[28] Organized into 'period sections' (ancient, medieval, sixteenth-seventeenth century, and nineteenth century, as well as a teachers' section), the Group's activities were centred in London, though Hobsbawm points out that there were efforts to establish regional branches that were partly successful. Through its members, the Group did actively seek to 'popularize' the historical research and perspective that they were developing, especially on such occasions as the tercentenary of 1649.

The 'modern' historians of the Group were naturally most anxious to pursue and make known the history of the British labour movement and, no doubt, were encouraged in their efforts by the British Communist Party. And yet this was the one field in which constraint was felt in relation to the Party. As Hobsbawm has stated on a number of occasions, there were problems in pursuing twentieth-century labour history because it necessarily involved critical consideration of the Party's own activities.[29]

In addition to members' individual studies and publications, the Group also planned and began a few collective efforts at research and publication. Most significantly, its members began to publish, in 1948-9, a series of volumes of historical documents (with introductions and annotations) covering different periods of British history, with the intention of popularizing their historical perspective and studies. Inspired by, and under the general editorship of, Dona Torr, the series was titled 'History in the Making' and four volumes were issued: *The Good Old Cause 1640-1660* (edited by Christopher Hill and Edmund Dell); *From Cobbett to the Chartists* (edited by Max Morris), *Labour's Formative Years* (edited by J. B. Jeffreys), and *Labour's Turning Point* (edited by E. J. Hobsbawm).[30]

Two other projects which were undertaken but which never reached publication stage – at least not in the form originally intended – were a Marxist history of the labour movement and, in response to a suggestion by Dona Torr, the 'entire history of British capitalist development'. In both cases conferences were held to initiate the work but no books appeared. Nevertheless, it should be remembered that, while the Group did not necessarily accomplish the ambitious projects which were discussed, in several cases the research initiated and papers written as prospectuses provided the basis for studies carried out later by members on their own. Additionally, we should note the Group's volume. *Democracy and the Labour Movement*, edited by John Saville with the assistance of George Thomson, Maurice Dobb, and Christopher Hill.[31] This collection of essays in honour of Dona Torr includes a number of outstanding – indeed seminal – papers indicative both of the quality of the scholarship of the Group's members and, to some extent, the nature of projects to be pursued in the years to come. For example, among the contributions to the volume are Christopher Hill's 'The Norman Yoke' and Eric Hobsbawm's 'The Labour Aristocracy in 19th Century Britain'. (These will be discussed in the chapters on Hill and Hobsbawm.)

In this context the 'powerful influence'[32] of Dona Torr in the 'making' of the British Marxist historians should be acknowledged. Born in 1883, Torr was the daughter of a canon of Chester Cathedral.[33] Completing her studies for a degree in history at University College London, she became a journalist, first at the *Daily Herald,* then at the *Daily Worker.* She was a founding member of the Communist Party in 1920 and has been described as a devoted Marxist scholar. In addition to serving as general editor of the series, 'History in the Making', Torr edited *Selected Correspondence of Marx and Engels* (1934); a Supplement to an English edition of *Capital* (vol. I) (1938); *Marxism, Nationality and War* (2 vols) (1940); and *Marx on China* (1951).[34] But her most important work, which was not fully completed at the time of her death in 1957, was *Tom Mann and His Times*.[35] In this last book, Torr not only sought to present the life and times of that working-class radical, socialist and activist of the labour movement, but also to link the struggles of the period of his life, 1856-1941, to a long history of struggle for democratic rights in England, originating in the seventeenth century.

Christopher Hill notes that though Torr was not one of the original initiators of the Group, 'she was at once at home in it, for it gave her the sort of intellectual stimulus of a specifically academic historical kind that she had hitherto lacked'. However, he adds: 'In fact, she knew more, had thought more about history than any of us; moreover, she put her work, learning, and wisdom at our disposal.' In the foreword to *Democracy and the Labour Movement,* Saville and his co-editors explain the important nature of Torr's influence and contribution:

> She has taught us historical *passion.* For her the understanding of the historical process is an intense emotional experience....
> ... All of us can recall fierce arguments with her, words sharpened by the fact that she made us know that something important was at stake. She made us feel history in our pulses. History was not words on a page, not the goings on of kings and prime ministers, not mere events. History was the sweat, blood, tears and triumphs of the common people, our people.[36]

Thus, Torr must surely have influenced the younger British Marxist historians in their development of 'people's history' as history from the bottom up. She herself indicated her conception of the role which socialist historians ought to perform by way of a quote from the nineteenth-century labour figure William Newton, which she used to open *Tom Mann and His Times:*

> It must be our task, our duty, to keep green the memory of our order, to record its struggles, to mark its victories, point to fresh conquests, and to gather from defeats the elements of success. ...... We should see then that the world grasps civilization with the rough large hand of the labourer, not with the slim gloved fingers of the noble.[37]

Furthermore, as Hill states in commenting on her 'caustic wit, which she tried (usually successfully) to reserve for her seniors or equals,' Torr was opposed to the economism which had been all too prevalent in Marxist thought. Specifically, she opposed 'what she called the '"catastrophic school"' of Marxists, those who believed that conditions in England must get far worse before serious change was possible, and who rather welcomed the prospect'.

Hobsbawm acknowledges that the modern historians felt constrained from working on the period since the establishment of the Communist Party. Yet he remarks that 'in the years 1946-56, the relations between the Group and the Party had been almost entirely unclouded'. This, he points out, was due to the fact that the historians 'were as loyal, active, and committed a group of Communists as any, if only because we felt that Marxism implied membership of the Party. To criticize Marxism was to criticize the Party, and the other way round.'[38] He also acknowledges that on some issues there was a tendency to allow assumptions to dictate the terms of historical debate, for example, regarding 'Absolutism and the English Revolution'. By this, Hobsbawm probably means that Marx's own writings were sometimes treated more as 'models to be applied' than as 'hypotheses to be explored or tested'. Nevertheless, he insists that 'the net result of our debates and activities was enormously to widen rather than to narrow or distort our understanding of history'. This was possible, he contends, because 'even during the most dogmatic Stalinist period, the authorized versions of Marxist history were concerned with genuine historical problems, and arguable as serious history, except where the political authority of the Bolshevik Party and similar matters were involved'. Moreover, he states that 'there was no "'party line'" on most of British history,' at least as far as they were aware at the time.[39]

It is also important to note that while members of the Group (with the support, naturally, of the Party) saw one of their tasks to be to criticize non-Marxist historical studies, they did not seek to isolate themselves from non-Marxist historians. In fact, they sought to 'build bridges' with non-Marxist historians who shared common interests and sympathies. The most significant product of that effort was the journal *Past & Present,* the first issue of which appeared in the Cold War climate of 1952. (Originally published twice a year, the journal is now a quarterly, and the hundredth issue was that of August 1983.) The initiative for the journal came from members of the Group, specifically Dobb, Hilton, Hill, Hobsbawm and the late John Morris (who is recognized as being the chief protagonist in organizing the journal). But *Past & Present* was not published by the Group or the Party. Nor was it intended to be a journal limited to Marxist historical studies – and it never has been. In fact, the editorial board has always included a number of non-Marxist historians and historical social scientists, such as historian Lawrence Stone, sociologist Philip Abrams and anthropologist Jack Goody.[40]

Quoting the fourteenth-century Arab scholar Ibn Khaldun, *Past & Present*'s editors indicated in the first issue what were to be the concerns of the new journal. They wrote that 'our main task...is to record and explain [the] "transformations that society undergoes by way of its very nature". Such a study cannot but prompt some general conclusions, whether or not we call them "laws of historical development" – though we shall be poor historians if we underrate their complexity.' Originally subtitled *a journal of scientific history* (which has since been dropped), *Past & Present's* editors distinguished their intentions from those of social scientists, especially structural-functional- ists. In their view, social scientists too often modelled their theoretical practices after those of the natural and biological sciences and, thus, lost touch with the 'historical specificity' of social life: 'Each form of human society, and each individual phase therein, has its own special laws of development.' Moreover, and this was important – lest 'laws of historical development' be read as implying some transcendental force or the predetermination of historical development – they also wrote that 'men are active and conscious makers of history, not merely its passive victims and indices'.[41]

Though not all of the editors' original intentions have been accomplished in equal measure (e.g. their interest in articles on the Third World), *Past & Present* has definitely become one of the leading journals of historical studies and has itself been a principal means by which social history and historical sociology have (re-)emerged as central to those disciplines. Joined in later years by Victor Kiernan and E. P. Thompson, Hill, Hilton and Hobsbawm have remained active in leadership roles with the journal. Hill is President of the Past & Present Society, and Hilton and Hobsbawm are Chair and Vice-Chair respectively of the editorial committee. Their collective work on the journal shows their comradeship and friendship which has persisted in spite of their respective decisions on whether or not to remain in the Communist Party in light of the events of 1956-7.

In early 1956, as a result of Khrushchev's speech on 'Stalinism' to the Twentieth Congress of The Communist Party of the Soviet Union, the Soviet invasion of Hungary later that year, and the failure of the British Communist Party to oppose it (and, at the same time, to democratize itself), thousands of British Communists left the Party. These included Rodney Hilton, Christopher Hill and E. P. Thompson, along with many others of the Historians' Group. Maurice Dobb and Eric Hobsbawm, however, stayed in. Though he did not leave the Party, Hobsbawm was active in the efforts of during the period 1956-7, which involved many members of the Group, to influence the Party leadership and effect 'democratic' changes in the Party's practices and policies. He observes that members of the Historians' Group were 'prominent among the critics of the official Party attitude at the time' and 'the three most dramatic episodes of "opposition" – the Reasoner, the publication of a letter by a number of intellectuals in The New Statesman and Tribune, and the Minority Report on Party Democracy at the Twenty-fifth Congress of the CPGB, were all associated with Communist historians (Saville, Thompson, Hilton, Hill, Hobsbawm, among others)'. To take note of the *Reasoner* in particular; Saville and Thompson organized the journal in 1956 to provide a vehicle for discussion and dissent within the Party, but the Party leadership reacted by suspending them from membership. Saville's and Thompson's response was to resign, and the *Reasoner* became the *New Reasoner* (a forerunner of the *New Left Review*).[42]

Hobsbawm hypothesizes that the historians were as active as they were in dissent and opposition because 'the crucial issue of Stalin was literally one of history: what had happened and why had it been concealed.' Since 'historical analysis was at the core of Marxist politics,' they were necessarily moved to action, especially since it was clear that the Party leadership was denying the necessity of such an analysis.[43] Hobsbawm concludes his article by observing that after 1956-7, the Historians' Group continued, but not as before, for too many of its members had left the Party. He briefly indicates what he believes to have been the

Group's major achievements, emphasizing their contributions to social history, especially history from below and, as subjects, labour history and the English Revolution.

The third article noted above is 'Culture and the Historians', written by Richard Johnson of the Centre for Contemporary Cultural Studies at the University of Birmingham.[44] Johnson's article was written as part of a larger project on the relation of British historical writing to social theory, politics, and 'popular memory', involving, in particular, a critical evaluation of the formation of the British Marxist historical tradition.[45] It is significant that, for much of the time during which the project was being pursued, the dominant theoretical perspective at the Centre was 'structuralist-Marxism' as formulated by the French philosopher Louis Althusser (to which and to whom reference will be made on several occasions in this book, especially in the chapters on Dobb's and Thompson's work).

In 'Culture and the Historians', Johnson examines the work of the British Marxist historians in terms of what he effectively recognizes as a particular 'structure of feeling'[46] in British socialist historical and social studies in the late fifties and sixties, which continues into the seventies. (Under 'socialist', Johnson includes Marxist and non-Marxist studies.) He argues that, in the post-1956 period, British socialist social historians and writers increasingly focused on and emphasized *cultural* relations and practices (for several historically specific reasons, such as the events of 1956 themselves, and the supposed 'embourgeoisement' of the British working class). This, he states, represented a shift both in Marxist historical studies, i.e. away from *economic* structure and relations, and in labour historiography, i.e. away from merely institutional studies. At the same time, he points out, 'culture' (as a concept) was broadened or, better, revised to comprehend the 'social' and the 'popular' as opposed to merely the 'literary-artistic' and the 'elite'.

Amongst the historians whom Johnson includes as part of this late fifties and sixties' structure of feeling are Hilton (whom Johnson views as being only partially involved), Hill, Hobsbawm, Saville and Thompson. He also includes such scholars as Asa Briggs, for works like his edited *Chartist Studies*;[47] Richard Hoggart, for *The Uses of Literacy*;[48] Raymond Williams, for *Culture and Society*;[49] among other books; and the American historian Eugene Genovese for *The Political Economy of Slavery*[50] and later studies.

The significance of Johnson's article and the related studies done by his colleagues at the Centre is to call attention to the wider socialist scholarship and discourse in post-1956 Britain and the relation of the British Marxist historians to it. This is especially important since several of the Marxist historians were actively involved in the formation of the early New Left, by way of such organizations as the Campaign for Nuclear Disarmament (CND), along with other historians, social scientists, and writers who were not themselves Marxists (at least not at the time, e.g. Raymond Williams, who has had a special intellectual relationship with Marxist thought).[51] Were Johnson and his colleagues merely insisting that the work of the British Marxist historians in this period needed to be considered in the context of the early British New Left, involving a change in emphasis in their historical studies, there would be little problem. However, they argue more than that. They assert that the work of Hilton, Hill, Hobsbawm, and Thompson in these years broke with the problematic of the pre-1956 period and, especially, with the perspective of Maurice Dobb. They argue that the British Marxist historians came to develop, after 1956, their own approach to historical study which they term 'cultural Marxism' or 'culturalism' and that this represented a break with the 'structural' and 'economic Marxism' of Dobb as presented in his historical work *Studies in the Development of Capitalism*.

The development of culturalism, Johnson argues, seems to

involve the rejection, or at least the avoidance, of the essential Marxist proposition that social being determines social consciousness, and also the important 'master category' or concept of 'mode of production'. According to Johnson and his colleagues, this is due to the British Marxist historians' efforts to overcome the base-superstructure model and their focus on class, understood in the 'reduced form' of class as class consciousness. In effect, then, it is being argued that the British Marxist historians have broken with several of the central tenets of Marx's thought and that, while Dobb, Hilton, Hill, Hobsbawm and Thompson might represent a historiographical tradition, they certainly do not represent a theoretical one. If anything, it is argued, they have made up two theoretical traditions, 'economism' and 'culturalism'.[52]

Johnson and his colleagues insist that much was lost in the development of culturalism and that it is necessary to restore to British Marxist historical studies the structural and, to some extent, economic concerns which characterize the work of Marx and Dobb. Yet they indicate that such a restoration should not be by way of a return to Dobb's 'theory' for it is too 'economistic'. Rather, they suggest that a dialogue be established between what they call 'humanistic' and 'cultural Marxism' and the structuralist-Marxism of Althusser and his followers.[53] Moreover, they seem confident that structuralists have much more to offer to the proposed theoretical dialogue than do the historians, for one of the supposedly major problems with culturalism is that it eschews theory and 'abstraction' in favour of 'empiricism' and 'lived experience'.

The assertion of a break has not gone unchallenged. For example, there was a heated exchange in the journal *History Workshop,* which was instigated by an article published there by Johnson, entitled 'Thompson, Genovese, and Socialist-Humanist History'.[54] In this paper Johnson examines the historical writings of those two 'culturalists' as evidence of the supposed break between Dobb and the younger historians. Curiously, there is one contribution to the exchange which indicates that perception of the supposed break is not limited to structuralist-Marxists. Simon Clarke, responding as a 'humanist' to the structuralism of Johnson, accepts the thesis of a break but rejects Johnson's evaluation of it. That is, Clarke agrees with Johnson that Hilton et al. have broken with the economism of Dobb in the course of developing culturalism; but in contrast to Johnson, who faults the younger historians for making the break, Clarke commends them for it – though he adds that they have not necessarily gone far enough![55] Yet another critic, Keith Tribe, argues (outside *History Workshop*) that, in fact, the work of the British Marxist historians from Dobb to Thompson has been characterized by continuity in 'their pre-eminent concern with economic relations in the periods that they study'.[56]

My own position – as opposed to those of Johnson/ Clarke and Tribe – is that the relationship between Dobb and Hilton et al. is characterized neither by a break between economism and culturalism nor by a continuity in terms of a concern for economic relations. Rather, I shall argue in the chapters which follow that while there may have been a change in emphasis from the work of Dobb to the work of his younger colleagues, it is just that, a change not a break. Moreover, the continuity is not in their concern for economic relations but for class relations and struggles in their totality.[57] Thus, if we must call the theory of class determination something, it should be neither economic nor cultural Marxism but *historical, social* or (to borrow a term which will appear in Chapter 2 in regard to the work of Robert Brenner) *political* Marxism,[58] for its emphasis on the historical forms and determinations of class struggle.

Chapter 2

Maurice Dobb and the Debate on the Transition to Capitalism

First of all, certain mechanisms occurring between the fifteenth and eighteenth centuries are crying out for a name all their own. One word does come spontaneously to mind: capitalism. Irritated one shoos it out the door, and almost immediately it climbs in through the window. There is no adequate substitute for the word ... it undoubtedly has the disadvantage of dragging countless controversies and discussions along after one. But the controversies – whatever their merit – cannot be avoided; we cannot carry on discussions and behave as if they did not exist. Fernand Braudel[1]

Maurice Dobb's *Studies in the Development of Capitalism*[2] was first published in 1946. Here, Dobb tested and extended the hypotheses and analyses proposed by Marx regarding the origins and development of capitalism (and industrialization) as a historically specific mode of production. *Studies* opened a continuing debate on the transition from feudalism to capitalism, which was to involve economics, sociology, historical and development studies, and Marxist theory, and which furthered the development of concepts such as the mode and relations of production, class structure and struggle, and totality. I will argue in this chapter that Dobb's *Studies* was an original and significant contribution to the development of the theory of class determination, and the theoretical tradition of the British Marxist historians, both in itself and through the later work which built on this approach.

Of course, the issue of the 'transition' has by no means been limited to Marxist studies. The dramatic and world-historical changes which took place between the fifteenth and nineteenth centuries have been, to varying degrees, the objects of study and subjects of controversy of all the 'historical sciences'. In fact, from the outset of the modern social science disciplines, the transition to capitalism and industrialism has been a major issue.[3] For example, in *The Wealth of Nations*,[4] the first classic of modern economics, Adam Smith presented a discussion not only of how capitalism worked, but also of how it came into being. The history of capitalist development which he offered involved the expansion of trade and commerce by way of the 'market mechanism', the pursuit of self-interest and competition, the development of the division and specialization of labour – which increased the productivity of labour – and capital accumulation. Later Saint-Simon, a founding figure of sociology, presented a theory of the new social order based on the rise of scientific knowledge and 'industrial forces' (a theory which led him to a political argument in support of the coming to power of specifically 'productive classes' in the new societies still taking shape).[5] Such themes were, of course, also dealt with by Marx (whose writings on them will be considered later in the chapter), though in a somewhat different formulation.

In the late nineteenth and early twentieth century, the development of capitalism remained an important issue, perhaps the core issue of social theory. For example, it can be argued that for Max Weber the 'origins of capitalism were the focus of his concern from his doctoral dissertation on medieval trading companies, through his research on the changes in the agrarian social structure of eastern Germany,[6] to his classic *The Protestant Ethic and the Spirit of Capitalism*[7] (to be considered later). Clearly, Durkheim's work *The Division of Labour in Society*[8] is also a treatise on the subject, as it discusses the movement from more primitive mechanical to more complex organic solidarity, and the concomitant development of the division of labour, not only in industry and the economy but in society as a whole.

Today, even outside Marxist discussion, the emergence of

capitalism remains an important issue in the social sciences. The terms in which non-Marxist discussions of the subject are conducted are, however, usually quite different from those used by Marxists. For example, there is the language of modernization theory, the key terms of which are 'traditional' and 'modern'. This theory has been most significant amongst certain circles of social and economic history and development studies,[9] and is related to the theory of industrial society, which has characterized sociology in particular.[10] Both modernization theory and the theory of industrial society originate in specific interpretations of the work of Durkheim and Weber; and in their emphases on complexity and rationality they frequently separate themselves from the historical and critical approaches to change and development originating in the work of Marx. As Raymond Williams points out, the avoidance of the very word 'capitalism' has not been a mere avoidance of terminological dispute but is, rather, a political action.[11] For Marxists (and others too), however, capitalism remains the issue.

The continuing interest amongst Marxists and non-Marxists in this topic is understandable. It is not just that the historical changes involved are intellectually fascinating, although that in itself could explain much of the interest. But, more significantly, it remains a subject of scholarly attention because of its political significance. Interpretations of the emergence of capitalism have practical consequences because particular political strategies regarding, for example, economic development in the Third World, are formulated on these interpretations. Also, since we ourselves are still living in the epoch of capitalism, an understanding of the origins and development of this epoch is consequential to our own sense of the possible – in terms of both continuity and change.

Maurice Dobb

Maurice Dobb (1900-76) was, in his own words, 'an unsuccessful schoolboy who showed no prowess at games and little proficiency at classics (the main subject of his education),' and 'his academic interest was only aroused in his last year at school when he was allowed to specialize in History'. In 1919, however, between school and entering Cambridge University, he read several 'unorthodox writers such as Marx, Hobson, Bernard Shaw and William Morris,' and 'there was born in him the desire to study economics,' which he did. Nevertheless, in his study of economics he continued to pursue his first interest, in the form of economic history.[12]

It was also in the year between leaving school and entering university that Dobb became an active socialist, first as a member of the Independent Labour Party and, from 1922, of the Communist Party. His commitment to socialism and the labour movement led him to actively support and participate in the National Council of Labour Colleges and the Labour Research Department – experiences which surely had an impact on his understanding of Marxism.

Upon completing his degree,[13] Dobb spent two years (1922-4) at the London School of Economics as a research student. By this time he had come to consider himself a Marxist. The research topic he pursued at LSE was the 'history and theory of capitalist enterprise', which provided the material for an article, 'The Entrepreneur Myth' (1924),[14] and his first book, *Capitalist Enterprise and Social Progress* (1925)[15] (a work he later called 'rather unsuccessful'). In these works we find the first statement of concerns which Dobb was to take up most fully twenty years later in *Studies:* the origins and development of capitalism as a historical and theoretical problem, and the necessity of a class analysis of capitalism's history and functioning.

At the end of 1924, Dobb returned to Cambridge as a lecturer in economics and taught there until his retirement (being appointed a Reader in 1959). In the late twenties he visited the Soviet Union, which inspired him to write *Russian Economic*

Development since the Revolution (1928), rewritten 20 years later as *Soviet Economic Development since* 1917..[16] His interest in Soviet economic development was later extended to include Third World development issues, on which he wrote several pieces, e.g. *Economic Growth and Underdeveloped Countries* (1963).[17]

In addition to his work on the Soviet Union and continuing activities with the Labour Colleges and Research Department, Dobb wrote a number of books, pamphlets and articles in the late twenties and thirties. Amongst the works of this period is his pamphlet *On Marxism Today* (1932).[18] In this still-relevant essay, Dobb makes it quite clear that he sees Marxism as *historical* materialism. He emphasizes that knowledge of history is only realizable by way of the study of historical experience. That is, it cannot be gained 'in intuition or in *a priori* logic'. This is not a rejection of theoretically informed historical study in favour of empiricism, however. In fact, one of the central concerns of the essay is theory. Dobb seeks to contrast historical materialism with idealism and, more essentially, economism. Indicating concerns which were to be taken up more fully by the other British Marxist historians, he writes that when a Marxist sets out to explain history in materialist terms, he 'does not intend to erect an abstract separation of events into "material" and "ideal", the former playing an active, and the latter only a passive role in historical causation'. Such a conception of the historical process may satisfy the 'economic determinist' but, for the Marxist, it is 'entirely barren and unreal'. To the extent that the process of history involves 'ideas', Dobb insists that 'they are "facts" of historical experience as much as mechanical inventions or property relationships, and they enter into the historical process in the same way as any other "facts"'. But this is not to say that history is indeterminate. He argues that history has been substantially governed by the struggles between classes.

He also discusses experience and agency, two important

terms in the vocabulary of the British Marxist historians: 'Historical experience is a moving process in which man himself is an active agent. The "reality" of history, if it has a meaning, can only mean the totality of history itself: and precisely in activity – in making history – does man establish his relation to the objective world and learn what history is.'[19]

As a politically committed Marxist and university economist, Dobb worked under two sets of interrelated pressures. On the one hand, his membership of the Communist Party, however politically essential and intellectually stimulating, was also a constraint. For example, on the publication of *On Marxism Today*, Dobb was reprimanded in the *Daily Worker* for having 'distorted Marxism' by failing to recognize the absolute priority of the base over the superstructure; this was not an isolated episode.[20] On the other hand, as Eric Hobsbawm has recounted, Dobb was isolated as a Marxist at Cambridge and as an academic economist he was viewed as marginal. This perception of Dobb and his work was probably due to his insistence, derived in great part from his Marxism, that economics had become much too narrow and that it was necessary to return the discipline to its historical and critical origins in classical political economy. Furthermore, Dobb argued that Marx was very much a part of that tradition.[21] Thus, Dobb often found himself criticized by academic economists for being polemical and sociological, and by 'orthodox' Marxists for being too ready to integrate his work into academic economics.

Before turning to an examination of *Studies*, note should be made of an essay which Dobb wrote in 1937, entitled, 'The Economic Basis of Class Conflict'.[22] In this paper, Dobb discusses the origins of the concepts of class conflict and class in France and England around the time of the French Revolution; reviews the Marxist concept of class and class conflict and its relevance to contemporary economic and social analysis; and presents a theory of class conflict based on the fusion of the short-term sectional interests of workers with their long-term class interests.[23] It is true that the essay narrowly focuses on 'the economic basis of class conflict', and that it presents a simple sociology of class consciousness and conflict derived from Marx himself. Nevertheless, a reading of it indicates that Dobb places more emphasis on class conflict and the relations between classes than he does on *class* as a thing or a structure and, just as important, that he avoids the elitist and demeaning imputation of 'false consciousness' to the working class. The absence of the imputation of 'false consciousness' from Dobb's work (and also, as we shall see, from the work of the other British Marxist historians) was probably the product of his activities with the Labour Colleges.

Studies I: Definitions and Theories

Capitalism represents a development of meaning in that it has been increasingly used to indicate a particular and historical economic system rather than any economic system as such. Raymond Williams[24]

In the first chapter of Studies, entitled simply 'Capitalism',[25] Dobb discusses the several meanings given to the word, both in everyday use and historical studies, and presents what he considers to be the specifically Marxist approach to the subject and to historical study in general. He notes three definitions of capitalism and theories of its origins in particular.[26] (Page references to Studies will be indicated in the text in parentheses.) First, he presents the definition proposed in the writings of Werner Sombart and Max Weber, which has come to be known as the 'spirit of capitalism'. Sombart locates the basis of capitalism in a particular unity of the 'spirit of enterprise' or adventure and the 'bourgeois spirit' of calculation and rationality (p. 45). Whereas the spirit of enterprise is understood to involve a 'synthesis of the greed for gold, the desire for adventure, [and] the love of exploration', the bourgeois spirit is thought to be made up of 'calculation, careful policy, reasonableness and economy'.[27]

Of particular significance and continuing controversy in sociology and economic history is the work on capitalism by Max Weber.[28] In his writings Weber seeks to differentiate modern capitalism from capitalisms of the past and other geographic regions.[29] Contrary to Sombart, Weber writes in *The Protestant Ethic and the Spirit of Capitalism* that 'the impulse to acquisition, pursuit of gain, of money, of the greatest possible amount of money has nothing to do with capitalism'. As he points out, such an 'impulse . . . has been common to all sorts and conditions of men at all times and all countries of the world'. Rather, capitalism is identified by Weber as entailing the 'restraint, or at least a rational tempering of this irrational impulse'. Thus, the definition of capitalism which Weber offers is the 'pursuit of profit, and forever *renewed* profit, by means of continuous rational capitalist enterprise'.[30] With this conception of the uniqueness of modern capitalism, Weber goes on to locate its origins in the Reformation and the rise of Protestantism, specifically the world of Calvinism and Puritanism.

The second major approach to capitalism which Dobb presents identifies it with production for the market, particularly distant markets. For example, the Belgian historian Henri Pirenne locates the origins of capitalism in the twelfth century (p. 6), amongst a developing class of merchants. Pirenne writes that, 'the capitalistic spirit made its appearance simultaneously with commerce ... it began in conformity with the stimulus which it received from the outerworld – with long range trading and the spirit of big business. . . . ... Those who initiated and directed and expanded the commerce of Europe were a class of merchant-adventurers.' Thus, for Pirenne, capitalism equals commerce. In fact, he makes it very clear that he rejects the theory that the capitalist spirit was in some way related to Puritanism or Protestantism. He insists that there is no mystery as to the social origins of capitalism. It began with a 'greedy merchant class – not among God fearing Calvinists', and the main objective of that class was the 'accumulation of wealth'.[31]

The third definition of capitalism which Dobb presents is the one advanced by Marx. In this case, it is defined as a particular 'mode of production', understood to be not merely the state of technique, i.e. 'the state of the productive forces', but 'the way in which the means of production were owned and to the social relations between men which resulted from their connections with the process of production' (p. 7). Marx writes in *Capital:*

> In themselves, money and commodities are no more capital than the means of production and subsistence are. They need to be transformed into capital. But this transformation can itself only take place under particular circumstances which meet together at this point: the confrontation of, and the contact between, two very different kinds of commodity owners; on the one hand, the owners of money, means of production, means of subsistence, who are eager to valorize the sum of values they have appropriated by buying the labour-power of others; on the other hand, free workers, the sellers of their own labour – power, and therefore the sellers of labour.[32]

Marx further explains that his definition of 'free workers' excludes 'slaves and serfs', who were themselves part of the means of production, and 'self-employed peasant proprietors', who themselves owned the means of production. The characteristic social relationship of production of capitalism is, therefore, according to Marx (and Dobb), the wage contract. But what was (or were) the origin(s) of the capitalist mode and relations of production for Marx?

Marx (and Engels) do note a relationship between capitalism and Protestantism.[33] It is also quite evident throughout Marx's writings that he recognizes a historical connection between European expansion – by way of conquest and commerce – and the rise of the capitalist mode of production. For example, in *Capital* he states that:

There can be no doubt – and this very fact has led to false conceptions – that the great revolutions that took place in trade in the sixteenth and seventeenth centuries, along with the geographical discoveries of that epoch, and which rapidly advanced the development of commercial capital, were a major moment in promoting the transition from the feudal to the capitalist mode of production. The sudden expansion of the world market, the multiplication of commodities in circulation, the competition among the European nations for the seizure of Asiatic products and American treasures, the colonial system, all made a fundamental contribution towards shattering the feudal barriers to production.[34]

However, though these historically dramatic changes were 'fundamental', they were not, according to Marx, sufficient to *create* the capitalist mode of production. For as he proceeds to explain, the development of capitalism 'in its first period' took place only where 'conditions' had already been created for it in the medieval period. The conditions to which Marx is referring existed specifically where capitalist relations of production were already in formation as a result of the process of primitive accumulation, this being, 'nothing else than the historical process of divorcing the producer from the means of production. It appears as "primitive" because it forms the pre-history of capital, and of the mode of production corresponding to capital.'[35]

For the origins of capitalism in the primitive accumulation process, Marx directs us to English history – the enclosure movement (and the seventeenth-century revolution):

> In the history of primitive accumulation, all revolutions
> are epoch-making that act as levers for the capitalist class
> in the course of its formation: but this is true above all for
> those moments when great masses of men are suddenly and
> forcibly torn from their means of subsistence and hurled
> onto the labour-market as free, unprotected and rightless
> proletarians. The expropriation of the agricultural producer,
> of the peasant, from the soil, is the basis of the whole process.
> The history of this expropriation assumes different aspects
> in different countries and runs through its various phases
> in different orders of succession, and at different historical
> epochs. Only in England, which we therefore take as our
> example, has it the classical form.[36]

Dobb indicates that the 'justification of any definition must
ultimately rest on its successful employment in illuminating the
actual process of historical development: on the extent to which
it gives a shape to our picture of the process corresponding to
the contours which the historical landscape proves to have'
(p. 8). Especially, he writes, we need a definition to describe
and analyze the 'modern world of recent centuries' (p. 9).
Dobb's primary criterion for choosing a particular definition
of capitalism is historical specificity and, for that reason, he
rejects the 'spirit of capitalism' and 'capitalism as commerce'
definitions. He contends that neither definition is restrictive
enough to limit capitalism to any single historical period. Thus,
to make use of either one involves a danger in that it would
likely lead to the conclusion that 'nearly all periods of history
have been capitalist, at least in some degree' (p. 8).

More was involved, however, in his choice of definition.
Studies is intended to be not merely a work in economic history,
but also a work of 'historical economics'. Dobb is quite self-

conscious about this and he acknowledges in the preface that he will most likely upset both economists and historians. That is, he is fully aware of the fact that economists usually have little interest in historical questions and historians have little interest or even respect for historical studies which are not derived from fieldwork or archival research. Nevertheless, he says he was 'encouraged to persevere by the obstinate belief that economic analysis only makes sense and can only bear fruit if it is joined to the study of historical development'. Moreover, he contends that even economists who are concerned with contemporary problems must surely be permitted to ask questions of historical data. Now an argument for the historical approach to economic issues, in particular economic development, *may* seem quite reasonable today but at the time of Dobb's writing, the social sciences were characteristically ahistorical, or even anti-historical (and becoming more so), and it was not often that historians took up such problems.

Late in the first chapter Dobb goes on to state that his choice of the Marxian approach is due not only to its historical perspective and specificity but also because it is more encompassing of historical reality. Pursuing the criticisms he had made in the thirties, Dobb explains that economists have focused too narrowly on 'exchange-relationships as an autonomous territory for a special science of economics', which debilitated any serious historical study (pp. 28-30). Of the absurd nature of disciplinary boundaries he writes that it is necessary to 'abolish... .... the existing frontier between what it is fashionable to label as "economic factors" and as "social factors"' (p. 32). The Marxist approach, however, by considering the mode and social relations of production, is a *political economy,* enabling the student of capitalism to study its development not merely as an economy in the limited sense but as a society in the broad sense.

Again, Dobb's concern is not merely to correlate a given historical epoch (the modern) and mode of production (capitalism) – an essential though limited activity. His interest is in the historical *development* of capitalism, that is, in a *dynamic* study of capitalism.[37] He notes that a conception of history which characterizes historical epochs in terms of their 'predominant type of socioeconomic relationship' necessitates a theory of history which can explain not only periods of 'gradual and continuous' change, but also those periods when 'the *tempo* is abnormally accelerated, and . . . . . . continuity is broken, in the sense of a sharp change of direction in the current of events'. This latter 'tempo' of change, he writes, corresponds to the 'social revolutions which mark the transition from an old system to a new one' (pp. 11-12). Such a theory would stand in contrast to those which 'see change as a simple function of some increasing factor, whether it be population or productivity or markets or division of labour or the stock of capital'. Moreover, it would have to recognize that 'society is so constituted that conflict and interaction of its leading elements, rather than the simple growth of some single element, form the principal agency of movement and change' (pp. 12-13). The theory Dobb offers is that of class structure and struggle, i.e. class determination: 'history has been to-date the history of *class societies:* namely, of societies divided into classes, in which either one class, or else a coalition of classes with some common interest constitutes the dominant class, and stands in partial or complete antagonism to another class or classes' (p. 13). By class, with 'some common interest', Dobb does not have in mind any simple conception of class based on income level or even source of income in any narrow sense, but something more fundamental: 'the relationship in which the group as a whole stands to the process of production and hence to other sections of society' (p. 15).

Dobb's definition of capitalism as a historically specific mode and relation of production, the wage relationship, is thus in conformity with his theory of history and social change, i.e. of class structure and struggle. Yet we should note that his theory of change does not posit any simple determination by the mode of production as 'base'. Although he writes on economic development as an economist, his theory of change is not reducible to technological or economic determinism. In fact, his theory of social change portends discussions currently taking place in history and the social sciences regarding the relations between technology and social structure (in the workplace and out)[38] and can be read as a warning against the resurgence of Marxism as techno-economic determinism.[39] Dobb states (p. 23):

It would be a mistake to suppose that. . . social relations were the passive reflection of technical processes and to ignore the extent to which changes in them exercised a reciprocal influence, at times a decisive influence, upon the shape of development. They are, indeed, the shell within which technological growth itself proceeds . . . any change in the circumstances affecting the sale of that crucial commodity labour-power, whether this concerns the relative abundance and scarcity of labour or the degree to which workers are organized and act in concert or can exert political influence, must vitally affect the prosperity of the system, and hence the impetus of its movement, the social and economic policies of the rulers of industry and even the nature of industrial organization and the march of technique.

Studies II: On the Transition to Capitalism

Traditional obstructions are not overcome by the economic impulse alone. Max Weber[40]

What were the origins of capitalism and when and where did it first develop? What was the relationship between capitalism and the 'preceding' mode of production, feudalism? In relation to the first set of questions, Dobb follows Marx closely. That is, he dates the capitalist era from the sixteenth century in England. He argues that it was in this period (specifically, the latter half of the sixteenth and the early seventeenth century), that 'capital began to penetrate production on a considerable scale' (p. 18). The 'production' to which he refers was, in particular, manufacturing activities both in the advanced form of 'capitalist and hired wage-earners' and the 'less developed form' which we know as the 'putting-out system'.

Regarding the issues of the historical role of merchant capital and whether or not there was a historical period which might be termed 'merchant capitalism', Dobb is also in agreement with Marx.[41] That is, while merchant capital had in some places performed a historically progressive part in contributing to the dissolution of feudalism, the 'appearance of large-scale trading and of a merchant class' does not constitute capitalism: 'We must look for the opening of the capitalist period only when changes in the mode of production occur, in the sense of a direct subordination of the producer to the capitalist.' In fact, Dobb argues, because the 'fortunes' of the merchant class will most likely be dependent on the 'existing mode of production, it is more likely to be under an inducement to preserve that mode of production than to transform it' (pp. 17-18). It should be noted that Dobb (again, like Marx) acknowledges a development of capitalism, prior to that of late sixteenth-century England, in the Netherlands and certain Italian cities around the fourteenth century. However, in this first 'appearance', capitalism remained a subordinate mode of production within pre-capitalist societies.

Following the development of capitalism as a mode of production in late sixteenth-century England, Dobb indicates two 'decisive moments' in its history. The first he situates in the upheavals of seventeenth-century England, a period of crucial 'political and social transformations' which he compares to the French Revolution of 1789 and the Russian Revolution of 1917: 'Where a new class, linked with a new mode of production, makes itself the dominant class, and ousts the representatives of the old economic and social order who previously held sway' (p. 22). (This decisive moment was, and has been, the subject of much controversy amongst Marxist and non-Marxist historians, involving Christopher Hill in particular, as we shall see.) The second decisive moment was the industrial revolution of the late eighteenth and early nineteenth century, which was predominantly of economic importance, but not insignificant politically.[42]

Yet, Dobb asks, had there not been a third decisive moment, 'marking the disintegration of Feudalism?' In Chapter 2 of *Studies,* entitled 'The Decline of Feudalism and the Growth of Towns', Dobb defines feudalism, as he does capitalism, as a mode of production. That is, he does not focus on the juridical relation between lord and vassal, nor on the relation (or its absence) between production and the market, but on the socio-economic relation between lord and peasant. He equates feudalism with serfdom: 'an obligation laid on the producer by force and independently of his own volition to fulfil certain economic demands of an overlord whether these demands take the form of services to be performed or of dues to be paid in money or in kind' (p. 35). Working with this definition, Dobb situates the crisis of the feudal order in the fourteenth century. But this was not the end of feudalism which, he argues, persisted until the upheavals of the seventeenth century. The two-hundred-year interval did witness changes in the feudal relations of production and even the development of a petty mode of production 'in the urban handicrafts and in the rise of well-to-do and middling well-to-do freehold farmers' (p. 20). But the relations remained feudal in character and the petty mode of production remained subordinate to the still-dominant feudal mode.

Having discounted the impact of trade and the role of merchant classes for compromising with feudal society once its privileges had been won, Dobb does not present a theory of the disintegration of feudalism in which capitalist *production* provided the chief agency of that disintegration. Although he argues that capitalist relations grew out of the disintegration of feudalism he sees the *cause* of the disintegration of feudalism as having been internal to that mode of production itself. Specifically, Dobb argues that the disintegration was brought about by the inefficiency of feudalism as a system of production, exacerbated by the 'growing needs of the ruling class for revenue'. That is, while feudalism was characterized by a low productivity of labour due to the methods in use and the lack of incentive to labour, the needs of the feudal ruling class for an increasing revenue to support growing military and military-related activities compelled them to intensify pressure and impose 'novel exactions on the producer' (pp. 42-5). The ever-increasing demands on the peasantry led many to leave their lands for the towns or for new regions to be colonized, and the long-term effect was to exacerbate the tendency to soil exhaustion and declining productivity. This, in turn, led to the further impoverishment of the peasantry and population decline. The result was the feudal crisis of the fourteenth century and changes in the feudal relations of production. The changes often involved a shift from predominantly labour-services to money payments by the peasants and/or the renting-out of demesne lands.

In his discussion of the changes, Dobb observes that the reaction of the European nobility to the fourteenth-century crisis varied from country to country and region to region. He acknowledges that whether or not the lords of the different countries and regions responded to the changing circumstances with concessions to the peasants or with renewed coercion (and the degree to which they did either one successfully) was determined to a great extent by political and social factors. Such factors included the 'strength of peasant resistance, the political and military power of local lords, and the extent to which the royal power sought to strengthen seigniorial authority . . . or to weaken [it]' (pp. 51-2). But Dobb insists that 'in deciding the outcome economic factors must have exercised the deciding influence'. The specific economic factor which determined the disposition of the lord to shift from labour services to a money payment (i.e. commutation) and the profitability of such a change if he was forced into it, was 'the abundance or scarcity, cheapness or dearness of hired labour' (p. 54). Thus, Dobb's explanation of the decline of feudalism is based on its inefficiency as a mode of production and focuses on the relations of exploitation between lord and peasant, though admittedly in a rather narrowly economic way. (I will return to this point later in the chapter.)

In detailing the rise of capitalism, 'which did not grow to any stature until the disintegration of Feudalism had reached an advanced stage' (p. 181), Dobb discusses the growth of towns and the emergence of the bourgeoisie. He reiterates his position that while the merchant classes contributed to the decline of feudalism as 'parasites on the old order' they were ultimately a conservative force not a revolutionary one. He then goes on to explain the actual rise of capitalism out of the subordinate petty mode of production by way of the primitive accumulation process. (This is discussed in chapters entitled 'The Rise of Industrial Capital', 'Capital Accumulation and Mercantilism', and 'Growth of the Proletariat'.)

Quoting Marx, Dobb presents the 'really revolutionary way' in which capitalism developed as occurring when 'a section of the producers themselves accumulated capital and took to trade, and in course of time began to organize production on a capitalist basis'. This was in contrast to the situation in which 'a section of the existing merchant class began to "take possession directly of production"'. For the second way was merely transitional, 'becoming eventually "an obstacle to a real capitalist mode of production and declin(ing) with the development of the latter"' (p. 123).[43] Thus, Dobb points out that in the sixteenth century mercantile capital moved into agricultural and manufacturing activities but, more importantly, that by the early seventeenth century there had emerged, in both agriculture and manufacturing, 'capitalist' classes from amongst the producers themselves.

Though Dobb does not treat the changes in agriculture adequately (as he later acknowledges in the debate with Paul Sweezy), he does make reference to the effects of the enclosure movement. He writes of how, in the course of the sixteenth century, many smallholding peasants were dispossessed of their lands and forced into the ranks of the rural proletariat or semi-proletariat. At the same time, however, there arose a class of richer peasants or yeomen farmers, being the top stratum of the peasantry as it became differentiated by its relation to resources and the operation of the market. As this richer class of peasants prospered, they increased the size of their landholdings either by rental arrangements or outright purchases. Quite often they became money lenders on a local scale and, as their own holdings grew, they necessarily hired wage-labour from amongst the 'victims of enclosures or from the poor cottages'. Furthermore, the changes wrought in agriculture by these yeoman farmers were not merely socio-economic but also technical. For, while they were seeking to improve their individual economic positions, they appear also to have been involved in pioneering most of the improvements and innovations in methods of cultivation which appeared in that period. Similarly, in manufacturing there arose a 'capitalist' class out of the ranks of the craftsmen, which carried out its activities through both domestic industry (the putting-out system), in order to evade the restrictions of the guilds and, to a lesser extent in the early stages, 'manufactories', i.e. workshops.

The development of the capitalist mode of production, both

in agriculture and industry, depended, of course, on the growth of a proletariat and accumulation of property – the means of production – in the hands of a 'capitalist' class. While Dobb follows Marx in acknowledging the importance of enclosures to the process of primitive accumulation, both for the accumulation of property and the creation of a proletarian class, he seems to be most interested in explaining the development of the capitalist mode of production in its industrial form. He argues that it is necessary to see the accumulation process as involving two phases: first, the transfer and concentration of property and, second, a phase in which 'the objects of the original accumulation were realized or sold (at least in part) in order to make possible an actual investment in industrial production' (p. 182).

Dobb asserts that it was the development of capitalist relations in agriculture and manufacturing and the emergence of a capitalist class which led to the struggles and upheavals in seventeenth-century England in which the feudal mode of production and social order were finally overthrown and the capitalist mode of production became dominant. Acknowledging the complexity of the struggles in town and countryside and in the composition of the opposing sides he, nevertheless, discusses the class configuration of the revolution in the following manner (p. 170):

Speaking generally, it seems true to say that those sections of the bourgeoisie that had any roots in industry, whether they were provincial clothiers or merchants of a London Livery Company who had used their capital to organize the country, were wholeheartedly supporters of the Parliamentary cause.... On the other hand, those elements who were farthest removed from active participation in industry, who had invested in lands and titles and become predominantly *rentier* and leisured . . . felt their interests tied to the stability of the existing order and tended to give their support to the King.

Of course, the ultimate political outcome of the upheavals was the Restoration. But Dobb insists on the politico-economic significance of the 'bourgeois revolution' in seventeenth-century England. He argues that the changes brought about in the revolutionary decades allowed for, and stimulated, a dramatic acceleration in the accumulation of capital and its investment in industrial enterprise during the ensuing half century. This capital accumulation was, he notes, particularly impressive when viewed in comparison to what was happening elsewhere in Europe. In this way, the English Revolution provided the necessary foundation for the Industrial Revolution.[44] In the chapters which follow, Dobb discusses the Industrial Revolution, but those chapters have not been the subject of much discussion.

The Debate on the Transition

The controversial nature of Dobb's interpretation of the transition to capitalism is evidenced by the exchange which followed the publication of *Studies* and by the continuing debate[45] on the subject which traces its origins, critically or otherwise, to the work by Dobb[46] This is of interest: (1) as a 'testimony' to the controversial nature of the 'history' which Dobb had presented; (2) because it forced Dobb to clarify, reconsider, defend and/ or amend several of his ideas and arguments; and (3) because it indicates the directions which later studies and discussion of the origins and development of capitalism were to follow and, thereby, provides a clearer sense of the contributions which Dobb's work has made to historical studies and social theory.

The debate began with the 'Critique' of *Studies* offered by Paul Sweezy.[47] He takes issue with Dobb on several aspects of his work: the definition and nature of feudalism, and the cause of its disintegration; the character of the two-hundred-year 'interval' from the fourteenth to the seventeenth century; and the origins of capitalism and the pattern of the primitive accumulation process.

First, Sweezy questions the definition and conception of feudalism which Dobb presents. He criticizes Dobb for equating feudalism with serfdom and thereby failing to define feudalism as a *'system* of production', specifically, as a system of *'production for use'*. Sweezy argues that though feudalism is not to be equated with 'natural economy', it was, nevertheless, 'production . . . organized in and around the manorial estate' and 'markets are for the most part local and . . . long distance trade. . . plays no determining role in the purposes or methods of production'. Thus, it was a system of production for use because 'The needs of the community are known and production is planned and organized with a view to satisfying these needs' (*Transition,* p. 35). He acknowledges that it is true that feudalism was not a 'stable or static' system. That is, there were destabilizing elements in the feudal competition amongst lords for lands and vassals, and also in the tendency of population to increase faster than economic growth. He insists, however, that feudalism was a system which inhibited, if not prohibited, innovations in production activities *(Transition,* pp. 35-6).

Second, and very much related, Sweezy is critical of Dobb's explanation of the decline of feudalism. In particular, he faults Dobb's rejection of the growth of trade as the cause of that decline and, though he acknowledges that Dobb does show that the impact of trade was complex, he proceeds to present an alternative theory based on commercial expansion, especially long-distance trade. Sweezy argues that long-distance trade had been a 'creative force' because it had brought 'into existence a *system* of production for exchange alongside the old feudal system of production for use' (*Transition,*p. 42). Furthermore, emphasizing the impact of the former on the latter, the interaction of the two 'economies' instigated important changes in feudalism. For example, the exchange economy 'revealed . . . the inefficiency of the manorial organization of production'; led the 'members of the old feudal society [to] acquire . . . a business-like attitude toward economic affairs'; stimulated demand – and hence the need for increased revenue – amongst the members of the 'feudal ruling class'; and supported the rise of towns, which provided an alternative for the peasant-serfs (Transition, pp. 42-3). In sum, regarding changes in the feudal mode of production, 'Sooner or later, new types of productive relations and new forms of organization had to be found to meet the requirements of a changed economic order' (Transition, p. 45). Sweezy supports his theory by pointing to Eastern Europe, which was geographically removed from the changes taking place in the West and where the limited development of town life offered little alternative to the agricultural work-force. There, he observes, the lords were able to successfully impose the 'second serfdom'. It should be noted that for much of his theory, Sweezy is depending on the work of Henri Pirenne, and he clearly acknowledges this. However, he can, and does, refer to Marx for support as well.

Third, Sweezy questions Dobb's conception of the period from the fourteenth-century crisis to the seventeenth-century upheavals. He notes that in this period serfdom had virtually disappeared and yet Dobb, who himself equates feudalism with serfdom, argues that this period remained feudal. Contrary to this, Sweezy argues that the transitional period's system of production should be designated 'pre-capitalist commodity production', in which the 'predominant elements were *neither* feudal *nor* capitalist' (*Transition*, p. 49).

Sweezy's last major area of criticism concerns Dobb's analysis of the rise of capitalism. He finds two aspects of Dobb's presentation of the origins of capitalism inadequate. One is Dobb's discussion of the so-called 'really revolutionary way' to the capitalist mode of production, in which the capitalist class originates amongst the producers themselves. The other is Dobb's 'two phases' of the accumulation process, which Sweezy not only finds inadequate but, in its second phase, non-essential to the whole process.

In response to Sweezy's criticism of his definition of feudalism, Dobb has pointed out that while Sweezy's definition of a 'system of production' is based on the nature of the exchange relations, his own definition of a 'mode of production' is based on the social relations of production between the producers and their overlords. Furthermore, Dobb feels that, as a result of this definition, Sweezy insists too much on the conservative and static character of feudalism and, thereby, fails to recognize the importance of class struggle in determining its history and the changes which did occur.

On the decline of feudalism, Dobb has replied that, whereas he sees the process as the result of the *interaction* of internal and external forces – 'although with primary emphasis . . . upon the internal contradictions' – Sweezy's conception of feudalism necessarily leads him to search for an external force alone to explain its disintegration, i.e. long-distance trade (*Transition,* p. 60). With reference to the second serfdom in Eastern Europe, [48] Dobb points out that, in fact, the impact of long-distance trade was to strengthen serfdom in that region!

While Dobb continues to argue that the 'labour supply' was crucial in the shift away from serfdom on the estates, he insists, even more strongly perhaps than in *Studies,* upon the centrality of class forces. Thus, on the issue of the two-hundred-year interval, the third area of Sweezy's critique of *Studies,* Dobb defends his argument that feudalism had, indeed, persisted (though again he acknowledges that it had changed somewhat). He does so by posing a question: What was the ruling class of this period? His own answer is that it was still based on essentially feudal relations of production. He also raises the subject of the class-based nature of the state in this period, i.e. the question of the 'class basis of absolutism'.

Finally, Dobb defends his position on the 'really revolutionary way' to capitalism by citing evidence which shows that a most 'radical' group of the period, economically and politically, was the *kulak* or yeoman farmer class. This class, he insists, had arisen out of the peasantry itself. Though he does not reject his original argument, he is in some agreement with Sweezy's criticism of his presentation of the pattern of the accumulation process. In both these cases he urges additional research to test his propositions further.

In this exchange, we recognize the emergence and divergence of two kinds of Marxist analysis of economic history and development. One is decidedly *economic,* focusing on exchange relations, as in Sweezy's critique. The other is politico-economic, focusing on the *social* relations of production and directing us towards class-struggle analysis, as in Dobb's *Studies* and reply. But perhaps Dobb's contribution can be best illustrated by looking at the continuing debate on the transition, both in the immediate responses to *Studies* and later writings in historical and development studies (to be considered in the next section of this chapter).

Kohachiro Takahashi has responded quite critically, and at length, to the alternative definitions and theory of the transition offered by Sweezy.[49] In the process he makes some original points regarding the transition in Europe and elsewhere. For example, he discusses at length the relationship between production and the market, and its role in the disintegration of feudalism, and he argues, in support of Dobb, that the essential cause is, therefore, not trade or the market itself, in fact the structure of the market is conditioned by the internal organization of the productive system. But especially suggestive is Taka-hashi's brief discussion of the transition to capitalism in Prussia and Japan and the political consequences of 'the erection of capitalism under the control and patronage of the feudal absolute state' *(Transition,* p. 95). That is, he raises the subject of 'revolution from above', which some have argued led to the making of fascism in Germany and Japan. In this 'path to the modern world', as Barrington Moore Jr, refers to it, the respective feudal ruling classes were able to reassert their power and authority in the state and at the same time carry out or participate in the 'modernization' of the national polity and economy without confronting revolutionary upheavals 'from below' (as occurred in England and France).[50]

In response Dobb acknowledges that he had himself dealt inadequately with the changes in agriculture during the two-hundred-year interval. Yet he continues to assert that there was little direct connection between the decline of feudalism and the development of capitalism. The disintegration of the feudal mode of production, he insists, was already quite advanced prior to the emergence of the capitalist mode of production. In other words, the development of capitalism was a separate process from the disintegration of feudalism; not *external,* in the sense indicated by Sweezy but, nevertheless, separate.

Sweezy's response is directed at both Dobb and Takahashi. He continues to argue for the essential role of trade. But he also notes, in a way that presages the work of Immanuel Wallerstein on the modern world system, that: 'Historical forces which are external to one set of social relations are internal with respect to a more comprehensive set of social relations.' From this perspective the relationship between the expansion of commerce and long-distance trade and the disintegration of Western European feudalism looks quite different. That is, while the growth of trade was 'external to the feudal mode of production... it was internal to the European-Mediterranean economy' as a whole *(Transition,* p. 105). In response to Dobb's question about the ruling class during the fifteenth and sixteenth centuries, Sweezy writes that, since there were several kinds of property relations in this period, there must also have been 'several' ruling classes competing for power and authority. Thus, the struggles of the seventeenth century are to be understood as '*the* capitalist revolution' because they gave control of the state to the bourgeoisie and provided for its 'definitive ascendancy over the other classes' (*Transition,* p. 108).

In the 1950s, Rodney Hilton, Christopher Hill, and Eric Hobsbawm made contributions to the debate worth discussing here.[51] Hilton's contribution is an indication of the set of problems in medieval historical studies to which, as we shall see, he has dedicated himself. He takes up the question of the prime mover in feudalism and states that Paul Sweezy's position, that feudalism had no prime mover, is not only un-Marxist but, more importantly, it is historically inaccurate. He locates the fault in Sweezy's dependence on Pirenne's historical studies. While capitalism has been unique in its accumulation process, Hilton argues, it was not the first *class* society. That is, capitalism has not been the first form of society in which there has been surplus production over subsistence requirements *and* relations of exploitation. 'Feudalism is our problem,' he writes, and its 'principal feature . . . is that owners of the means of production, the landed proprietors, are constantly striving to appropriate for their own use the whole of the surplus produced by the direct producers' (*Transition,* p. 112). In answer to the question., *Why* did the feudal rulers strive to get as near the whole of the direct producers' surplus as possible? (which Sweezy had asked), Hilton moves beyond Dobb by asserting that the lords 'strove to increase feudal rent in order to maintain and improve their position as rulers, against their innumerable rivals as well as against their exploited underlings. The *maintenance of class power* in existing hands, and its extension if possible is the driving force in feudal economy and feudal politics. For this reason rent had to be maximized' (*Transition,* p. 114, my emphasis).

Hilton cites a few examples that support Takahashi's argument that the organization of production primarily structured the market rather than the reverse. (He says they are offered as suggestions for further research, not to put an end to discussion.) Furthermore, he presents the elements for a theory of the disintegration of feudalism based on the struggle over rent (i.e. class struggle), which suggest a more direct connection to the rise of *agrarian* capitalism than does Dobb's theory. (In an article several years later, Dobb does subscribe to Hilton's argument regarding the centrality of class struggle in feudalism. However, he does not pursue the connection which Hilton's essay seems to hypothesize.[52] This 'hypothesis' was to be pursued by Robert Brenner, as we shall see.)

Christopher Hill's comment on the debate takes issue with Sweezy's suggestion that there were '*several* ruling classes' in the fifteenth and sixteenth centuries. He insists that while there were competing and struggling classes, there was, and could be, but one ruling class, which until the seventeenth century was the feudal landlord class (i.e. the nobility). Furthermore, the power of the feudal ruling class was indicated in the absolute monarchy. This was a different form of the state than the feudal-estates monarchy which had preceded it, but it was still a feudal monarchy. This question of the class nature of 'absolutism' carries through the entire debate and becomes a subject of importance in the work on the transition by Perry Anderson (which will be discussed in the next section).

Eric Hobsbawm's contribution did not appear, as did the others, in the journal *Science and Society,* but in *Past & Present.*[53] In his article, Hobsbawm argues that what is known as 'the crisis of the seventeenth century' is, in fact, the last phase of the general transition from a feudal to a capitalist economy. He details the differential impact of the crisis, from the Mediterranean to north-western Europe, and from the Spanish colonies in the Americas to Eastern Europe, which, while it evidences the existence of a European European world economy, indicates in particular the central role of the social structures of the respective regions in determining its ultimate pattern. A particularly cogent example of the centrality of the social structures (i.e. class structures) in determining the impact of the crisis in a specific region, is that even in those countries where industry (and a 'business-class') had developed on a sufficiently large scale, as in Italy, the feudal social structure could effectively inhibit, or even prohibit, the development of or, rather, breakthrough to, capitalism.[54] Furthermore, the contradictory nature of the 'transitional' crisis was that while it had provided the essential basis for the industrial revolution in England and north-western Europe, it had strengthened feudalism in other regions, thereby delaying the progress of that same revolution as, for example, in Eastern Europe.

Recent Contributions to the Debate

The debate on the transition to capitalism which *Studies* instigated has continued not only in British and European scholarship, but also in Latin American and Third World, and even North American, historical studies. Discussed in this section are: the debate in Latin American studies between Andre Gunder Frank and Ernesto Laclau which reproduces the Sweezy-Dobb exchange to a great extent;[55] the work of Immanuel Wallerstein on the modem world system and Eugene Genovese on Southern United States slavery which, when examined together, can be seen as a further extension of the debate; and the recent contributions by Perry Anderson and Robert Brenner which emphasize political aspects of the transition. Through the continuing debate we not only see further evidence of the controversial nature of the argument presented by Dobb in *Studies,* but also further recognize the contribution he made to historical studies and theory.

The dominant interpretation of Latin American history and society for much of the post-war period was that of 'dualism'. Its basic thesis is that the development of the Latin American economies/societies involved a split or disjuncture within those societies, between the developed, modern, commercial, urban, industrial-capitalist regions and the backward, traditional, subsistence-oriented, agrarian-feudal regions, e.g. between southern and north-eastern Brazil, and coastal and highland Peru.[56] In radical opposition to the dualist perspective, or theory of underdevelopment, Andre Gunder Frank presented his theory of the 'development of underdevelopment' (also known as the dependency model). Frank argues that, in fact, the Latin American societies have been historically capitalist and that those regions which are termed 'feudal' are merely the regions which have suffered most the international process of capitalist underdevelopment. The counterpart to this has been the process of capitalist development in the North Atlantic metropolitan countries.[57] That is, Frank explains, Latin America has been capitalist since the conquest, insofar as it has been integrated (by way of Spanish colonialism) into the world capitalist system. Moreover, the most backward regions (e.g. highland Peru and north-eastern Brazil) were at one time the most important regions of Latin American economic and commercial activity. Thus, it is inappropriate to label as feudal those regions whose 'backwardness' is, in fact, a product of capitalism.

Frank's work is better informed historically than the work of the dualists, but it is still poor history and equally poor sociology. It is true that the Latin American societies had been involved in the world-economy from the time of the conquest. But it can be questioned:

(1) whether the world-economy was 'capitalist' at the time of the formation of the Latin American societies;
(2) even when the world economy became dominated by capitalist societies, were the Latin American societies, therefore, necessarily capitalist?
(3) was the involvement of the Latin American societies in

the world economy, capitalist or otherwise, necessarily the cause of underdevelopment?

These are the questions which Ernesto Laclau puts to the theory of the development of underdevelopment in his critique of Frank's work.[58]

Laclau argues, quite rightly, that while Frank is correct in his critique of dualism, his conceptions of feudalism and capitalism weaken his analysis; for Frank, like the dualists whom he is attacking, and like Paul Sweezy, defines systems or modes of production in terms of their relations to the market (in this case, the world economy, which Frank argues was capitalist). Thus, Laclau states that Frank's analysis is not Marxist (which is disputable), for were it a Marxist analysis, Frank would approach the question of 'feudalism or capitalism?' in terms of the social relations of production of the Latin American societies in whatever period he is considering; in which case, he would conclude that feudalism characterized those societies right through much of the nineteenth century. Essentially, Laclau is proposing Dobb's approach, as opposed to Sweezy's, to which Frank seems to subscribe. Laclau's conclusion is that Frank confuses 'mode of production' with 'economic system', i.e. 'the *capitalist mode of production* with *participation in a world capitalist economic system*'.

Furthermore, he states that while he agrees with Frank on the necessity of 'confront[ing] the system as a whole and show[ing] the indissoluble unity that exists between the maintenance of feudal backwardness at one extreme and apparent progress of a bourgeois dynamism at the other', and that 'development does generate underdevelopment', it is necessary to do so by 'bas[ing] our reasoning on relations of production and not only those of the market'.[59]

Laclau's critique of Frank is important, but at some points he moves very close to subscribing to Frank's *causal* level of analysis, the world economy, which would seem to make discussion of feudalism *vs.* capitalism a question of mere terminology.[60] But there is more to it than this. For Frank, participation in the world economy *determines* the social structures, cultures and economic development of the Latin American societies. Such an argument is economically deterministic, sociologically simplistic and historically wrong.

Following the lead of Dobb, Laclau, and Eugene Genovese (whose work will be discussed shortly), I myself analyzed the historical development of the Spanish American societies in terms of their similar, but respective, social relations of production and class relations in the context of the changing and developing world economy.[61] I argued that those societies were, in fact, characterized by *seigneurial* relations of production and forms of class structure and struggle which developed out of the conquest and colonial domination by a still-feudal, or seigneurial, Spain. Thus, the social structures of the Spanish American societies were not *determined* by the world economy but by the struggles to construct seigneurial relations of production by Spanish conquerors and colonizers. To paraphrase Marx, 'the *señores* created a world after their own image'.[62] Furthermore, the underdevelopment of the Spanish American societies was not *determined* by the world economy, but by the persistence of those seigneurial relations of production and class structures (which is not to say that the world economy has not contributed to Latin American underdevelopment).[63]

The importance of Dobb's contribution to historical and development studies is further shown by contrasting the writings of Immanuel Wallerstein with those of Eugene Genovese, for in their respective works we see an extension of this same debate. We also see further evidence of the consequences of Dobb's approach in the case of Genovese, and Sweezy's approach in the case of Wallerstein, regarding the persistence of economic determinism in Marxist historical studies and social theory.[64]

Immanuel Wallerstein has sought to develop a new model for understanding modern world history – the 'world systems' approach. Following Henri Pierenne, Paul Sweezy and, especially, Andre Gunder Frank, the *determinate* level of analysis in Wallerstein's work is the capitalist world economy which emerged in the 'long sixteenth century'.[65] He came to this model out of his efforts to define the concept 'social system' which, he argues, must be viewed from the level of the whole or 'totality', because the totality defines the parts.[66] The defining characteristic of the social system as totality, Wallerstein writes, is 'the existence within it of a division of labour, such that various sectors or areas within are dependent upon economic exchange with other areas for the smooth and continuous provisioning of the area'.[67] Based on this definition of a social system, Wallerstein argues that modem history (since the sixteenth century) has been the history of a 'world system', defined as 'a unit with a single division of labour and multiple cultural systems'. It has been a historically specific world system – the capitalist world economy – the essential feature of which is 'production for sale in the market in which the object is to realize the maximum profit'. The 'full development and economic predominance of market trade' emerged in sixteenth-century Europe. This was the system called capitalism.'[68]

The modern world system/capitalist world economy has been based on the unequal exchange between core, semi-peripheral and peripheral areas, with the core areas appropriating the surplus of the periphery. In the emergent world economy of the sixteenth century the core was North-Western Europe; the semi-periphery, Mediterranean Europe; and the periphery. Eastern Europe and the Americas. These structural positions of the world-economy hierarchy, corresponding at a general level to the division of labour of the social system, produced specific agrarian labour systems: tenancy and wage-labour in the core, sharecropping in the semi-periphery and slavery and 'coerced cash-crop' labour in the periphery. While the modes of labour control in the periphery might appear to be pre-capitalist relations of production, specifically slave and feudal (seigneurial), Wallerstein argues that they were capitalist because they were the products of the world system, the definitive totality, which is the capitalist world economy. The totality defines the parts: so the capitalist world economy makes the areas of the world system capitalist. Wallerstein neutralizes the issue of 'mode and relations of production' as opposed to 'economic system' which Laclau raises in his critique of Frank, by conflating the mode of production such that it *equates* with the world system/capitalist world economy. That is, the relations of production are to be understood as the relations of the world system.[69]

Frank's work, with its roots in Sweezy's argument, is clearly recognizable in Wallerstein's. Yet the influence of Fernand Braudel, the great *Annales* historian, is of equal importance in Wallerstein's work, especially regarding the temporal (historical) and spatial (geographical) dimensions of Wallerstein's world system (and is also, perhaps, the cause of Wallerstein's economic determinism).[70]

Wallerstein's work is theoretically interesting and suggestive and it has been attractive to sociologists (especially to history-starved American sociologists), but it is historically flawed,[71] and as sociology, like Frank's work, economically deterministic.[72] Wallerstein argues that the capitalist world economy not only defines and determines the relations of production and class structures in the narrow sense, but also determines politics and polities. For example, he writes that 'the different roles led to different class structures which led to different politics,' and the 'world-economy develops a pattern where state structures are relatively strong in the core areas and relatively weak in the periphery'. The economic determinism of Wallerstein's thought and the functionalism of his model of the modern world system are further evidenced in what he has to say about culture. He states that 'the social system is built on having a multiplicity of value systems within it, reflecting the specific functions groups and areas play in the world division of labour'. Finally, his conception of the role of ideology is most simplistic. He expresses it quite bluntly: 'it seems to be true in general that any complex system of ideas can be manipulated to serve any social or political objective'. As one historian puts it: 'Wallerstein's man is economic man and his mental equipment is apparently the mechanical product of his economic relationships.'[74]

To introduce Eugene Genovese in this context, we should note his critique of Frank, which is just as applicable to Wallerstein. He writes that the primary problem with Frank's work is its 'singular concern with *economics*', for 'it is one thing to argue that European capitalism has intruded itself into every part of the world and has exploited and subjugated the most diverse peoples, societies, and social systems; but it is quite another thing to argue that therefore every such people, society, and social system has become one more variant of bourgeois culture'.[75] Genovese's work on the 'slave South', though not a direct contribution to the debate on the transition to capitalism, is framed by and relevant to it.

In *The Political Economy of Slavery*,[76] Genovese presents an interpretation of the slave South as a society in crisis. Basing his analysis on the approach to history and economic development which Dobb presents in *Studies*, he argues that the pre-capitalist social relations of production, slavery, and class structure to which slavery gave rise – although admittedly commercial – prevented the economic development of the South by inhibiting the growth of a 'home'-market and immobilizing the mercantile and industrial bourgeoisies due to their dependence on the slaveholders. Later, in *The World the Slaveholders Made*, Genovese places the slave South in comparative perspective with the slave and seigneurial societies of Latin America and the Caribbean. In his introduction to the work he writes that his goal is 'to replace the current viewpoints which take the race question as their point of departure, with an alternative which takes the formation and development of social classes as its point of departure'. By means of class analysis he hopes to advance the study of the comparative history of slavery and, at the same time, to further 'the claims of the superiority of the Marxian interpretation of history'.[77] He emphasizes that he does not intend merely to replace an 'idealist' interpretation of history and society with a mechanical materialism. For, as he states elsewhere: 'if the case for materialism rests on a denial of the *totality* of human history and on the resurrection of an economic determinism brought to a higher level of sophistication, materialism has poor prospects.'[78] Thus, for Genovese, like Wallerstein, 'totality' is an important theoretical dimension. For Genovese, however, unlike Wallerstein the totality begins with the dialectic of people's experience as it is defined historically for them and by them in their specific class situations.

Early in his work Genovese indicates that he hopes to distance his class analysis from economic determinism and the base-superstructure model.[79] In his third book, *In Red and Black*, a volume of collected essays, his conception of totality becomes more apparent. Genovese's totality is derived from the Italian Marxist Antonio Gramsci – the historical bloc, 'in which precisely material forces are the content and ideologies are the form, though this distinction is purely didactic since the material forces would be inconceivable historically without form and the ideologies would be individual fancies without the material forces'.[80] Concerned with the development and crisis of a pre-bourgeois society and culture in the midst of a capitalist world economy, Genovese writes of Gramsci's historical bloc that 'a particular base (mode of production) will generate a corresponding superstructure (political system, complex of ideologies, culture, etc.), but that superstructure will develop according to its own logic as well as in response to the development of the base'.[81] The superstructure for Genovese is not merely a reflection of the base, it is also active.

At this point it would seem that Genovese is still somewhat trapped in the base-superstructure model. To fully comprehend his movement beyond that model it is necessary to consider his major work, *Roll, Jordan, Roll: The World the Slaves Made*[82] (which will be noted in relation to the work of E. P. Thompson). Regarding the issue of the transition to capitalism, however, what is important is that Genovese, in following Dobb (i.e. by focusing on the social relations of production and class structure to which it gives rise), is directed away from any simple determinism towards a fuller appreciation of the complex nature of historical reality. This is evidenced especially well in two recent essays on modern slavery, in which he discusses the economic, cultural and, in particular, political contradictions and crises which the slaveholders experienced (leading up to the United States Civil War), determined by their adherence to the social order of slavery which they had made in the context of a capitalist-dominated world.[83] In effect, through class-struggle analysis, as opposed to 'economic' or 'systems analysis', we are better able to appreciate not merely the order of things, but also the contradictions of human experience and the struggles – for good or evil – involved in resolving them.

Other contributions to the debate on the transition that are particularly relevant are those of Perry Anderson and Robert Brenner. They are especially interesting in that they both emphasize *political* aspects, though in quite different ways and with dramatically different results.

Perry Anderson's contribution is by way of two books, *Passages from Anticmity to Feudalism* and *Lineages of the Absolutist State*,[84] written from the perspective of structuralist (i.e. Althusserian) Marxism, with strong influences from Max Weber (for instance, with respect to the relationship between the classical world and capitalism, and the methodology of comparative historical sociology).[85] In *Passages* Anderson presents the history of the transition from the ancient social formation, in which the slave mode of production was dominant, to the medieval European social formation, in which the feudal mode of production was dominant. In *Lineages* he deals with the history of the development of absolutist states in the last phase of the feudal epoch, in relation to the rise of the capitalist mode of production.[86] He does this by way of a comparative historical sociology of Western and Eastern Europe.

In his focus on modes of production it would seem that Anderson is working from the model of Dobb and the British Marxist historians, but he plainly differentiates his approach from theirs. First, Anderson's structuralist perspective – though very much historically leavened – does move away from the British historians' emphasis on class relations and struggles, and efforts to supersede the base-superstructure model. Marxist structuralists argue that the mode of production is constituted by three levels – the economic, political and ideological – and that in any given historical moment a particular level may make a particular contribution to a historical outcome, *yet the economic level is ultimately (i.e. in the last instance) determining.* Working to some extent from this model, Anderson argues that pre-capitalist modes of production, in that they depend on extra-economic coercion for their functioning, must be *defined* via their 'superstructures', since these are what determine the type of 'extra-economic coercion that specifies them'. This is unlike capitalism, which is the 'first mode of production in history in which the means whereby the surplus is pumped out of the producer is "purely" economic in form'.[87]

Second, in what one commentator calls his 'eclectic Marxist' approach to the transition, Anderson focuses on the state for, in his words, 'secular struggles between classes [are] ultimately resolved at the *political* – not at the economic or cultural – level of society. In other words, it is the construction and destruction of

States which seal the basic shifts in the relations of production, so long as classes subsist.' Third, following from his focus on the state (which pertains more to later chapters than to the present one), Anderson argues that 'history from above' – of the intricate machinery of class domination is as essential as history from below. In this way, he criticizes the British Marxist historians and further differentiates his approach from theirs.[88]

At the same time, Anderson does present a history which occasionally parallels and intersects with that of the British Marxist historians. For example, regarding the decline of feudalism, Anderson argues – in partial opposition to Dobb but along with Hilton – that feudalism was, indeed, economically expansionary. One of the feudal dynamics was the struggle between lords and peasants which led to a process of land reclamation and, hence, economic growth. However, this pattern of expansion from the eleventh to the thirteenth centuries reached an 'ecological' outer limit and the feudal mode of production experienced its epochal crisis in the fourteenth century.[89] But this was not the end of feudalism, for out of the 'long crisis of European economy and society during the fourteenth and fifteenth centuries . . . there emerged in the West [in] the sixteenth century the Absolutist state'. Here Anderson is in agreement with Christopher Hill. The absolutist state was *'a redeployed and recharged apparatus of feudal domination,* designed to clamp the peasant masses back into their traditional social position – despite and against the gains they had won by the commutation of dues'. That is, it was not a balance or an 'arbiter between the aristocracy and the bourgeoisie', nor was it the tool of a rising capitalist class against the old feudal ruling class. Rather, he emphasizes, 'it was the new political carapace of a threatened nobility.'[90]

Yet we should not push the similarities too far, for there are significant differences. As we have noted, the struggle between lords and peasants was just one feudal dynamic. The *other* was the *'opposition* between town and country'. On this, at least one writer notes that Anderson goes even further than the British Marxist historians in asserting the persistence of feudal relations of production in the countryside, resulting from the power and protection provided by the absolutist state to the feudal aristocracy. Thus, Anderson inadequately attends to the changes which took place in the countryside and supports the theory which associates capitalist development with the activities of *urban* mercantile and manufacturing groups.[91] This is true, but it is not only his focus on the absolutist state which leads Anderson to that conclusion. It is already structured into his conception of the feudal mode of production *and* his emphasis on the 'political level'. That is, the opposition between town and country was made made possible by the 'dispersal of sovereignties . . . which freed urban economies from direct domination by a feudal ruling class'.[92] Such an argument is somewhat curious because Anderson is enthusiastic about the work of John Merrington. In his article 'Town and Country in the Transition to Capitalism',[93] Merrington demonstrates that 'European feudalism – far from constituting an exclusive agrarian economy – was the *first* mode of production in history to accord an autonomous structural place to urban production and exchange.'[94] But equally he demonstrates the conservatism of the towns, i.e. the urban bourgeoisie, and the importance of the prior, or at least concomitant development of, *capitalist agriculture* for *urban capitalist* development. On this point Rodney Hilton's essay, 'Towns in English Feudal Society', is significant. Here Hilton explains medieval urbanization in terms of the feudal agrarian political economy and is very critical of the idea of a feudal dynamic between town and country or antagonism between the burgess and feudal lord. Hilton shows how at every level urbanization was the consequence of the structure of agricultural activity. In short, the small market towns were determined by 'peasant simple commodity production within the framework of, and subject to, the demands of feudal lordship'. And the larger urban centres were the 'consequence of the disbursement of agrarian surplus by crown and aristocracy, and of the profits from the middleman function of large, middling, and small merchant capitalist'.[95]

Anderson argues that feudalism itself did not give rise to capitalism. He bases this argument on comparisons of the differential development of Western and Eastern Europe, and the differential development of European and Japanese feudalisms, concluding that 'what rendered the unique passage to capitalism possible was the *concatenation of antiquity and feudalism*'. That is, it was not a contradiction or impulse inherent in feudalism as a mode of production which gave rise to capitalism; otherwise we should expect to find evidence of the development of capitalism out of feudalism not only in Western Europe but in Eastern Europe and Japan as well. Yet we do not. The historical 'crux' which Anderson offers is the Renaissance: 'the double moment of an equally unexampled expansion of space, and recovery of time'. Clearly differentiating his work from that of the British Marxist historians, it is here that we find his theory of the rise of capitalism. He contends that the Renaissance represents three crucial moments. First, there was the 'rediscovery of the Ancient World' in the revival of urban civilization and Roman law, especially property law ('one of the institutional pre-conditions for the quickening of capitalist relations of production on a continental scale'). Second, there was 'the discovery of the New World', which Anderson seems to equate with the primitive accumulation process: 'Conducted and organized within still notably seigneurial structures the plunder of the Americas was, nevertheless, at the same time the most spectacular act in the primitive accumulation of European capital during the Renaissance.' Third, there was the 'rise of the European state-system' in the specific form of 'absolutism', which, though it effectively brought an end to the 'parcellization of sovereignty', extended the life of feudalism and the feudal ruling class. Moreover it permitted the 'spread of mercantile and manufacturing capitalism which tended to dissolve the primary feudal relations in the countryside'.[96] Thus in the end, whereas Dobb explains the rise of capitalism by way of a new class of industrial *and* agrarian capitalists, Anderson's 'rising bourgeoisie' is overwhelmingly, if not strictly, urban, and the primitive accumulation process, rather than being the class-structured land enclosures in England, as Marx argues, seems to have become for Anderson something akin to Wallerstein's.

Robert Brenner also emphasizes the political, but in a different sense, and with dramatically different results.[97] In a series of brilliant articles on the transition and capitalist development and underdevelopment, he carries Dobb's class-struggle approach further. In fact, his development of Dobb's approach is termed by one critic 'political Marxism'.[98] The first piece is 'Agrarian Class Structure and Economic Development in Pre-Industrial Europe'[99] (which instigated a symposium on the subject in the pages of *Past & Present*).[100] In it Brenner presents a critique of both the demographic, or neo-Malthusian, model (offered separately by M. M. Postan and Emmanuel Le Roy Ladurie)[101] and the commercialization model of 'long-term economic change in late medieval and early modern Europe'. He writes that studies based on 'objective' economic forces fall into three possible traps: (1) they 'abstract' the economic forces from the social or class structure for analytical purposes, in which case 'class structure tends, almost inevitably, to creep back in'; (2) they insert class structure 'in an *ad hoc* way, to comprehend a historical trend which the model cannot cover'; or (3) more often they integrate class structure in the model as a dependent variable, 'shaped by, or changeable in terms of, the objective forces around which the model has been constructed'. But, he argues, efforts such as these will necessarily fail because they are improperly constructed. For it is not demographic or commercial change which determines the long-term patterns and possibilities of economic growth and development but the 'structure of class relations, of class power', which does.[102]

Brenner states that his conception of class structure, derived from the work of Marx, involves 'two analytically distinct, but historically unified aspects'. The first is the relations of the direct producers amongst themselves; that is, their relations 'to one another, to their tools and to the land in the immediate process of production'. The second is the 'inherently conflictive relations of property', or 'surplus extraction relationship'. He explains that it is around the latter relationship that one defines 'the fundamental classes of society – the class(es) of direct producers on the one hand, the surplus-extracting or ruling class(es) on the other'.[103] The historical importance of this is that 'surplus extraction relations', once established, tend to impose rather strict limits and possibilities, indeed rather specific long-term patterns, on a society's economic development. Furthermore, he contends that 'class structures tend to be highly resilient in relation to the impact of economic forces; as a rule, they are not shaped by, or alterable in terms of, changes in demographic or commercial trends.'[104] Thus, to study the economic development of late medieval and early modern Europe, and the transition from feudalism to capitalism, it is essential to 'analyze the relatively autonomous processes by which particular class structures . . . are established and the class conflicts to which they do (or do not) give rise'.

Brenner then proceeds to his critique of the demographic and commercial models. He points out that they are incapable of accounting for 'contrasting lines of development in different places under similar constellations of economic forces.' What he means is that neither the demographic nor the commercial model can explain the different patterns of development in Western and Eastern Europe in the late medieval and early modern period. That is, neither can account for the fact that by the sixteenth century 'the same Europe-wide trends had gone a long way toward establishing one of the great divides in European history, the emergence of an almost totally free peasant population in Western Europe, the debasement of the peasantry to unfreedom in Eastern Europe.' One of the 'Europe-wide trends' to which Brenner is referring was the demographic decline which began in the fourteenth century (the crisis period of feudalism). Moreover, in the same way that the demographic and commercial models are unable to explain the 'great divide' between Western and Eastern Europe, they are incapable of explaining the different paths taken by France and England in the period from 1500 to 1750. With particular reference to the inadequacy of the neo-Malthusian model, Brenner observes that, whereas both France and England experienced population growth in this period, their respective patterns of agrarian economic development were quite different. In France there was an increase in the subdivision of landholdings and with it declining agricultural productivity. In England, however, there was a process of enclosure and consolidation of landholdings. These larger units were then leased out to tenant farmers who regularly employed agricultural workers on a wage basis. Moreover, associated with the reorganization of English agricultural production were 'major increases in agricultural productivity with truly epoch-making results'; specifically, the development of capitalism.

Thus, Brenner rejects the demographic and commercialization models (the latter of which Postan and Le Roy Ladurie themselves criticize and reject). But he also rejects the urbanization and 'economic factor' models. (The 'economic factor' model is the one offered by Dobb, i.e. regarding the labour market supply.) Instead, Brenner offers an explanation focusing on the decline *vs.* intensification of seigneurialism from the fourteenth to the sixteenth century. In particular, it is based on the different 'class-structured' capacities of the respective peasantries to resist landlords' efforts to enforce or intensify seigneurial relations and controls. Moreover, from this analysis, he argues – against Wallerstein – that:

> economic backwardness in Eastern Europe cannot be regarded as economically determined, arising from 'dependence' upon trade in primary products to the West, as is sometimes asserted. Indeed, it would be more correct to state that dependence upon grain exports was a result of backwardness; of the failure of the home market – the terribly reduced purchasing power of the mass of the population – which was the result of the dismal productivity and the vastly unequal distribution of income in agriculture, rooted in last analysis in the structure of serfdom.[105]

That is, population change and commerce may provide movement, but the movement is primarily class structured.

The decline of serfdom does not, however, explain the rise of capitalism. On this issue, Brenner again presents a comparative class-struggle and structure analysis, but this time of the differential development of England and France. He shows how the English peasantry 'was able by the mid-fifteenth century, through flight and resistance, to break definitively feudal controls over its mobility and to win full freedom,' but in the end failed to secure control of the land. Then he shows, with reference to the supportive role of the state, how the landlords were able to suppress widespread peasant rebellion in the first half of the sixteenth century and proceed to carry out enclosures. Thus, they were able to 'create large farms which they leased to capitalist tenants who could afford to make capitalist investments.' The three-tiered agrarian social structure enabled the tenants to carry out improvements and, in fact, *determined*, in relation to the market, that they had little choice but to do so if they were to maintain their positions. In France, on the other hand, the peasants had been able to secure possession of their lands against the lords and thereby inhibit the development of capitalism and economic development. Furthermore, the development of capitalist agriculture in England provided the basis for a 'symbiotic' process of economic growth and development in agriculture and industry. That is, the increased productivity of agriculture produced by the new mode of production allowed or forced labour to leave the land for industry (rural or urban), and, in the growth of the tenant and yeoman farmer class, provided the essential home market for English industry during the 'general crisis of the seventeenth century' of the European world economy.[106]

In the second article of the 'trilogy', Brenner presents a critique of the work of Sweezy, Frank, and Wallerstein. He argues that their *method* 'led them to displace class relations from the centre of their analyses', which seriously disables their studies and leads them to depend on a neo-Smithian (Adam Smith) behavioural model to explain the stimulus to economic development.[107] Again, in place of their trade-based theories of development and underdevelopment, he proposes the theory of class determination, i.e. the -structure and struggle approach.

Finally, in the third article, 'Maurice Dobb and the Transition from Feudalism to Capitalism', Brenner presents an appreciative critique of Dobb himself. He acknowledges Dobb's essential contribution but finds fault with him for not following his own prescribed method and theory. As Brenner points out, at crucial points in his analysis in *Studies,* Dobb resorts to a more economic mode of analysis than a class-struggle one. Thus, Brenner writes reprovingly that 'Dobb does not analyze the development out of feudal crisis in terms of the internal contradictions and class conflicts which he himself delineated: most especially between the development of a petty peasant production and feudal surplus extraction relations, between peasants and lords.'[108]

It can be argued, therefore, that Brenner's advance beyond

Dobb can be explained by the fact that he stays closer to Dobb's prescribed method than does Dobb himself. As a result, Brenner is able to show the intimate connection in England between the feudal class struggle and decline and the rise of capitalism in agriculture as being prior to, or at least the basis for, capitalist development in industry and the towns.

Dobb's Historical Perspective

The major historical work which was to influence us crucially was Maurice Dobb's Studies in the Development of Capitalism which formulated our main and central problem. Eric Hobsbawm[109]

To us, more than 30 years later, Dobb's *Studies* may not seem all that unusual now that we have acknowledged interdisciplinary studies, and now that Marxian studies have been granted some space in universities and colleges. However, in the period in which Dobb's book first appeared (the late 1940s), disciplinary boundaries were producing narrowly conceived studies of economic history and development, and Cold-War political and ideological boundaries were having a similarly oppressive effect. Dobb was far from writing 'total history' (he never claimed to be doing so), but he pushed economic history beyond economics. That is, Dobb's *Studies* did not propose an *economic* definition of capitalism or present an *economic* analysis of the transition to capitalism (as some critics assert).[110] Rather, it proposed a politico-economic definition and analysis showing the mode and social relations of production of the transition as historically specific. In fact, he was quite consciously seeking to shift the focus of study in economic history and development away from a narrow economism to a broader politico-economic perspective.[111] Even then, although he did not always adhere to his own method, the politico-economic perspective was intended to support a class-structure and struggle analysis.

This was significant, for it contributed to the development of an understanding of class as a historical phenomenon, as opposed to merely an economic or sociological category. Furthermore, in terms of Marxian studies, it represented a movement towards the reconceptualization of the 'totality' – away from the base-super-structure model towards the study of class relations as the core of materialist analysis.

As we have seen, Dobb's work was not only theoretically pioneering, but in so far as *Studies* reinvigorated research and discussion on the genesis of capitalism, it was historically pioneering as well. Though I have been somewhat critical of Wallerstein's and Anderson's contributions to the transition debate it is worth restating them. Each highlights particular inadequacies of Dobb's approach while, at the same time, also signalling its particular strengths. Wallerstein's world-systems approach is especially important in raising the subject of the making of capitalism as a world historical process. However much we may insist that the origins of capitalism were in the agrarian changes which took place in early modern England, the expansion of capitalism and its development into industrial capitalism has been a global process. While Dobb's work is not solely an analysis of the development of English capitalism, it does not examine the emergence of capitalism at the level of the world economy. Yet as we know, it is one of the strengths of Dobb's *Studies* that it represents an attempt to transcend a merely economic approach to the transition; to which Wallerstein's work would seem to lead. The significance of Anderson's structuralist approach is its focus on the state. His books place the question of the state at the centre of thinking on the process in which one mode of production is displaced by another. Here again, Dobb was not oblivious to the role of the state but, as in most Marxist historical studies (going back to Marx himself), the state is by no means treated adequately. Speaking 'politically', however, in contrast to the approach offered by Anderson, Dobb emphasizes class *struggle.* That aspect of his work was to be pursued even more emphatically by his fellow British Marxist historians, as we shall see in the following chapters.

Chapter 3

Rodney Hilton on Feudalism and the English Peasantry

The term 'feudalism', applied to a phase of European history, has sometimes been interpreted in ways so different as to be almost contradictory, yet the mere existence of the word attests to the special quality which men have instinctively recognized in the period which it denotes. Marc Bloch[1]

The debate on the transition to capitalism involved not only dispute about the definition and origins of capitalism, but also about the definition and characteristics (or the significance of specific characteristics) of feudal society and medieval history. For example, whereas Dobb argued that feudalism was a specific social relationship of production, Sweezy insisted that it was a system of production for use, in contrast to capitalism, which was a system of production for exchange. There was even a later contribution to the debate by the French historian, Georges Lefebvre, which stated that the word 'feudalism' was not appropriate to the discussion, because 'the specific characteristic of a feudal regime was the hierarchical relationship between a lord and his vassals rather than in the way a lord distributed fiefs to those vassals.'[2] Thus, at least in historical studies, feudalism has remained as controversial as capitalism.

Rodney Hilton is the British Marxist historian who has most actively pursued the study of medieval history and the feudal mode of production, focusing in particular on the historical experience of the English peasantry. As the author of numerous books and articles, Hilton has made, and continues to make, significant and original contributions to medieval historical studies. In particular, I will argue in this chapter that Hilton has contributed much to the reconceptualization of feudalism, not as a stable and static social order, but as one of contradiction, struggle and movement. He has provided not merely an analysis of feudalism as a class-divided society (a controversial-enough argument, as we shall see) but as a class-struggle society. In this way, his work has been important to the development of the theory of class determination. Furthermore, we see in Hilton's studies of feudalism and the English peasantry the conscious pursuit and development of 'history from below' which led him to confront the 'enduring myth of the passive peasantry'.[3]

Rodney Hilton

Rodney Hilton was born in Middleton, near Manchester, in 1916. He attended Manchester Grammar School and Oxford University. More so than the other historians under discussion, Hilton grew up in a politically active socialist family, his parents being militants of the Independent Labour Party before and after the First World War.'[4]

At Oxford (1935-9), Hilton read history at Balliol College. He says that he came to specialize in medieval history at university because his 'medievalist college tutors, specifically V. H. Galbraith and R. W. Southern, were much more inspiring than the modernists.' It was while at university that Hilton joined the Communist Party, of which he remained a member until 1956. He has also been active in a variety of other left political pressure groups and is currently a member of the Labour Party. Concerning the relationship between his interest in history, especially medieval studies, and his political commitments, he writes that 'as a communist I was interested in the potentialities for resistance to exploitation of the subordinated classes. It seemed sensible to begin with medieval peasants and craftsmen – of course within the general economic and social context of the time. I expected to move forward to modern times, but found myself too much involved in the study of medieval society as a whole.'

In the Second World War he served in the army in the Middle East and Italy (1940-6) and was afterwards appointed a lecturer in the School of History at the University of Birmingham, later becoming Professor of Medieval Social History. He remained at Birmingham until his retirement in 1982. Hilton's first article was 'A Thirteenth Century Poem about disputed Villein Services' (1941)[5] and his first book, based on his doctoral research at Oxford, was *The Economic Development of Some Leicestershire Estates in the Fourteenth and Fifteenth Centuries* (1947).[6] In the book, Hilton examines, at a regional level, the changes which occurred in the 'component parts of agrarian economy – the seigneurial estates, the peasant holding, and the social classes of the countryside – during the later Middle Ages.' By way of this study, which he notes 'was researched and written under the inspiration of Marxism', Hilton hoped to explore some of the aspects of change in the medieval social structure which led to the development of capitalism and the seventeenth-century revolution.[7]

In Chapter 2, I indicated that Hilton's contribution to the debate on the emergence of capitalism involved, in particular, the argument that feudalism was a *'class* society' and, furthermore, that the struggle between lords and peasants was the 'prime mover' of feudal society. That argument has been at the core of Hilton's work and, as such, has forced him to confront and deal with the prevalent conceptions of feudalism and the peasantry amongst historians and social scientists (and even those found in the work of Marx).

Historians and Social Scientists on Feudalism and the Peasantry

To dismiss peasant experience as belonging only to the past, as having no relevance to modern life, to imagine that the thousands

of years of peasant culture leave no heritage for the future simply
because it was seldom embodied in lasting objects – to continue
to maintain, as has been maintained for centuries, that peasant
experience is marginal to civilization is to deny the value of too
many lives. No line of exclusion can be drawn across history in
that manner, as if it were a line across a closed account.
John Berger, Pig Earth[8]

As a Marxist social historian, Hilton subscribes to a particular
(though not always agreed upon) conception of feudalism,
which he defines as 'the exploitative relationship between
landowners and subordinated peasants, in which the surplus
beyond subsistence of the latter, whether in direct labour
or in rent in kind or in money, is transferred under coercive
sanction to the former. This relationship is termed 'serfdom',
a term which causes some difficulties.'[9] This has not been the
commonly agreed upon conception of feudalism. When Georges
Lefebvre argued that the term was inappropriate, he was not
just quibbling, but indicating an aspect of the history of the
study of the Middle Ages. That is, it had become the practice
for several generations of medievalists to reserve the term
'feudalism' for discussion of the politico-military or legalistic
relationship between a lord and his vassals. Furthermore, this
practice was a reflection of the much more significant one of
narrowing the frame of reference in studies of medieval history
(though this was by no means unique to medieval studies) to
the elites or ruling class. History was not just written *from* the
perspective of the top but was also often limited to studies *of*
the top. Thus, as Hilton explains, 'when taken in this refined
sense, feudalism has little to do with the relationships between
lords and peasants (who probably constituted at least 90 per
cent of the population in the early middle ages), and strictly
speaking, lasted for only a couple of centuries.' He notes that
many historians have abandoned this restrictive conception of

the term, due especially to the work of Marc Bloch, a founder of the *Annales*. But he adds that the narrow interpretation remains very influential, in particular amongst English historians.[10]

The revival of a broader conception of feudalism in historical studies has not, however, necessarily led to a consensus that the European feudal social order ought to be conceived of as a form of *class* society. A representative example of an alternative to a class analysis of feudalism in historical studies is that offered by the French social historian Roland Mousnier. He argues that 'class stratification' is limited to societies characterized by the market economy. Thus, according to Mousnier, class stratification has only come to predominate in Europe and America in the period since the early nineteenth century. However, there had existed, for example in France, a 'society of orders, or estates' right through the early modern period (i.e. up to the late eighteenth century). Mousnier explains: 'In a stratification by orders, or estates, these social groups are, in principle, arranged hierarchically not according to the wealth and consuming capacity of the members and not according to their role in the production of material goods but according to the respect, honour and dignity attached by society to social functions which may have nothing to do with the production of material goods.' Furthermore, he asserts, 'There is thus a consensus which, owing to the circumstances in which society once found itself, decides what the most important social function is, and places a given social group at the top of the hierarchy.'[11]

Hilton argues that such a theory does not involve analysis but rather mere 'acceptance by the historian of the society's own evaluation of itself (or rather the evaluation of its ruling intelligentsia)'.[12] It reproduces the ideology that society was naturally divided into those who fight, those who pray and those who work, i.e. lords, clerics and peasants. But, of course, historians have not been alone in this conception of the feudal social structure. For, as Hilton points out, it has been 'reinforced by modern sociological theory', that is, the theory of social stratification originating in the work of Max Weber.[13]

Yet the study of the Middle Ages has increasingly involved broader analyses of the social structure. Thus we ought to note, at least briefly (along with Hilton's criticisms), the work of a few of the more important historians who have moved outside the narrow framework to present more extensive analyses of medieval feudalism. In this manner, we can better recognize not only the way in which Hilton has been part of a 'collective' effort to reconceive the history of medieval feudalism, but also the way in which he has made original contributions to such study, particularly regarding the historical experience of the medieval peasantry. In this context I will examine the work of Marc Bloch, M. M. Postan, and Georges Duby.

As Hilton himself indicates, Marc Bloch's work has been most influential in broadening the framework of studies of medieval feudalism.[14] Bloch had sought to present a 'total history' of European feudalism and, while he was not a Marxist (though it has been argued that he was greatly influenced by Marx), and did not explicitly propose a class analysis, his research was very concerned with lord-peasant relations, i.e. seigneurial relationships. In *French Rural History* (1931)[15] he presents an *agrarian* history which emphasizes the activities of the peasantry in relation to both the land and the lords. Later, in *Feudal Society* (1940), though he focuses on the lord-vassal relationship to a greater extent, lord-peasant relations are also considered. In fact, the very definition of feudalism which he offers in the work places the peasantry out in front: 'A subject peasantry; widespread use of the service tenement (i.e. the fief) instead of a salary, which was out of the question; the supremacy of a class of specialized warriors; ties of obedience and protection which bind man to man and, within the warrior class, assume the distinctive form, called vassalage; fragmentation of authority –

leading inevitably to disorder'.[16]

Bloch was most concerned with change: in *French Rural History,* with 'the continuity and development of agriculture and rural life from the Middle Ages to the present' and, in *Feudal Society,* with 'the rise and decline of a social structure'. In fact, his definition of history is 'the science of eternal change'.[17] Yet his work offers no theory of historical change and, in the end, remains 'more descriptive than explanatory.'[18] But, within his concern for the feudal social structure as a whole, there is the recognition of historical contradiction. Moreover, he provides an important hypothesis which Hilton often refers to appreciatively and, from a Marxist perspective, pursues with significant results. Bloch writes: 'To the historian, whose task is merely to observe and explain the connections between phenomena, agrarian revolt is as natural to the seigneurial regime as strikes, let us say, are to large-scale capitalism.' In this vein, although Hilton would probably not agree (as we shall see later) with Bloch's evaluation of peasant rebellions, he could not but endorse Bloch's recognition of the persistence and importance of peasant *political action*: 'Almost invariably doomed to defeat and eventual massacre, the great insurrections were altogether too disorganized to achieve any lasting result. The patient, silent struggles stubbornly carried on by rural communities over the years would accomplish more than these flashes in the pan. During the Middle Ages the consolidation of the village as a group and its recognition by the outside world was a constant preoccupation of peasant life.'[19]

The late M. M. Postan[20] wrote extensively on medieval social and economic history, particularly English agrarian history. As the author of the studies in *Essays on Medieval Agriculture and General Problems of the Medieval Economy,* for example 'The Economic Foundations of Medieval Economy' (1950), 'The Chronology of Labour Services' (1937), and 'The Charters of the Villeins' (1960), and *The Medieval Economy and Society* (of

England), he focused much of his research on the 'peasant base of the economy.'[21] Of particular importance is Postan's materialist, though non-Marxist, theory of the 'prime mover' of feudal society which is, thereby, a theory of medieval development. Postan is not alone in offering this interpretation which is, in Hilton's words, a 'persuasive . . . cogently argued demographic interpretation', and, more specifically, 'an ecological theory of history'.[22] As Postan states: 'Behind most economic trends in the middle ages, above all behind the advancing and retreating land settlement, it is possible to discern the inexorable effects of rising and declining population.' Here he makes a comparison between the medieval world and the underdeveloped countries of today, to the extent that 'the numbers of people on the land determined not only the performance of the economy as a whole, but the wellbeing of individuals.'[23]

As I mentioned in Chapter 2, Postan's theory of medieval development is the object of criticism in Brenner's *Past & Present* article on the agrarian basis of capitalist development. Brenner terms Postan's approach 'neo-Malthusian' (a description which Postan rejects) and, though he credits it with being an advance over the much too simple commercialization model, nevertheless he argues, it is inadequate to explain the regionally differential pattern of development in late medieval and early modern Europe.[24] Hilton's own criticism of Postan's approach, in spite of his appreciation of its emphasis on the peasantry, is that it concentrates too much on the 'relationship of the cultivator to the environment' and fails to adequately consider the 'relations between the cultivator and the exploiting landowner'.[25] Furthermore, Hilton argues, referring specifically to Postan's evaluation of the rebellion of 1381,[26] his demographic or ecological theory causes him to fail to appreciate the historical significance of peasant political action, as opposed to their production and reproduction. For example, Postan asserts that the Peasant Rising of 1381 was an ephemeral episode in the social history of late medieval England and was basically inconsequential in terms of accelerating or arresting the 'movement towards commutation of labour services and the emancipation of serfs'.[27] (Maurice Dobb's original explanation for the commutation of labour services was the demographics of labour supply, a position which he later seems to have amended as a result of the arguments presented by Hilton.)

Hilton also indicates his strong appreciation of the work of Georges Duby, noting the influence of Marx on Duby's work and urging Marxists to study it in turn.[28] Nevertheless, his major criticism of Duby's work is similar to his criticism of Postan's. That is, that it fails to adequately consider the peasantry as historically active, in the political sense of historical. Duby's work does involve class analysis, but not class-struggle analysis. It is not that he completely ignores peasants as historical actors. For example, in his extensive study *Rural Economy and Country Life in the Medieval West*,[29] Duby opens his concluding chapter, on peasants in the fourteenth century, with a discussion of popular revolts. However, as Hilton points out, Duby seems to limit peasant revolt and resistance to the particular crises of that century, as opposed to what Bloch and Hilton argue, i.e. that such conflict was inherent in the feudal-seigneurial order. This impression is reinforced by Duby's later work *The Early Growth of the European* Economy.[30] In this study of the formation and development of feudalism from the seventh to the twelfth century, he presents a theory of the 'prime mover' which focuses on the lord's exploitation of the peasantry (in the Marxist sense) and the technical improvements and increased production it instigated. In spite of his attention to lord-peasant relations as relations of exploitation, however, except for a few brief remarks, Duby 'does not pay the same attention to the efforts of the peasants to retain for themselves as much of the surplus to subsistence as was possible given the socio-political balance of forces.'[31]

Hilton, then, has not been alone in seeking to broaden the conception of feudalism in historical studies of the Middle Ages, nor has he been the only medievalist who has pursued studies of lord-peasant relations (in fact, there have been several classic studies of different aspects of medieval English agrarian history).[32] However, as the next section of this chapter will detail, Hilton is the historian of medieval feudalism who has most definitely focused on and argued for the recognition of the peasantry as political actors.

Of course, other disciplines of the social sciences have been involved in peasant studies – a field which has only really come into being since the late 1960s, as evidenced by the appearance of two periodicals: the *Journal of Peasant Studies* in Britain, and *Peasant Studies* in the United States. (Hilton is on the editorial board of the former.) Yet as Hilton stated early in the growth of this field (1973), there were aspects of the social sciences' approach to peasant studies which inhibited potential contributions, that is, in terms of historical studies and class analysis. In fact, as Hilton himself seemed to argue, social scientists actually tended to 'de-historicize' and/or 'de-class' the peasant experience.[33]

Social scientists in general have shown very little interest in pursuing historical studies until quite recently. Anthropological studies of peasants, for example, were most often pursued at the village or community level and thus tended to view the peasants in isolation from the larger politico-economic and power-structure relationships which they were involved in and subject to. Isolated both in time and space, it was practically impossible to recognize peasants as political actors. The result was the development of models of peasant culture and/or psychological types which presented peasants as, 'by nature', politically and economically conservative.[34] Furthermore, economists working in development studies too readily projected their own highly questionable (historically and theoretically speaking) models of 'economic man' onto peasants; and sociologists and political scientists just simply ignored peasants or occasionally lumped them together with other agrarian social groups as 'low-status rural cultivators'.[35]

There were exceptions to the pattern. For example, there were the studies by Eric Wolf, *Peasant Wars of the Twentieth Century*, and Barrington Moore Jr, *Social Origins of Dictatorship and Democracy: Lord and Peasant in the Making of the Modern World*.[36] But these works appeared in the late sixties and thus actually represent the start of the expansion of peasant studies which has occurred during the last ten years, involving historical and class analyses and viewing peasants as political actors[37]. Considering the history of this century at least, such studies have been a long time in coming.

There is one other approach to peasant studies which ought to be indicated in this context. This is the 'theory of peasant economy', which originates in the work of the Russian agricultural economist A. V. Chayanov, whose studies The Theory of Non-Capitalist Farming and Theory of Peasant Economy are based on research in Russia before and after the 1917 Revolution.[38] Basile Kerblay has summarized Chayanov's argument: 'peasant motivations are different from those of the capitalist; they aim at securing for the needs of the family rather than to make a profit'. Of central importance to his theory is 'the notion of balance between subsistence needs and a subjective distaste for manual labour (dis-utility) for this determines the intensity of cultivation and the size of the net product'. From this he proceeds to argue that 'at the national level peasant economy ought to be treated as an economic system in its own right.'[39] Daniel Thorner, the economist, took Chayanov's theory and based a historical model on it. He presents the peasant economy as a specific historical formation, defined by the following characteristics: '(1) roughly half of the total population must be agricultural; (2) more than half of the working population must be engaged in agriculture; (3) there must exist a State power and a ruling hierarchy; (4) there is a division between town and countryside . . . five percent of the population . . . be resident in towns; and (5) the unit of production is the peasant family household.'[40]

According to Hilton, there are two major problems with this theory, or model. First, intended as a basis for historical and comparative analysis, it actually inhibits such studies as it 'effectively merges all pre-industrial societies together'. In this way it differs little from the modernization approach which divides history, quite simplistically, into traditional and modern societies. Second, the theory of peasant economy, again like the modernization approach, fails to adequately consider the relations between peasants and the specific classes which have exploited and dominated them and which they have supported, and resisted, historically.[41]

Class Struggle, Feudalism and the Peasantry

It should be obvious that the peasants of the sixteenth century, like those of other eras, were far from being the inert, loutish 'sack of potatoes' Karl Marx once unfortunately labelled them. Emmanuel Le Roy Ladurie[42]

This brief survey indicates not just the too-long absence of class analysis in studies of feudalism and the peasantry, but also, in those cases where a class, or at least socioeconomic, analysis is offered, the tendency to present the peasantry in a merely one-dimensional fashion, i.e. as agriculturalists. Hilton does not reject such efforts, but he finds them inadequate. In his own work, he pursues and presents a class-struggle analysis of medieval history, like the other British Marxist historians on their respective periods. In this way he has developed a theory of the 'prime mover' (i.e. of social change) in feudalism and of the role of the feudal peasantry and its historical contribution.

Although clearly influenced by Marx, Hilton's studies are quite different from Marx's own of feudalism and, especially, of the peasantry. As Eric Hobsbawm states: 'It is generally agreed that Marx and Engels' observations on pre-capitalist epochs rest on far less thorough study than Marx's description and analysis of capitalism. Marx concentrated his energies on the study of capitalism and he dealt with the rest of history in varying degrees of detail, but mainly in so far as it bore on the origins and development of capitalism.' Furthermore, Hobsbawm points out, the medieval social class in which Marx was particularly interested was (the development of) the bourgeoisie, not the peasantry.[43]

Regarding the latter, in most of his writings Marx evidences a rather low estimation of peasants as a social class. In fact, there are the oft-quoted lines, in *The Eighteenth Brumaire of Louis Bonaparte,* which raise doubts as to whether or not peasants are, in his terms, even to be considered a class. He writes, regarding the French peasants: 'The small peasant proprietors form an immense mass, the members of which live in the same situation but do not enter into manifold relationships with each other. Their mode of operation isolates them instead of bringing them together.' And he continues several lines later: 'In so far as millions of families live under economic conditions of existence that separate their mode of life, their interests and their cultural formation from those of other classes, they form a class. In so far as these small peasant proprietors are merely connected on a local basis, and the identity of their interests fails to produce a feeling of community, national links or a political organization they do not form a class.'[44]

Hilton himself rightly observes that Marx's remarks should be read as Marx intended them, that is, as historically specific to mid-nineteenth-century France. Nevertheless, if Marx was not always against the peasantry, as some have argued,[45] the best that might be said, perhaps, is that he was ambivalent on the subject.[46]

It should be added, however, that Engels was more interested than Marx in pre-capitalist societies, particularly in feudalism and the peasantry. This is indicated by his study *The Peasant War in Germany*.[47] Contemporary with Hilton's early research there was the work of the Soviet historian E. A. Kosminsky. As editor of the English edition of Kosminsky's *Studies in the Agrarian History of England in the Thirteenth Century*, Hilton has discussed the importance of his work, the influence of which is recognizable on Hilton's own.[48]

Like Marx, then, Hilton has been interested in the historical relationship between feudalism and capitalism; unlike Marx, however, Hilton has been especially interested in the medieval peasantry. In this regard, he also recommends the comparative historical study of the peasantry and provides a definition for such a purpose:

(1) They possess, even if they do not own, the means of agricultural production by which they subsist. (2) They work their holdings essentially as a family unit, primarily with family labour. (3) They are normally associated in larger units than the family, that is villages or hamlets, with greater or lesser elements of common property and collective rights according to the character of the economy. (4) Ancillary workers, such as agricultural labourers, artisans, building workers are derived from their own ranks and are therefore part of the peasantry. (5) They support super-imposed classes and institutions such as landlord, church, state, towns by producing more than is necessary for their own subsistence and economic reproduction.[49]

As indicated in his criticisms of Postan's and Thorner's work, and his definition of the peasantry as a class, Hilton insists on the importance of studying the medieval peasantry in relationship to the lords. It is not that the peasants' specifically agricultural activities and family unit or household are less important, 'but if we are to analyse, not a self-contained "peasant economy" (which has probably never existed) but the *feudal* economy of the middle ages, we must consider other elements in the social structure.' Thus, it is essential to analyse the lordship because 'it is within the lordship that the two main classes of feudal society meet for the transfer of the surplus.'[50]

Hilton's own studies, from *The Economic Development of Some Leicestershire Estates,* through his post-war study of 'Social Structure of Rural Warwickshire in the Middle Ages' (1950),[51] to his later books, *A Medieval Society: The West Midlands at the End of the Thirteenth Century* (1966)[52] and *The Decline of Serfdom in Medieval England* (1969), consistently examine the peasantry in relation to the lords. This is not because Hilton views the lords as having been all-determining, which Duby's work seems to imply, for he does not: 'These lords, with their armed retainers and their far-reaching private or public jurisdictions, had by no means complete control even over the servile peasantry. In particular their military and political power was not matched by their power to manage the agrarian economy.'[53] Rather, it is because the 'most striking of the contradictions' of feudalism was to be found in the lord-peasant relationship. That is, as Hilton argues, the 'prime mover' of feudalism was the lords' efforts to maximize their receipt of feudal rent, i.e. surplus, for the maintenance and, if possible, extension of class power.[54]

As Hilton acknowledges, this is still inadequate. The maintenance of class power was not just in terms of intraclass competition and conflict, it was, even more so, based on the need to maintain class power *over* the peasants in particular. But the peasants, the very source of feudal rent, did not necessarily accept the lords' demands passively. The 'prime mover', then, was not merely the lords' demands for feudal rent, but the struggle between lords and peasants over that rent. This was not just the case, he argues, during the later Middle Ages, on which his own work focuses. It was equally true in earlier periods: 'The conflict between lord and peasant rather than simply the exploitation of the peasant by the lord was the "motor" of early medieval society.'[55]

Although much of Hilton's work might be described as politico-economic studies of medieval feudalism, he by no means reduces the struggle between lords and peasants to merely economic concerns, as we shall see. We can look at the concluding remarks to his essay, 'Capitalism: What's in a Name?' which appeared in the inaugural issue of *Past & Present*. Speaking in particular of historical study of the transition, he states that:

> Since men make their own history, the historian must know what part the political and social consciousness of the various classes played in advancing or retarding the tempo of capitalist development. Since that consciousness is by no means a direct reflection of the economic activity of these classes, the historian cannot but concern himself with law, politics, art and religion. Neither feudalism nor capitalism are understandable simply as phases in economic history. Society and its movement must be examined in their totality.[56]

Not limited to an elaboration of the relations of exploitation, Hilton's studies of medieval feudalism move beyond class analysis to class-struggle analysis. Moreover, Hilton himself is one of the first of the group to have presented the perspective of 'history from the bottom up' in his studies. In the introduction to their book *The English Rising of 1381*, Hilton and his co-author, H. Fagan, admonish the authors of previous studies of the Rising for having allowed themselves to be taken in – consciously or unconsciously – by the biased perspectives of the literary and official sources of the period. They declare that, in contrast to such studies, they are seeking to 'redress the balance by reconstructing the inadequately recorded motives and aims, not of the oppressors, but of the oppressed'. They add that their efforts are motivated by both historical and contemporary concerns. That is, they have written the book not only to correct and reassess the history of the Rising, but also 'to present to the British people one part of their own tradition of struggle for popular liberties.'[57] Later, in *A Medieval Society,* a book intended for scholarly readers (as opposed to a more popular audience), Hilton restates the necessity of pursuing history from the bottom up. He writes that when viewed from the perspective of the 'village, hundred, and county', much of what medieval historians have traditionally concerned themselves with was actually much less significant than it might appear to have been from the 'writings of national chroniclers, or the records of the central government.' Thus, he adds, 'by looking from the bottom upwards we might get a more accurate picture of the whole of society, and of the state, than if we look at society from on high.'[58]

Class-struggle analysis and his approach to history from the bottom up have led Hilton to a necessary confrontation with the 'myth of the passive peasantry'. Much of his work is devoted to the study of medieval peasant movements as class struggles, from his first article, 'A Thirteenth Century Poem on Disputed Villein Services', and the classic 'Peasant Movements in England Before 1381' (1949)[59] (as well the already cited work on the 1381 Rising), to his most important work, *Bond Men Made Tree: Medieval Peasant Movements and the English Rising of 1381* (1973).[60] The significance of Hilton's work is not just that he indicates the historical and geographical extensiveness of the occurrence of medieval peasant movements: 'Peasant movements of all sorts occur during the formative period of feudal society, during the period of trade and urbanization in the twelfth and thirteenth centuries, during the period of extreme population pressure before about 1350, as well as during the critical years of the later Middle Ages.' Nor is it merely that he persuasively links peasant movements to the feudal social structure – as Bloch suggests – as opposed to simply being the product of crises: 'It would appear from these facts that while local or short-term economic and political difficulties could well be precipitating causes of peasant movements, the basic factor must be found in the nature of the relations of the principle classes concerned, peasants and lords.' But rather, what is significant in Hilton's work is that he shows that peasant movements as *class struggles* were consequential to medieval social change and development and, in their aims, both purposeful in the historically specific terms of the Middle Ages and significant as contributions to later historical periods and generations' struggles.

Hilton writes that the aims of peasant movements 'can almost entirely be summed up as the demand for land, for freedom, and for the reduction or abolition of rents and services'. He points out that these demands have not been limited to the medieval peasantry, but in their particulars were historically specific to medieval Europe. For example, the demand for land did not usually seek the breakup and redistribution of estate lands, but rather sought to secure peasant access to and control over pastures, woodlands and waters against 'the assertion of seigneurial rights by lords... ... to overriding property rights'. Moreover, Hilton explains, in the medieval context, the demands for (1) the reduction or abolition of rents and services, and (2) freedom were not economic and political issues, respectively, but were most often linked together.[61]

To argue that peasant movements (i.e. 'common action in pursuit of aims which are specific to peasants as a class') were consequential to medieval social change and development is not, of course, to argue that they were 'successful'. But neither should the contrary assumption be made – as it so often has been – that because they were not necessarily successful, they were, therefore, inconsequential. Moreover, to argue that medieval peasant movements were consequential is not to imply that they were all of equal extent (in time or space), intensity and importance. They varied historically in (dialectical) relation to the changing feudal society.

Hilton divides the history of medieval Europe into three broad phases; (1) sixth to tenth century – the feudalization of Western Europe; (2) eleventh to early fourteenth century – a period of growth and expansion; and (3) the fourteenth to fifteenth century – a period of crisis and then recovery, and the beginnings of a new period of European development. But these phases can be roughly collapsed into two: early and late medieval. In these terms, he finds that 'most' of the peasant movements of the early Middle Ages, were 'localized geographically and limited in scope'. By this he means that they were generally movements of single villages seeking to affect the balance of relations with the individual lords to whom they were subject. They did not, however, seek the restructuring or abolition of those relationships. He adds that the most such movements could accomplish was to secure the form of autonomy and self-government which the urban communes had. This was in itself no small achievement. Where this did occur it was almost always under the leadership of the wealthier villagers.[62]

Obviously, an important element in medieval (if not all) peasant movements was village-community cohesion. I have emphasized Hilton's insistence that analysis focus on the lord-peasant relation, but he also gives much attention to the structure of the peasant village and intra-class peasant relations.[63] For, as he himself notes, it was the network of relationships in the village community that mediated between the lord and individual peasant households. Village community relationships were not just an essential part of the everyday problem of material survival but also an important variable in the peasants' confrontation – from resistance to rebellion –

with the lords. It should be added, as Hilton himself indicates, that although the medieval peasant community was not characterized by equality, the degree of inequality amongst the peasants of a particular village or locale was 'strictly limited'. For most of the medieval period 'poor smallholders and richer peasants were, in spite of the differences in their incomes, still part of the same social group, with a similar style of life, and differed from one to the other in the abundance rather than the quality of their possessions'.[64]

Whereas the earlier peasant movements can be termed localized or a continuous series of guerrilla actions, the peasant movements of the later Middle Ages were on the scale of risings or rebellions: 'Whole regions containing many villages are involved and aims are proclaimed – or are at least implicit in peasant actions, which subvert existing social and political relationships'. The changes are attributed to a series of developments in medieval society, e.g. the growth of the apparatus and jurisdiction of the state, and the expansion of trade and communications.[65]

Hilton argues – against Postan's demographic model, for example – that the late medieval peasant movements were consequential as class struggles, from the continuing village-level resistance to the uprisings. He offers an alternative explanation of the 'crisis of feudalism' in terms of late medieval class struggle, stating that the crisis was neither one of subsistence, nor was it caused by the 'scissors effect of rising industrial and falling agricultural prices'. The crisis of the feudal social order had begun prior to the 'arrival of the bubonic plague, even before the great famines of the second decade of the fourteenth century'. These events, or processes, were significant in the development of the crisis. Nevertheless, Hilton insists that at its core the crisis of the social order was a crisis in the 'relationships between the two main classes of feudal society, which had begun before the demographic collapse and continued, even in some altered forms, during and after it'.[66] That is, the late medieval peasant movements – *as class struggles* – were actually *the* determinants of the 'crisis of feudalism'.

There were not only changes in the scale of peasant movements in the late Middle Ages, but also changes in the realm of ideas and social mentality. Such changes often resulted from peasant involvement in other, not specifically peasant, mass movements. The ideological driving force of many of these other mass movements was, of course, religion. This was the case, for example, in the 'people's crusades' to liberate Jerusalem.

Surveying the peasant movements of the late Middle Ages, Hilton notes that the mass movements which caused the greatest concern were actually instigated by the feudal lords or governments themselves. Many of the most significant of the late medieval movements began as peasant responses to actions by their feudal rulers which had 'altered the customary relationships or disappointed normal expectations to the detriment of the peasant class as a whole, rich and poor'. In this way the movements appear to have been 'conservative'; the peasants could not 'accept the abandonment of traditional roles by anyone of the orders of the society – whose basic structure they [did] not, to begin with, challenge'.[67]

This leads to the issue of the 'dominant ideology thesis' (which will reappear in my studies of the other historians and be considered again in Chapter 7). That is, did the ruling class's ideology determine the world-view of the peasantry, as some have argued, or, to the contrary, did the peasants have an autonomous, i.e. separate, culture?[68] Hilton argues that, contrary to widely held assumption, the culture of the medieval peasantry was not separated from that of the medieval European ruling class any more so than the culture of the modern working class of capitalist society is separated from those of the middle and upper classes. There was, of course, a cultural separation between lords and peasants in the Middle Ages. It was not, however, specific to the separateness of peasant from the rest but something which 'was specific to the class divisions within society'.[69] Hilton further writes that 'for the most part, in so far as one has evidence at all, the ruling ideas of medieval peasants seem to have been the ideas of the rulers of society as transmitted to them in innumerable sermons about the duties and the characteristic sins of the various orders of society.' But this should not be pushed too far. Peasant 'conservatism' should not be construed as indicating that the peasants accepted the social order *as it was given by the lords,* nor that the dominant ideology determined in any complete sense the world-view of the peasants. For, as Hilton adds, pointing to the likely possibility of a more complex and contradictory world-view than the above statement might indicate: 'To what extent those ideas were mingled with those derived from the ensemble of archaic beliefs and practices which entered into the religion of rural communities is unknown and perhaps unknowable.'[70]

In *A Medieval Society* Hilton provides an example of a more 'complex' peasant world-view, determined not only by the 'dominant ideology' but also by peasant 'memory'. He grants that in the thirteenth century the peasants of the West Midlands of England probably accepted the seigneurial social structure, 'the institutions of lordship, and the ownership of great estates', as if they had been there since the start of time itself. 'But,' he adds, 'within this aristocratic framework, ancient peasant communities still doubted the legality of the absolute disposal by the lord of the commons, still doubted whether any man except slaves could be treated as unfree, still doubted whether lords had the right to increase or change rents and customary services.'[71] In further explanation of medieval peasant conservatism, at the same time directing us towards a class-differential interpretation of medieval culture, Hilton notes that 'peasants, even more than lords, tended to cling to custom

116

even when, without knowing it, they were constantly seeking to mould custom to suit their own interests'.[72] Moreover, there were even circumstances in which the actual acceptance by the peasantry of their own traditional role in the feudal social order could generate a *'consciousness* which was antagonistic to other social classes'.[73]

Class struggle, culture, ideology and now consciousness: did medieval peasants ever develop *class* consciousness? Did they, in their conflicts with the lords, ever move beyond struggles over the specific content of the medieval order and feudal relationships – which were not insignificant – to confront the feudal society as a whole, perhaps articulating a vision of an alternative social order? Hilton argues that moments of class consciousness did develop, however briefly. The Continental peasant movements of the late Middle Ages, e.g. the Jacquerie in 1358, the Tuchin Movement in France from the 1360s to the end of the century, and the fifteenth-century wars of the *remensas* in Catalonia (he does not include the German Peasant War in his survey), did evidence the emergence, among some of the participants, of a consciousness of class. However, it was a 'negative class consciousness in that the definition of class which was involved was that of their enemies rather than of themselves'. By negative class consciousness Hilton means a 'bitter hatred of the land-owning nobility, sometimes even of all the rich or well-to-do'.

More significantly, in the English Rising of 1381 (often called the Peasants' Revolt) there emerged a 'positive class consciousness', a recognition of the 'mutual interests of peasants and other basic producers' and, to some extent, 'the formulation of a long-term programme of political action'.[74] The 1381 Rising 'was *initiated* from within peasant society...... [but] its social composition was much wider'.' It may have begun as a peasant rebellion but it was soon joined by others – artisans and merchants of small towns and traditional rural craftsmen (smiths, cobblers, carpenters).[75] It was not, therefore, even limited to participants from the countryside alone but involved townsmen as well. In fact, expressed in the social categories of the medieval period: 'it was a broadly-based popular uprising of the third estate (but excluding the London merchant capitalists) against the other two components of the tripartite society of the middle ages, not a movement of all social groups against a narrow governing clique.' Clearly, the producing classes also knew their enemies. As Hilton observes, there is no evidence 'of even the beginnings of an alliance between the rebels and any group which had a part to play in the accepted political game'.[76]

Chief among the demands put forth by the rebels at Mile End and Smithfield in June 1381 was the abolition of serfdom. There was also a demand made for the elimination of all peasant obligations to landowners, both monetary and personal. But the movement also seems to have possessed a long-term programme of political action involving a conception of an alternative society and how to achieve it. Hilton states that the peasants and their allies envisioned a popular monarchy, a state where there would be no hierarchy or social classes standing between the people and their king. In other words, there would be no feudal ruling class owning lands and controlling law and administration. In fact, Hilton notes, some of the rebels had in mind to establish county or regional monarchies rather than a single monarchy with a king distant from the people. The making of laws and the administration of justice were somehow to be taken care of by the people. The church was to be reorganized in a similar fashion: there was to be 'a people's church whose basic unit would be the parish, again with no intermediate hierarchy between Christians and the single bishop or archbishop who, as head of the church, was the ecclesiastical equivalent of the people's king.' Thus, the rebels sought freedom and equality (at least in political terms). Though some things were to be held in common, they appear to have imagined 'a regime of family ownership of peasant holdings and artisan workshops, with the large scale landed property of the church and the aristocracy divided among the peasants'.[77]

This is important, because historians and others have too often viewed the aspirations of the movement as 'sermon-induced, hallucinatory fantasies'. For example, Norman Cohn describes those involved in the 1381 Rising as 'fanatical *prophetae* mixed with disoriented and desperate masses on the very margin of society'.[78] Hilton rejects such an interpretation. The *prophetae* – John Ball and his fellow clerics (poor priests, chaplains and parish clerks) – were, as Hilton states, the 'medieval equivalent of the radical intelligentsia'.[79] Furthermore, he argues: 'What is remarkable is the way that their vision of a society of free and equal men and women fused with the ancient peasant demand for freedom of status and tenure, in the formulation of a programme which, though entirely incapable of realization, given the historical forces at work in the late middle ages, did challenge root and branch the ideas of the ruling class.'[80]

In addition to the 'radical Christian tradition', the peasant and artisan rebels of 1381 were also influenced by legal thought. This may seem surprising, but peasants did employ lawyers to present petitions and argue their cases in the courts. The arguments which the lawyers made regularly asserted that 'freedom was man's natural condition'. Thus, Hilton suggests that since peasants had a clear sense of what free status meant in practice, they must have been 'reinforced in their desire for freedom by listening to their lawyers' arguments'.[81]

The rising failed to bring about the popular and egalitarian monarchy, but it was consequential. Though it did not succeed in ending landlordism, it seems to have been responsible for forcing an end to the feudal reaction following the Black Death. Moreover, it contributed, along with the struggles which continued after it, to the decline of the feudal-seigneurial regime in England and, thereby, helped the development of agrarian capitalism. And 'from this, in turn, industrial capitalism sprang.'[82]

Before concluding this chapter, I should mention another area of medieval history in which Hilton has been working during the past few years – urban history. He has published several pieces of work in which he considers the issues (1) of whether or not the separation of town and country in the medieval period represented a central contradiction of feudalism, and (2) the extent to which urban social conflicts were class conflicts and, moreover, threatening to the feudal social order.[83]

Basically (as I mentioned in Chapter 2), Hilton argues that, while the differences between town and country were significant and consequential to medieval life, towns were, nevertheless, an 'integral part of feudal society', not 'nonfeudal islands within a feudal sea'. Thus, though he recognizes the importance of disputes and quarrels between urban elites and seigneurial lords, he continues to maintain that the 'dynamic . . . of feudal society' is not to be found in some town-country or burgess-feudal lord antagonism; it is to be found first in the antagonism between lords and peasants in the act of the appropriation of the unretained portion or surplus of peasant production.' Hilton does indicate another contradiction, however, 'in the distance between family-based peasant and artisan production and the feudal and merchant capitalist appropriators',[84] which raises the issue of 'urban class conflict' alongside agrarian class conflict. On this he shows that there was an 'inherent class conflict between merchant capital and small-scale craft industry in medieval urban society', although adding that peasant struggles 'posed a much greater threat than did [those of] the townsmen'.[85]

Hilton's writings on medieval urban history represent merely the beginnings of his work on the subject. He is currently engaged in a major study of urban social history focused on the West Midlands of England, where he has done research before, on lords and peasants (A Medieval Society).

Peasant Contributions to History

Rodney Hilton has not been alone in seeking to broaden the framework of analysis in medieval historical studies. But as Eric Hobsbawm appreciatively writes, regarding the development and recent growth of class-struggle analysis and interpretation of feudalism and the peasantry, it has been a 'lonely fight that Rodney Hilton has been fighting for a long time'.[86]

I have argued in this chapter that what Hilton presents in his studies of medieval history is a dynamic analysis of feudalism in terms of the theory of class determination. That is, it is Hilton's thesis that the 'prime mover' of medieval social change and development was the class struggle between lords and peasants. Pursuing a class-struggle analysis, Hilton necessarily confronts the myth of the passive peasantry. In this way, he offers an alternative view of the medieval peasantry. Hilton shows that medieval peasants, as opposed to being merely agriculturalists, were makers of history in the political sense of the term. In other words, medieval peasants were not just historically significant in the 'Braudelian' (environmental-materialist) sense of the *longue durée* but, more importantly, they were consequential to the course of history as the story of 'who rides whom and how?'[87] In what can be read as almost a summary of the role of medieval peasant movements, Hilton writes that 'peasant resistance was of crucial importance in the development of the rural communes, the extension of free tenure and status, the freeing of peasant and artisan economies for the development of commodity production, and eventually the emergence of the capitalist entrepreneur'.[88]

The foregoing quote, of course, emphasizes the political economy of change and development – Hilton's main, but by no means sole, concern. As he himself acknowledges, 'medieval peasantries must be understood not only as "peasantries" but in the context of the institutions and culture of medieval feudal society'.[89] (In this regard, as an example of his interest in medieval cultural questions, we ought to note his much-contested, but still relevant, essay, 'The Origins of Robin Hood' (1958),[90] in which he presents a class-struggle analysis of the Robin Hood legends.)

This brings us to the issue of the medieval peasants' contribution to history and later generations' struggles. There are two studies which direct us *towards* a recognition of the medieval peasants' contribution to history but, for separate reasons, fail themselves to acknowledge it. First, there is the previously cited book by Barrington Moore Jr, *Social Origins of Dictatorship and Democracy*. In this work, Moore is interested in the historical bases of twentieth-century liberal democracy, fascism, and communism. He seeks the origins of these modern socio-political forms in the outcomes of the class struggles between lords and peasants. Although he goes much further than most historians and social scientists in presenting the peasant role in the making of the modem world, Barrington Moore nevertheless concludes that peasant revolts have been repressed far more than they have succeeded. For them to succeed requires a somewhat unusual combination of circumstances that has occurred only in modern times. 'Success itself has been of a strictly negative sort. The peasants have provided the dynamite to bring down the old building. To the subsequent work of reconstruction they have brought nothing.'[91] But Barrington Moore's approach is based on a too-narrow conception of historical contribution, suggesting that it is to be equated with 'success' in class struggle, and in the end he reinforces the attitude that the medieval peasants' contribution was limited to their self-sacrificial demise in the early modern or modern epoch.

Published more recently, there is *The Origins of English Individualism*, by Alan Macfarlane,[92] which has been widely discussed and, in some quarters, well-received. In it, Macfarlane argues that historians and social scientists have been mistaken in their assumption that it was in sixteenth- and seventeenth-century England that modern individualism originated. On the contrary, he asserts, the origins of individualism are much further back in English history. He finds that the necessary socio-economic basis for individualism – specifically a market economy in land and labour – existed in England long before the sixteenth century, in fact, at least since the thirteenth century. Thus, Macfarlane directs attention back to medieval agrarian life. The problem in this case, however, is that his work is seriously flawed – definitionally, analytically and historically. For example, because he fails to consider the social relations of production between lords and peasants, Macfarlane literally ends up defining the medieval English peasantry out of existence in favour of a model of medieval England as a petty-bourgeois social order.[93] Furthermore, though he criticizes the economic determinism of other perspectives and theories, he essentially offers an economically deterministic theory of his own – that is, that capitalism, in the narrow sense of the market economy, produced individualism. Thus, it might be said that, for Macfarlane, the contribution of the medieval peasantry was, in essence, to have not existed at all.

Hilton's argument, however, offers a dramatic alternative to historians' and sociologists' traditional conception of the origins of individualism. If *equality* and *liberty*, or *freedom*, are at the core of the modern concept of individualism,[94] then it is not to the bourgeoisie that we ought to attribute its origins. 'The assertion of freedom against feudal subordination was not, as is often supposed, a specific contribution of the bourgeoisie,' but rather, Hilton contends, it was the contribution 'of the peasantry of the feudal era'.[95] That is, 'one of the most important if intangible legacies of medieval peasants to the modern world is the concept of the freeman, owing no obligation, not even deference, to an overlord.'[96] (I will return return to this argument in Chapter 7.)

Hilton's theory of the origins of 'individualism' – as idea, value, or cultural practice – is derived from a class-struggle analysis and history from the bottom up. It is very far removed from economic determinism and the base-superstructure model. Ideas, values and cultural practices are not merely 'superstructural' but an integral dimension of the class struggle.

Chapter 4

Christopher Hill on the English Revolution

In the works of man we have to distinguish between those which hardly concern more than a particular, tiny group of men and those which, extending beyond the boundaries of tiny groups, tend to unite them or at least steer them all in the same direction. Religions do this in so far as they are not the closed religions of small groups forbidden to non-members of the group. So do great ideologies and doctrines which spread beyond frontiers and bring together men of all groups. And political works too – organizations, revolutions or movements of conquest and expansion together with all their consequent annexations and resistances. Lucien Febvre[1]

Following Rodney Hilton, in terms of a chronological division of labour in British Marxist historical studies, is Christopher Hill, whose domain is seventeenth-century England. In terms of both the quantity and quality of his work, Hill must be considered one of the greatest historians to work in the English language in the twentieth century. Over more than a forty-year period he has written many outstanding works, including *Society and Puritanism in Pre-Revolutionary England* (1964),[2] *Intellectual Origins of the English Revolution* (1965),[3] *The World Turned Upside Down: Radical Ideas During the English Revolution* (1975),[4] and *Milton and the English Revolution* (1979).[5] This represents merely a small part of his work now in book form![6]

Notably, like Hilton, Hill participated in the debate on the transition from feudalism to capitalism and the focus of his life's work, the English Revolution – like Hilton's medieval feudalism – has been an important topic in that debate. Indeed, the English Revolution has been a subject of controversy not only in Marxist studies of the rise of capitalism, but in British historical studies in general.[7]

In this chapter I will look at Hill's contributions to seventeenth-century studies with reference to both these fields. He has presented two major theses in his writings, both of which I will examine. First, that the English Revolution was a 'social revolution' and, specifically, a *bourgeois* one. Regardless of the modifications which he has made to this thesis over the years, Hill has persistently and effectively argued that the Revolution dramatically furthered the development of capitalism. Second, that the English Revolution, in addition to having been a bourgeois revolution and, so, capitalist in its consequences, was also a democratic one although this aspect of it was defeated. Concerning both theses, I will show that Hill's interpretations of the struggles and upheavals of seventeenth-century England have been developed in terms of the British Marxist historians' theory of class determination, that he has pursued a class-struggle analysis of seventeenth-century English society. Moreover, his work on the 'century of revolution' has not been limited to political economy or even political sociology, but has involved the development of a sociology of culture and ideas of seventeenth-century England, as well. And I will argue that Hill has, thereby, made major contributions not only to the historiography of the English Revolution, but also to the development of the theory of class determination. He has shown that class struggle and experience are not just economic or political, nor even politico-economic, but rather social in the broadest sense. Finally, Hill's work has involved the pursuit of history from the bottom up with significance for both the study of the seventeenth century and the development of the theory of class determination.

Christopher Hill

John Edward Christopher Hill was born in York in 1912. His upbringing was middle class and Nonconformist. He attended

St Peter's School, York, and in 1931 he entered Balliol College, Oxford, to read history. Upon graduating he was made a Fellow of All Souls College, Oxford (1934-8) and, from 1936 to 1938, he held a lectureship in the History Department at Cardiff. Prior to going to Wales he spent a year in the Soviet Union studying the work of Soviet historians on British history, especially the seventeenth century, which he later introduced to English readers by way of several articles.[8] And following the trip, he joined the Communist Party.

Hill returned to Balliol College in 1938 as a Fellow and Tutor in Modern History. During the War he served in the army and then worked at the Foreign Office (due to his knowledge of Russian and the Soviet Union). In this period, he authored *The Two Commonwealths* under the pseudonym of K. E. Holme.[9] (K. E. = Christopher Edward in Russian, and Holme = 'hill' in Russian.)[10] He returned to Oxford and Balliol following the war. From 1958 to 1965, Hill was university lecturer in sixteenth- and seventeenth-century history and in 1965 he was elected Master of Balliol College, a position he held until his retirement in 1978. Since retiring, he has held visiting professorships at the Open University, the Australian National University and Rutgers University.

Acknowledged as the dominant figure in studies of the English Revolution today, Hill states – somewhat in jest, but not completely so – that his interest in the seventeenth century was 'all due to T. S. Eliot, who got me interested in metaphysical poetry'. (It was Eliot who wrote, 'in the seventeenth century a dissociation of sensibility set in, from which we have never recovered'.)[11] Thus, Hill adds, 'in trying to understand that I found I had to understand the conflicts of the age.' Furthermore, directing attention to the connection between his intellectual/ historical interests and his developing political commitment, Hill notes that he became: 'fed-up with the insular complacency of English and especially Oxford history – Anglo-centred, all about liberty and the constitution, the English Revolution = "the interregnum", something that really never happened. I wanted to show that England's peaceful gradualist evolution after the seventeenth century was the consequence of what had happened then.'

Hill's Marxism developed at university, but not only out of his studies. He recalls that it was also a response to the political and economic situation in the thirties:

[S]lump, dreadful unemployment, danger of World War II, apparent successes of the USSR – the usual things. I would stress, since such horrors have become all too familiar since, that all this came as a terrible shock to middle-class English children brought up to assume that even if England was just not still top nation, still it was stable and secure. The bottom fell out of our universe in 1931, the year I went up to Balliol. And there, the influence of undergraduate friends – a great deal of Marxist discussion went on in Oxford in the early thirties. Marxism seemed to me (and many others) to make better sense of the world situation than anything else, just as it seemed to make better sense of seventeenth-century English history.

In this context, it should be added that it is clear that Hill's 'productive period' has been since he left the Communist Party in 1957. Nevertheless, he himself states that the period 1946-56 (his years in the Historians' Group) involved 'discussions which were much the greatest stimulus I have ever known'. Thus, in the developmental sense, while Hill's writings of the forties and early fifties are necessarily discussed prior to his later studies, I do not see 1956-7 as a *break* in his work. First, because the problems which Hill has pursued since the mid-fifties were indicated in his earlier writings; and second, because his approach to those problems developed during the earlier years.

At the same time, however, I do not contend that Hill's work
has remained the same from the forties to the eighties. Rather,
as this chapter will show, his work developed as it took up new
problems and, in the process, modifications were made, even at
the level of theory. But none of this should be too surprising in
a scholarly career of over forty years.

A final biographical point regarding Hill's Nonconformist
background: Raphael Samuel,[12] Rodney Hilton, and Christopher
Hill himself, note a connection in the life-histories of several
historians (Hill, E. P. Thompson and Sheila Rowbotham)[13]
between Nonconformism (in the way of upbringing or education)
and Marxism. In this, Nonconformism should not be read in a
narrowly religious sense but in the sense of a 'culture' as, for
example, the way in which Hilton intends it when he writes in
his 'reminiscence' of Hill, himself, and the Communist Party
group at Balliol College in the late thirties: 'I think that many [of
us] had a strong Nonconformist upbringing, or (as in my case)
deliberately irreligious, though with all the cultural attributes
of Nonconformity. In fact, it was not difficult for people with
this sort of background to become Communists.'[14] In Hill's case,
beyond the possible political links, the connection between
Nonconformism and his intellectual interests and commitments
can also be seen in his studies of seventeenth-century England,
from *Economic Problems of the Church: From Archbishop Whitgift
to the Long Parliament*[15] to *The World Turned Upside Down* and,
perhaps especially well, in his own work ethic and the volume
of his scholarship.

Civil War Studies and the Bourgeis Revolution Thesis

*One who studies the development of social theory can hardly hope
to avoid the criticism which is brought against those who disturb
the dust in forgotten lumber-rooms. If he seeks an excuse beyond
his own curiosity, he may find it, perhaps, in the reflection that the*

past reveals to the present what the present is capable of seeing,
and that the face which to one age is a blank to another be pregnant
with meaning. R. H. Tawney[16]

Hill's early writings drew on the statements on the English
Revolution found in the writings of Marx and Engels, which
are numerous, but dispersed, and the studies being done by
Soviet historians on the political and economic history of the
period.[17] It was Hill's intention that the Marxist interpretation
of history should provide for the reintegration of the study
of the English Revolution, which had splintered into several
narrow specialisms and associated perspectives. The early
development of Hill's work ought to be considered, then,
in light of the contemporaneous state of both 'academic' and
Marxist historical studies of the seventeenth century.

The dominant paradigm for generations of British historians
was the Whig interpretation of history, perhaps especially
regarding the upheavals of the seventeenth century. Depending
on the specific articulation of this approach, the English Civil
War, or Revolution, was presented as a constitutional, political
or religious conflict. It was viewed as a struggle for liberties,
defined in constitutional or narrowly political terms or, as in
the 'Gardiner thesis'[18] (which became dominant in the late-
nineteenth and early-twentieth century), it was a religious
struggle – the 'Puritan Revolution'.

In the period when Hill first began to develop his view of
the English Revolution (the late thirties and forties), the Whig
interpretation and the Gardiner thesis, though still important
and influential, were, however, no longer predominant. This
was due in good part to the work of R. H. Tawney (1880-1962),
whose writings were most effective in showing the inadequacies
of purely constitutional or religious analyses of the Civil War
and seventeenth-century England.

Tawney was one of Britain's leading historians and social

essayists of this century and he wrote several works of importance to seventeenth-century studies.[19] His particular interest was in the rise of capitalism (though it was not necessarily conceived of in Marxist terms). He sought to re-examine the political and religious conflicts of the Civil War in relation to the economic history of the sixteenth and seventeenth centuries. The works for which he is most noted in this area are his books *The Agrarian Problem in the Sixteenth Century* and *Religion and the Rise of Capitalism*, and his seminal article, 'The Rise of the Gentry, 1558-1640'.[20] In the first study, Tawney presents an analysis of the development of rural capitalism in England, and, in the second, he re-examines the issue which Weber pursues in *The Protestant Ethic and the Spirit of Capitalism*[21] (Hill offers his own argument on this issue, which will be considered later in this chapter.) In 'The Rise of the Gentry', which generated a major controversy in seventeenth-century studies,[22] Tawney presents a 'sociological' analysis of the Civil War wherein political power was realigned in relation to the economic power structure which had been developing as a result of changes in the agrarian economy.[23]

The impact of such studies, not to mention the changed political and economic situation in Britain, was to force a reconsideration of the struggles which had occurred in seventeenth-century England as having involved not just a conflict of constitutional principles, or differing conceptions of liberty, but also conflict over material interests. (In this sense, although Tawney was a Christian socialist not a Marxist, he appreciated and was influenced by Marx.) Thus, Tawney's work, in seeking to broaden the historical perspective on the Civil War, enlarged the very scope of seventeenth-century studies, and in so doing effectively challenged the Gardiner thesis of the Puritan Revolution. Yet his work did not provide a new, integrative thesis. It was in this context that Hill offered his own interpretation.

Although the bourgeois revolution thesis has (rightly) come

to be associated with Hill's work, he did not develop the thesis in isolation, nor was he the only British historian to present it. The view that the English Revolution was a bourgeois one developed, of course, among Marxist historians. There were the statements by Marx and Engels and the research of the Soviet historians which Hill was active in presenting to English readers. And most important amongst British Marxist historical writings of the time, there were the studies by A. L. Morton, *A People's History of England*,[24] and Maurice Dobb, *Studies in the Development of Capitalism*.[25]

A People's History of England was written by Morton to present a popular, comprehensive, Marxist interpretation of English history. It is a 'people's history' in the double sense that it is intended for a popular audience, as opposed to a merely academic one, and its class-struggle analysis involves elements of a history from the bottom up, not just a history of the monarchy and upper classes. Not surprisingly, the upheavals of the seventeenth century figure prominently in Morton's book. The interpretation he offers is that 'in spite of all that has been said to the contrary it cannot be too strongly insisted upon that the Civil War *was* a class struggle, *was* revolutionary, and *was* progressive'.[26]

Hill's first significant essay, *The English Revolution, 1640*,[27] was published in 1940. In it, he too presents the bourgeois revolution thesis: 'the English Revolution of 1640-60 was a great social movement like the French Revolution of 1789. The state power protecting an old order that was essentially feudal was violently overthrown, power passed into the hands of a new class, and so the freer development of capitalism was made possible.' Furthermore, he continues, 'the Civil War was a class war, in which the despotism of Charles I was defended by the reactionary forces of the established Church and conservative landlords. Parliament beat the King because it could appeal to the enthusiastic support of the trading and industrial classes in town and countryside, to the yeoman and progressive gentry, and to wider masses of the population whenever they were able by free discussion to understand what the struggle was really about.'[28]

Clearly, such an interpretation was bound to be controversial in terms of 'academic' historical studies of the Civil War, but it was also controversial to Marxists. Hill's essay sparked off a very lively exchange among Marxist historians regarding (1) the whole issue of the characterization of the mode of production of sixteenth- and early seventeenth-century England, and (2) the class basis of the absolute monarchy in England.[29] Although discussion of the first issue was limited to British Communist historians, it did, thereby, contribute to Dobb's writing of *Studies* and to the debate which followed its publication.

As the above quotation from *1640* states, Hill's argument at this time was that the pre-Civil War social order was 'essentially feudal' and that the Civil War, as a class war resulting in revolution, brought an end to that social order and the state which had maintained it. That is, the Revolution was bourgeois because it resulted in capitalism replacing feudalism. Although it was basically this position and later (in a much-refined version) Dobb's that held sway amongst British Communist historians,[30] opposition to it came from such outstanding Marxists as Jurgen Kuczynski[31] and Victor Kiernan.[32] And, although Hill continues to support the thesis that the English Revolution was a bourgeois one, he has now dropped his assertion that sixteenth-century England was necessarily feudal.[33]

Hill has insisted that he was not merely interested in an economic mode of analysis nor such an interpretation of the Civil War. He points out that Tawney and others, who were themselves influenced by Marx (whether or not they acknowledged it), had already gone some way in showing that the Civil War had involved conflicts over material interests.[34] What Hill did develop is a *social* interpretation of the English

Revolution which is not simply political, economic or religious, but rather comprehensive of all these. He writes: 'we must widen our view so as to embrace the total activity of society. Any event so complex as a revolution must be seen as a whole. Large numbers of men and women were drawn into political activity by religious and political ideals as well as by economic necessities.'[35]

The English Revolution as a Bourgeois Revolution

In the history of primitive accumulation, all revolutions are epoch-making that act as levers for the capitalist class in the course of its formation. Karl Marx[36]

If we are to appreciate his contributions, it is important that we understand what Hill intends by the thesis that the English Revolution was a bourgeois revolution. His most recent writings show that he does not mean that it was a revolution 'made by or consciously willed by the bourgeoisie'.[37] Rather, he means that the 'revolution...... cleared the way for the capitalist development that made it possible for England to become the country of the first Industrial Revolution.'[38] Furthermore, in arguing that the English Revolution paved the way for the accelerated development of capitalism, he does not mean that it involved merely polihtico-economic change any more than constitutional, political or religious change: 'a Revolution embraces all aspects of social life and activity'.[39]

It is true that the most basic element of Hill's thesis has always been that the Revolution radically furthered the development of capitalism (and, thereby, industry) and, also, that he has always insisted that it must be comprehended as a totality. However, the bourgeois revolution thesis has not always been limited to such an argument, nor has Hill always been effective in presenting an analysis of the Revolution which has appreciated it in its totality. While his basic argument has remained – from his early writings to his most recent – he has made modifications to it.

In his early efforts to present a class-struggle analysis of the seventeenth century (e.g. *1640)*, Hill presented the Revolution as an epochal confrontation between two clearly defined and self-conscious classes – the aristocracy and the bourgeoisie – representing feudalism and capitalism, respectively. It was a bourgeois revolution, then, not just in terms of its consequences, but also because it was made – if not consciously willed – by the bourgeoisie (a 'new class of capitalist merchants and farmers'), both as an effort to wrest political power away from the feudal aristocracy and monarchy, and to further the development of capitalism (i.e. that class's own economic interests).

However, in the course of his research and writing, Hill altered this presentation. He has not ceased to view the English Revolution as epochally important, but he now sees its significance in its determination of the *course* which British capitalism was to take, not so much whether or not capitalism would in the end be victorious over feudalism. Thus, he has come more recently to describe the Revolution in the following way: 'Two conceptions of civilization were in conflict. One took French absolutism for its model, the other the Dutch Republic.'[40] Or, as on another occasion: 'The English Revolution, like all revolutions, was caused by the breakdown of the old society; it was brought about neither by the wishes of the bourgeoisie, nor by the leaders of the Long Parliament. But its *outcome* was the establishment of conditions far more favourable to the development of capitalism than those which prevailed before 1640.'[41] The modifications which Hill has made to his thesis are the result of his continuing development of a class-struggle analysis.

The historical theme which frames Hill's work is, then, the rise of capitalism. In England, *agrarian* capitalism developed through the course of changes wrought by class struggles between landlords and peasants during the late medieval period, but its further growth and development into industrial capitalism was not so assured.

In *Reformation to Industrial Revolution: A Social and Economic History of Britain, 1530-1780* (1969),[42] Hill examines this period of transition as that of 'the making of modern English society', always stressing the *interaction* between politics and economics. He does not analyze the changes (and continuities) in English society during these 250 years merely as adaptations to the development of capitalism, conceived of as an autonomously determining realm of economic activities, but as outcomes of actions and struggles among classes. Early in the work, Hill introduces the social classes of sixteenth-century, pre-revolutionary England. There was the landed ruling class, which was composed in the first place of the aristocracy, but also increasingly included the gentry. 'On top' as well was the wealthy merchant class, especially of London. Then there was the group beneath the large land-owning and merchant families which Hill calls the 'middle' class, made up of 'most merchants, richer artisans, the independent peasantry (yeomanry) and well-to-do tenant farmers'. On the bottom were the lower orders, or propertyless, who depended on wage labour and/or charity for their survival. This last group, with segments of the 'middle sort', made up the 'common people'. Hill then proceeds to present the transformation of English society in the areas of agriculture and agrarian relations, industry, government, trade and foreign policy, and religion and intellectual life by way of a class-struggle analysis. For example, regarding agriculture and agricultural relations, he points out that although peasant uprisings occurred throughout the sixteenth and into the seventeenth century, the ever-increasing differentiation amongst the peasantry inhibited any 'successful' peasant rebellion because better-off peasants tended to share the 'outlook and interests of gentlemen and merchants rather than of landless labourers and subsistence husbandmen'.[43] Thus, a major result of the English Revolution was the furtherance of the process of enclosure and, thereby, the expansion of agrarian capitalism, which provided the necessary accumulation of capital for industrial development.

The first two major monographs which Hill wrote, *Economic Problems of the Church* (1956) and *Society and Puritanism in Pre-Revolutionary England* (1964), as well as numerous articles,'[44] especially 'Protestantism and the Rise of Capitalism',[45] take up the relationship between religion and class (in light of the development of capitalism) and its contribution to the making of the English Revolution. Although he rejects Gardiner's Puritan Revolution thesis, Hill recognizes that religion was too important an institution in sixteenth- and seventeenth-century England – materially and otherwise – to be reduced to either the merely economic or the merely ideological.

Though Hill calls *Economic Problems of the Church* an economic study, it is, in fact, a *politico-economic* study of the English Church in relation to the development of capitalism in the sixteenth and seventeenth centuries. Hill shows that the Church, which was as much an economic and political institution as a religious one, was confronted with a series of major problems as a result of the economic developments of the period, which included the plundering of the Church's property as part of the English Reformation. He goes on to argue that the way in which the Church hierarchy sought to resolve those problems, or contradictions, contributed significantly to the formation and alignment of the two sides in the Civil War. He writes: 'It was the retrogressiveness of the hierarchy's solutions, their unacceptability to the social groups which the House of Commons represented, that forced the bishops into that close co-operation with the government which reached its height under Laud, [Archbishop of Canterbury, 1733-45] and brought church and state down together.'[46]

In order to pre-empt the criticism that a Marxist interpretation was merely economic determinism, Hill points out that he had pursued a (politico-)economic study of the English Church because it had yet to be adequately considered in Civil War studies. Moreover, he adds that the Church was a convenient *starting place* for a reconsideration of the role of religion and ideas in the English Revolution. He also indicates the direction that much of his later work in this area takes: 'All I would suggest', he writes, 'is that revolutions are made not only by the great symbolic figures whom posterity recollects, but also by nameless masses of men and women. The higher flights of theory may have passed them by. They expected, however, that political ideas or platforms of church government should be rooted in experience.'[47]

Where Economic Problems of the Church is a study of why some men, for non-theological reasons, would oppose the English Church as it was constituted, *Society and Puritanism in Pre-Revolutionary England* is a companion study of why, also for non-theological reasons, they would support Puritanism or 'become' Puritans themselves. In the first chapter, Hill considers the problem of defining a Puritan in sixteenth- and seventeenth-century England. He warns us away from a too-narrow religious conception (and also from projecting our modern notion of Puritans as 'killjoys' onto the period), and explains that the term had religious, political and social connotations to contemporaries. In religious matters Puritans wanted reforms in the Church, i.e. they were not separatists – at least not until 1640. In politics, they were opposed to the Court and its policies, and favoured Parliament, i.e. the Commons. (Hill adds a warning that we should not draw too sharp a distinction between religion and politics in this period.) And socially, Puritans were those of a particular rank or social class, i.e. the middle sort of people or, as Hill termed them in this book, the 'industrious sort of people – yeomen, artisans and small and middling merchants'. The actual focus of *Society and Puritanism* is the body of doctrines and practices that was labelled Puritanism and its appeal to the middle, or industrious, sort of people.'[48] In this long, yet fascinating, study Hill presents a veritable sociology of knowledge of the relationship between the middle sort of people and the values and practices of Puritanism. He deals with such subjects as the importance of preaching and lecturing to Puritan congregations, and the social and political consequences of Puritan efforts to control such appointments; the Puritan elevation of the Sabbath (Sabbatarianism) as a day of rest and meditation, and the denigration of the traditional Saints' Days and festivals – to assure 'the liberty of working six days in the week'; the emphasis on self-discipline, which prepared Puritans 'for intense and devoted activity in all spheres of life, and for actions requiring great political courage'; the Puritan work ethic, which he points out was double-edged, i.e. the dignity of labour appealed to the 'smaller employers and self-employed men', but was potentially subversive for 'it was possible to conclude that idleness should lead to expropriation: no labour, no property'.[49] He also considers the Puritan attitudes to charity and the poor (and the control of the two), the political role of the Church, and the changing conceptions of community, household and family, and the individual. The development of such practices and values, Hill argues, confronted the Church's own efforts to restore its position of dominance in English political and religious life.

A particular characteristic of Hill's work is that he recognizes and draws out the connections between seemingly discrete areas of social activity and cultural practice. Moreover, he explains the inherent tensions and potential contradictions of Puritan experience, practices and ideas in the context of the class structure and struggles of sixteenth- and seventeenth-century England. In this regard, *Society and Puritanism* may be Hill's best book. One cannot read this study without having to reconsider the one-dimensional images traditionally associated with Puritanism. On the one hand, the conception of a relationship between Puritanism and the development of English capitalism is confirmed by Hill. On the other hand, he also indicates how those very same aspects of Puritan thought and practice which contributed to capitalist development were potentially subversive of it, in that they pointed towards radical democracy. (The development of the radical-democratic aspect of Puritanism is taken up by Hill in his later studies, as we shall see.)

Society and Puritanism might, then, seem like a confirmation of the thesis offered by both Max Weber and R. H. Tawney, regarding the relationship between Puritanism and capitalism. But, actually, Hill is recomposing their thesis. Whereas the Weber-Tawney thesis tends to 'put the *ideas* in the forefront of any explanation of the great social changes which took place in England',[50] Hill starts by switching the order of priority. Of particular relevance in this regard is his article, 'Protestantism and the Rise of Capitalism' (originally written, in fact, for a volume honouring Tawney).[51] Here Hill reconsiders the 'Protestant ethic' thesis and offers his own version of it (at the same time he offers a hypothesis on the source of modernm individualism). He compares the Protestant doctrine of justification by faith with the Roman Catholic doctrine of justification by works. He points out that Protestants criticized Catholics for the *ritualistic* nature of their performance of so-called 'good works', which seemed to be fostered by the Catholic Church itself. In contrast, Protestants believed that the spirit in which a man acted was more important than the actions themselves; that is, 'a good man made a good work, not a good work a good man.' Moreover, the only *person* who could judge the motives, intentions, and faith involved was the believer himself, as opposed to a priest of the Church. The believer, then, had to 'look inward to his own heart', a practice which gave to Protestantism its fundamentally individualist bias. At the same time, there was nothing specifically characteristic of Protestantism which automatically generated capitalism. Its significance was that it 'undermined obstacles which the more rigid institutions and ceremonies imposed'. The middle sort of people might be 'convinced in their hearts that industry was a good work, for the common good . . . But men did not become capitalists because they were protestants, nor protestants because they were capitalists.' Rather, 'in a society already becoming capitalist, protestantism facilitated the triumph of the new values.' In other words, the Protestant emphasis on 'frugality, hard work, [and] accumulation' was not due to something uniquely inherent in Protestant theology but was a 'natural consequence of the religion of the heart in a society where capitalist production was developing'. Moreover, protestantism had different 'effects' in different countries and among different classes. As Hill points out, the very same sets of ideas and principles which appealed to the middle class in England also appealed to quite different discontented groups in other societies, 'like the gentry of Hungary and Scotland, or the plebeians of the Dutch towns'. Moreover, 'protestant churches were established in Scandinavia [and] central Europe' but they apparently 'made only slight and incidental contributions to the development of capitalism'.[52]

Hill's work on the social bases of ideas in sixteenth- and seventeenth-century England, especially the ideas which appealed to the middle sort of people, is not limited to religion but includes his study of the *Intellectual Origins of the English Revolutions*.[53] In this work, Hill considers the development of the new ideas in, and new conceptions of, science, history and the law, and their contributions to the making of the English Revolution. He does so by focusing on the pivotal figures of the period in those areas: Francis Bacon, Walter Raleigh, and Edward Coke. Thus, for example regarding Bacon's work, Hill argues that his essential contribution was to synthesize and systematize the practice and thought which had been developing during the sixteenth century in scientific and medical studies, with the very active support of the middle sort of people, especially in London around such alternative centres as Gresham College ('alternative', that is, to the conservative Oxbridge universities). Bacon emphasized the empirical and experimental approach to knowledge and, thereby, 'elevated to a coherent intellectual system what had hitherto been only the partially spoken assumptions of practical men'. In this way he 'caught the optimism of the merchants and craftsmen, confident in their new-found ability to control their environment [after 1640 especially], including the social and political environment: and their contempt for the old scholasticism'. Similarly, Raleigh, in respect to history and historical consciousness, and Coke, in his assertion of the primacy of common law and its elevation to the level of a national myth, synthesized and articulated ideas and perspectives which appealed and gave 'confidence' to the middle sort of people: 'All three provided ideas for the men who hitherto had existed only to be ruled, but who in the sixteen-forties would help to take over the government. Together with the Puritan sense of destiny and emphasis on self-help, they prepared men for revolution.'[54]

Hill pursues studies of the middle sort of people in particular because it was this class (though not alone) that turned the Civil War into a revolution. They did not start the Civil War, nor consciously will that it would result in a social order conducive to the further development of capitalism, but they turned that struggle into the English Revolution. (On the question of who started the Civil War, Hill states that it began as a struggle between two factions of the landed ruling class. Each of the factions was defined in part by its respective relationship to the Crown – a Crown unable to govern in the traditional way, yet unable to transform itself.)[55] Hill seeks to show that the middle sort of people, who supported Parliament against the King and his supporters, did not act merely out of economic interest but were motivated by ideas and values which had developed out of the totality of their class experience – economic, political, religious, etc. Again, they did not consciously will a revolution to further capitalism. But out of the upheavals to which they contributed, and which their leaders sought to master, changes were wrought by 1660 in the political and social structure which, regardless of what was intended by those who instigated them, had the effect of making possible a dramatic acceleration in the development of English capitalism.[56]

Again, it should be noted that these studies indicate both change and continuity in Hill's thesis from his earlier to his later writings. They indicate change in that Hill's conception of a bourgeois revolution is modified. It no longer necessarily refers to confrontation between a *feudal* aristocracy and a *capitalist* bourgeoisie. At the same time, however, there is continuity in Hill's basic argument that the English Revolution was a bourgeois revolution in that its outcome decisively favoured the development of capitalism.[57]

The further development of Hill's class-struggle analysis has led not only to modifications in the bourgeois revolution thesis, but also in his conceptualization of the totality of class experience. He has always been especially interested in the culture and ideas of the century of revolution, as his references to the early influence of T. S. Eliot and his comments on Milton et al. in this early work indicate.[58] Yet in his early writings, in spite of his sincere interest in the thought of the period, the social totality is often theorized in terms of the base-superstructure model: 'the economic stage of development determines ultimately both the political superstructure and the ideology of that society.'[59] Later, as in the studies of the middle class, he sought to present a sociology of culture and ideas which remained materialist, but was no longer harnessed to that model. Thus, in *Intellectual Origins of the English Revolution,* he warns against economic determinism: 'a sociological approach to intellectual history carries its own risks. Marx himself did not fall into the error of thinking that men's ideas were merely a pale reflection of their economic needs, with no history of their own; but some of his successors, including many who would not call themselves Marxists, have been far more economic-determinist than Marx.' At the same time, he writes, 'It seems to me that any body of thought which plays a major part in history – Luther's, Rousseau's, Marx's own – "takes on" because it meets the needs of significant groups in the society in which it comes into prominence.'[60]

More recently, in an essay on the problem of the relation between economics and culture for the history of ideas, Hill indirectly indicates his conception of class-struggle analysis. He states that 'economic history is essential to historians of culture because culture is a class phenomenon'.This would seem to mean that class relations are determined by the social relations of production, but also that a class-struggle analysis must necessarily appreciate the totality of class experience. Furthermore, he writes, 'all history should be cultural history, and the best history is.' That is, the social relations of production are themselves determined by the struggle between classes, which is as much cultural as it is economic, *viz.* the theory of class determination.[61]

The English Revolution as a Defeated Democratic Revolution

The poorest he that is in England hath a life to live as the greatest he; and therefore truly, sir, I think it's clear that every man that is to live under a government ought first by his own consent to put himself under that government; and I do think that the poorest man in England is not at all bound in a strict sense to that government that he hath not had a voice to put himself under. Colonel Rainsborough at the Putney Debates[62]

Although this section focuses on those writings in which Hill has emphasized the defeated democratic struggles of the English Revolution, it would be wrong to differentiate too sharply between these and his studies of the middle sort of people which have already been discussed. *Society and Puritanism* and *Intellectual Origins of the English Revolution* are not merely about the middle class in relation to nascent capitalism, but also note the radical-democratic reality or potential of the values and practices of Puritanism and the scientific-intellectual thought of the time. Hill himself always emphasizes that they were all part of a 'single revolution'.

Within that single English Revolution, however, Hill identifies two linked, but distinct, revolutions, one of which succeeded, while the other failed. The one that succeeded was the bourgeois revolution which concluded with the forceful ejection of James II from England in 1688. In the course of this revolution there was 'the civil war of 1642-6, the trial and execution of King Charles I, the proclamation of the English Republic, [and] the abolition of the House of Lords'. Politically, it meant that the efforts of the Stuart kings and their bishops to create an absolutist regime had been defeated. Moreover, it made crown and church subservient 'to Parliament (representing the gentry and merchants) and to the common law (adapted to the interests of the propertied classes)'. It also, of course, ensured the further development of capitalism.

Had the other revolution succeeded, Hill argues, we would have had a very different England. This revolution began when the troops of the New Model Army, whom Parliament had mobilized to fight the King, began to have aspirations of their own. With the London Leveller party, they proposed the redistribution and extension of the 'Parliamentary franchise to all men, or nearly all men, reforming the law in the interests of the middling sort'; the establishment of 'security of ownership' for the small as well as the large property holders; and the institutionalization of the religious freedom which had emerged in the period after 1640. Nevertheless, Hill contends, this movement was of momentous importance, for 'it was this radical movement which forced the trial and execution of the King as a traitor to the people of England'. Moreover, in the midst of the unprecedented freedom of the decade or so after 1640, this movement actively instigated vigorous and fascinating discussions on a whole range of subjects. Though the participants articulated their positions in religious terms, the ideas and pronouncements were often 'revolutionary'. As Hill sums up: 'Levellers called for political democracy. Diggers for communism. Ranters for free love. Others called in question the common law, the Bible, the existence of heaven and hell, God and the devil.'[63]

This revolution, Hill argues, would have been the revolution of the 'common people'. The term appears to encompass elements of both the middle and the lower orders. Hill has not, however, written extensively on the common people nor pursued a general sociology of their way of life, though he has said, in invitation to younger historians, that 'we know far too little about those who lived in mud houses, ate rye and bran bread, and got a high proportion of their calories (if they were lucky) from home-brewed beer'.[64] Rather, what he has studied are the radical groups of the Revolution and the ideas articulated by them. He stresses that they have too often been marginalized by historians who have been more interested in narrowly political or religious aspects of the seventeenth century. Hill has sought to show that the ideas articulated, fought for, and/or *practised* by those groups were politically and culturally meaningful and consequential in seventeenth-century terms and that they contributed decisively to the making of modern history.

Hill has had a long-standing interest in both history from the bottom up and the radical groups of the English Revolution, especially the Levellers and Diggers. This is seen even in his early writings. In one of the early essays, he says that the development of a Marxist approach to history has not only academic but also political value in that 'it alone, can restore to the English people part of their heritage of which they have been robbed'. He laments the fact that, whereas for the French, 1789 seems to mean a great deal, for the English 1640 has little meaning: 'The Jacobins are still alive in France today: not the Levellers in England.' Hill places the blame for this historical amnesia on the part of the English with historians, and he censures them for continuing to propagate the notion that the English Revolution was a Puritan one. The problem is that the Puritan revolution theory emphasizes 'the differences between our seventeenth-century forefathers and present-day Englishmen, between their struggles and ours. So school children find the most enthralling episodes in the history of their country boring. Marxism by showing the unity of society, the class basis of political and ideological conflicts can make the past live again.'[65] This, of course, had been the intention behind Morton's *A People's History of England,* and became an important aspect of the work of the Communist Party Historians' Group. In fact, as previously noted, it was for the Group's volume, *Democracy and the Labour Movement,* that Hill wrote his classic essay, 'The Norman Yoke',[66] which provides further evidence that we should not see 1956-7 as a 'break' in Hill's work.

'The Norman Yoke' is a classic piece both for the substance of its argument and because it represents – as an approach to the history and sociology of ideas – one of Hill's most important contributions to the theory of class determination. For it offers an analysis of the history of the Norman Yoke theory in terms of the class-differential ways in which it was interpreted. Just as Hill warns against the assumption that men's ideas are 'merely a pale reflection of their economic needs,' he also warns against the assumption that the ideas of the ruling class are necessarily the ideas of the ruled, even if it *appears* to be so for a period of time. He writes: 'The fact that the same words can signify different things at different times should help us also to grasp that the same ideas can point to different conclusions for different classes at the same time.'[67] (He adds that, unfortunately, 'historians always, by the nature of the surviving evidence, tend to find ruling class views the easiest to recapture in any society: the viewpoint of the underdog has to be reconstructed painfully and piecemeal'.)

Hill discusses the Norman Yoke theory as the specifically English version of the 'theory of lost rights', or myth of a Golden Age, which has 'existed in nearly all communities'. It is a theory that took many forms and that left a lot to be desired as an actual historical account of the Norman Conquest and subsequent history. Hill summarizes it as follows:

> Before 1066 the Anglo-Saxon inhabitants of this country lived as free and equal citizens, governing themselves through representative institutions. The Norman Conquest deprived them of this liberty, and established the tyranny of an alien King and landlords. But the people did not forget the rights they had lost. They fought continuously to recover them, with varying success. Concessions (Magna Carta, for instance) were from time to time extorted from their rulers, and always the tradition of lost Anglo-Saxon freedom was a stimulus to ever more insistent demands upon the successors of the Norman usurpers.[68]

The most important aspect of the essay is that Hill examines the Norman Yoke theory in terms of the class-differential interpretations of it. He explains that at the outset it appealed to 'all the underprivileged'. It even appealed to the merchants and gentry who, though they were becoming very much a part of the dominant class, nevertheless stood second, in status, to the 'feudal' aristocracy and absolute monarchy, which, according to the Norman Yoke theory, had been introduced into

England by the Norman Conquest. In fact, the Royalist version of the theory justified absolutism and feudal prerogatives by the fact of the Conquest. These merchants and gentry 'felt their property endangered by arbitrary government, arbitrary taxation, and the enforcement of feudal payments,' and they saw the 'common law', which, according to their conception of the Norman Yoke, had survived the Norman Conquest, as 'the embodiment of Anglo-Saxon liberties'. Represented by the conservative Parliamentarians, they proposed that to end the Norman Yoke it was merely necessary to abolish the repressive monarchy, in favour of the rule of common law.

Another version of the Norman Yoke theory was advanced by the Levellers. Representing 'the small proprietors of town and countryside', the Levellers were radical democrats. For them, the abolition of monarchy was insufficient to rid England of Normanism. Rather, it was necessary to carry out both drastic political and legal reforms, including a wide extension of manhood suffrage. For the Levellers, the victory of Parliament needed to be followed up by making Parliament itself more representative of the English people.[69]

There was still another version of the Norman Yoke theory, put forward by the Diggers – the 'spokesmen for the dispossessed' and the 'most radical group of all.' In this version, if England was to be cleansed of Normanism and a true commonwealth established, it was necessary not only to institute political and legal reforms, but also to put an end to 'all feudal survivals and property in land'.[70]

In *Antichrist in Seventeenth-Century England* (1971), a work reminiscent of 'The Norman Yoke', Hill pursues the 'Antichrist myth' through its several transformations in English history prior to and during the 1600s. He traces it to its origins in the Middle Ages as a subversive and heretical doctrine; pursues it into Reformation England, where it was propagated by church and state in a 'respectable' version which declared that the

Antichrist was the Pope in Rome; and then follows it immediately thereafter to its re-emergence in the late sixteenth century as a subversive idea, when Puritans began to see the Antichrist in the Church of England. In this last permutation the myth was used to mobilize the common people against the bishops and royal absolutism in the 1640s. But even that was not the end of the story. Prior to the Civil War the simple equation of the Antichrist with the crown and its high clerics was sufficient to harness the support of the 'revolutionary Utopians of the lower classes' to the cause of the Parliamentary opposition. But after victory in the Civil War was secured it became quite clear that, whereas the lower-class radicals were anxious to carry out a broad campaign against the Antichrist, the 'sober leaders' of the Parliamentary opposition had only been looking 'to get rid of antichristian bishops'.[71] Among those who argued that a social revolution was necessary to rid the earth of the Antichrist was Gerrard Winstanley, a leader and spokesman of the Diggers, and a figure whom Hill takes up at greater length in what many regard as his most exciting book. *The World Turned Upside Down: Radical Ideas During the English Revolution.*

In this book Hill looks directly at the English revolution 'which never happened, though from time to time it threatened.' Had it actually happened, it 'might have established communal property, a far wider democracy in political and legal institutions, might have disestablished the state church and rejected the protestant ethic.' *The World Turned Upside Down* is a study of the radical movements of the common people – the Levellers, the Diggers, the Ranters and other religious groups – which emerged in the 1640s and 1650s, when 'literally anything seemed possible'.[72]

The Levellers sought political democracy, that is, a wide extension of the Parliamentary franchise. Winstanley and the Diggers or, as they called themselves, the True Levellers, wanted to extend these demands to include economic democracy by way of land reform leading to common cultivation:

> The poorest man hath as true a title and just right to the land
> as the richest man.... True freedom lies in the free enjoyment
> of the earth.... If the common people have no more freedom
> in England but only to live among their elder brothers and
> work for them for hire, what freedom then have they in
> England more than we can have in Turkey or France?[73]

The Diggers went so far as to carry out land invasions in which,
having successfully occupied the land, they would proceed
with collective cultivation as, for example, at St George's Hill
in 1649.[74]

Hill also looks at the Ranters. This was a group which at first
sight does not appear to have had any 'politics'. But, Hill shows,
the Ranters' ethic 'involved a real subversion of existing society
and its values'. They believed that the earth had been created
for man, and that all men were equal. Moreover, many Ranters
preached that there was no heaven or hell, no afterlife and that
'all that matters is here and now'. They emphasized the unity
of God's creation and love and, in fact, regularly preached and
practised 'free love'. In the end, Hill urges us to see the Ranters'
ideas as a 'negative reaction' to the development of capitalism.
He describes their movement as 'a cry for human brotherhood,
freedom and unity against the divisive forces of a harsh ethic
enforced by the harsh discipline of the market'.[75]

Hill makes it clear from the outset of the book that it is written
from what he calls 'the worm's eye view'. His intention is to
reconsider the radical religious groups which had traditionally
been viewed as the 'lunatic fringe' by historians of the English
Revolution, and thereby show that they and their ideas were
politically and culturally meaningful in the historically specific
terms of the seventeenth century. 'Upside down is after all a
relative concept,' Hill tells us. He asks if we have not become

so used to comprehending the developments of the last three centuries as the only way things might have been that we are unable to be 'fair to those in the seventeenth century who saw other possibilities'. But, on the assumption that we are still capable of historical empathy, he suggests that we consider the possibility that many of the radicals' seemingly outlandish and utopian views 'are not necessarily opposed to order; they merely envisage a different order'. Furthermore, Hill believes that such reconsideration would both enable us to 'obtain a deeper insight into English society' of the seventeenth century, and might also speak to the age in which we live. In the same fashion that the establishment of 'political democracy' in England brought a new appreciation of the Levellers in the late nineteenth and early twentieth century, Hill suggests that 'the Diggers have something to say to twentieth-century socialists.' In fact, he continues, 'now that the protestant ethic itself, the greatest achievement of European bourgeois society in the sixteenth and seventeenth centuries, is at last being questioned after a rule of three or four centuries, we can study with a new sympathy the Diggers, the Ranters, and the many other daring thinkers who in the seventeenth century refused to bow down and worship'.[76]

Yet these radical groups of the common people were not only 'meaningful' or 'reasonable'[77] in seventeenth-century terms, they were also consequential. They were both a radical force in the revolutionary decades (1640s-50s) – pushing the Parliamentarians further than they would have gone in the Civil War – and they contributed to later struggles. Though it was the fear of a resurgence of revolutionary activity among the common people that reunited the propertied classes and thus instigated the Restoration in 1660, 'without the pressure of the radicals the Civil War might not have been transformed into a Revolution'.[78] The ideas of the radicals, along with the much more successful ideas of the bourgeois revolution, also contributed to the radical tradition and, thus, to later struggles in England, America and France.[79]

Hill's century of revolution is, then, a period of class antagonism, of class conflict and struggle. But what about those historians who reject Hill's argument that the seventeenth century can be understood in these terms either because they do not believe classes existed before industrial capitalism or because, as Peter Laslett argues in *The World We Have Lost*,[80] only the ruling class was *conscious* of itself as a class in seventeenth-century England? Hill responds, first, that, 'I think of class as defined by the objective position of its members in relation to the productive process and to other classes. Men become conscious of shared interests in the process of struggling against common enemies, but this struggle can go a long way before one can call it "class consciousness".'[81] Second, he claims that the supposed consciousness of the members of the landed ruling class of sixteenth- and seventeenth-century England was necessarily determined by their own awareness of the class antagonism, tension and struggle, which characterized the society they ruled and which could potentially break through to rebellion.[82] Furthermore, it needs to be remembered that their experience of class antagonism was expressed, not surprisingly, in seventeenth-century terms, and thus quite often in specifically religious terms. 'Indeed,' Hill writes, 'it is perhaps misleading to differentiate too sharply between politics, religion, and general scepticism.'[83]

The Legacy of Revolutionary Ideas

Hill's studies of the seventeenth century[84] include writings on three individuals in particular from the revolutionary decades – Oliver Cromwell, John Milton and Gerrard Winstanley. In *God's Englishman: Oliver Cromwell and the English Revolution* (1972) he is not uncritical of Cromwell and his policies, but his appreciation of the man is evident. In the same way that Hill

laments the defeat of the democratic revolution, but nevertheless recognizes the historical legacy of the English Revolution – even as bourgeois – he acknowledges the significance of Cromwell. Actually, his book makes clear why Cromwell has been perceived as personifying the Revolution. He was Puritan and gentry; he both defeated the 'backward-looking loyalists' and suppressed the radicals, and thereby presided over the changes which laid the groundwork for the further development of England as a capitalist society and the expansion of British capitalism on a world scale. Yet the Cromwell to whom Hill seems particularly drawn is 'the boisterous and confident leader of the IMOs...
. . . whose pungent, earthy truths echo down the centuries'. He asserts that, for as long as people struggle over questions of liberty and equality, the struggles and actions of Oliver Cromwell will remain enthralling and controversial.[85]

Milton and the English Revolution is one of Hill's major studies. In it he examines Milton and his work firmly in the context of the seventeenth century and the Revolution with which he was so intimately involved. Most importantly, Hill sees Milton in relation to 'two overlapping circles'. One circle stands for traditional Puritan thought and the other for the ideas of the radical groups. Milton, he argues, drew his ideas from both circles, but his own ideas make up yet a third circle. The originality of Hill's work is his insistence that Milton must be recognized as 'living in a state of permanent dialogue' with the ideas of the radicals. He does not argue that Milton was a member of one of the radical groups, but while Milton was not a Leveller or Ranter he was definitely drawn to many of their ideas.[86] (In particular, among the radical groups, Hill sees Milton's ideas as being closest to the Muggletonians.)[87]

Yet the seventeenth-century figure whom Hill most appreciates is the Digger leader, Gerrard Winstanley. His writings on Winstanley include a lengthy discussion in *The World Turned Upside Down;* a substantial introduction to a selection of Winstanley's tracts which he edited, entitled *The Law of Freedom and Other Writings* (1973);[88] and a short monograph, entitled *The Religion of Gerrard Winstanley* (1978).[89] Hill claims that, though Winstanley's thought was influenced by an image and the values of a disappearing 'village community', it points towards the socialist and communist thought of the age of industrial capitalism. He says that it is characteristically modern in that it recognizes that 'state power is related to the property system and to the body of ideas which supports that system'. Moreover, he continues, Winstanley realized that political freedom ultimately depended upon economic equality and, thus, to establish freedom it was necessary to eliminate private property and wage labour. Hill grants that Winstanley did not create the first blueprint for a communist society but, he argues, Winstanley's work was original in that it was written at the zenith of a revolution, in the language of the common people, with the intention of calling the 'poorer classes to political action'.

The special affection for Winstanley which is evident in Hill's writings is due in great part to the originality of Winstanley's thought and his efforts to put them into practice. It also seems to be due to the fact that Winstanley's writings enable Hill to declare that England was not only the source of the 'starting texts' of 'conservative-individualist and liberal-democratic' thought, but also of socialist-communist thought. Moreover, Hill not only sees Winstanley's thought as pertinent to the history of ideas, but as having things to say to both socialist and Third World struggles today.[90]

The work which Hill is currently pursuing deals with the question of what happened to the radicals and their ideas following the revolutionary decades. This is of interest to more than just intellectual historians. Hill's analysis of the revolutionary decades has already shown that, given the opportunity, lower-class expressions of grievances and visions of alternative social orders can be most articulate. Thus, it is quite possible that before 1640 and after 1660 the same sentiments are there but expressed in different ways, and in different places. The theoretical conclusion is that 'we should not exclude the possibility that a class-dominated society may contain an egalitarian society struggling to get out; nor assume that the hegemony of one set of values excludes the possibility that other values exist, at a lower social level, or in the interstices, geographical or social, of an apparently homogeneous society'.[91]

Eric Hobsbawm, in the course of discussing the 'legacy' of the original Communist Party Historians' Group, comments on Hill's particular contribution: '[An] advantage of our Marxism – we owe it largely to Hill . . . was never to reduce history to a simple economic or 'class interest' determinism, or to devalue politics and ideology . . . [and] the serious concern with plebeian ideology – the theory underlying the actions of social movements – is still largely identified with historians of this provenance, for the social history of *ideas* was always (thanks largely to Hill) one of our main preoccupations.'[92]

Hill's work has made a major contribution to the British Marxist historians' theory of class determination and their efforts to overcome the base-superstructure model with its tendency to economic determinism. For, in his efforts to show that the English Revolution was not merely a political, religious, or economic revolution but 'embraced the whole of life', Hill clearly demonstrates the centrality of culture and ideas to a class-struggle analysis. Though he recognizes the historical determination of productive relations, he does not reduce history to determination by 'the base'. Rather, his class-struggle analysis involves study of the way in which life was structured by changing relations of production; the ways in which those structured experiences were understood and expressed in seventeenth-century terms, 'intellectually', and otherwise; and the ways in which they were developed or resisted, defended or attacked, secured or accommodated in class – though not necessarily fully 'class-conscious' fashion, thereby contributing in turn to the structuring of experience and ultimately determining the reproduction *or not* of the productive relations.

Of especial importance, I would argue, are Hill's studies of the class-differential interpretation of ideas in seventeenth-century England, which demonstrate that culture and ideas, or ideologies, are not so one-dimensional as we have often thought, nor the common people, or lower classes as simple. As he put it in *The World Turned Upside Down:*

Something analogous [to the English Revolution] occurred during the French Revolution. Middle-class revolutionaries proclaimed the Rights of Man, and seem to have been genuinely taken aback when the Fourth Estate claimed that they too were men. The distinction between active and passive citizens fulfills the same function as that between godly and ungodly . . . both justification by faith and the Rights of Man suffer from the same inescapable contradiction: in order to give the not-yet privileged confidence to fight against the old-type of inequality it is necessary to appeal to that in them which unites them against the privileged: their common humanity, the equality before God of those who believe themselves to be elect.[93]

Chapter 5

Eric Hobsbawm on Workers, Peasants and World History

To think everything historically, that is Marxism.... Born out of colonization and the 'world market', capitalism has universalized history. It has not unified it, certainly – this will be the task of another mode of production. It is in this perspective that the historian's ultimate ambition must lie. 'Universal history' belongs to yesterday. Its time is not yet over. There is something laughable about these remarks one now hears so frequently: 'We know too much', 'There are too many specialists', the world is 'too big' for any one man, one book, or one teaching-method to tackle 'universal history'. This implicit encyclopaedism is the polar opposite of the notion of 'reasoned history', 'total history' or – simply – the 'concept of history'. Pierre Vilar[1]

Eric Hobsbawm has been referred to as the premier Marxist historian working today.[2] This is due, no doubt, to the impressive array of subjects to which he has made significant contributions – in particular, labour history, peasant studies and world history. Whereas Rodney Hilton, Christopher Hill and Edward Thompson have worked primarily in British historical studies (Maurice Dobb's 'historical' writings beyond *Studies in the Development of Capitalism* and the history of economic thought were on Soviet economic development), Hobsbawm's writings have ranged geographically from Britain and Europe to Latin America. Moreover, while his major writings have focused on the nineteenth century, he has also written on the seventeenth, eighteenth and twentieth centuries. Beyond his extensive historical studies, he has also written articles and reviews on contemporary politics and society, historiography and social theory, and art and cultural criticism.³ (In fact, for more than ten years, Hobsbawm wrote as a jazz critic under the pseudonym of Francis Newton.)⁴

Although, as will be indicated, Hobsbawm has been less willing than the other British Marxist historians to reject the base-superstructure model, nevertheless I would argue that his work has been very much a part of the development of their theory of class determination. For not only has class-struggle analysis, pursued from the perspective of history from the bottom up, been central to Hobsbawm's historical studies but, as a result of this, he has 'opened up' new areas of study, such as 'primitive rebels', and transformed old ones, e.g. labour history and even, to some extent, world history. He has, in this way, contributed to the theory of class determination by broadening what we consider to be 'class experience', to be 'political', and to be subject to the determination of class struggle.

Eric Hobsbawm

Eric John Ernst Hobsbawm was born in the summer of 1917 in Alexandria, Egypt. His mother was Austrian and his father English (the son of a Russian-Jewish immigrant to the East End of London). Not long after he was born, Hobsbawm's family moved to Vienna (1919) and later to Berlin (1931), where they lived until Hitler came to power (1933). They then settled in England. Hobsbawm attended St Marylebone Grammar School (London) and went on to King's College, Cambridge, to read history.⁵ He has written that he considered himself a Marxist even as a schoolboy and that his pursuit of historical studies was because he answered exam questions in 'unexpected ways', and thus did well at it. At Cambridge he found himself among other Marxist students – from whom, he says, he learned more than from most professors – and was an active member of the Communist Party.⁶ His studies were interrupted by the War, during which he served in the education corps, returning afterwards to Cambridge to complete his degree.

In 1947 Hobsbawm was appointed a lecturer in history at Birkbeck College, University of London, becoming a Reader in 1959, and Professor of Economic and Social History in 1970 (a position he held until his retirement in 1982). From 1949 to 1955, he was a Fellow of King's College, Cambridge. He is currently a visiting professor at the New School for Social Research in New York.

While Hobsbawm has clearly been one of the *British* Marxist historians, the importance of his central European background should not be ignored. In an essay titled 'Intellectuals and Class Struggle', in which he discusses the making of the young French revolutionaries of May 1968 in Paris in historical and comparative perspective, Hobsbawm also comments on his own 'social biography'. He states that he sees himself as a survivor of the now all but extinguished 'Jewish middle-class culture of Central Europe after the first world war'. The demise of the pre-war social order, the Soviet Revolution, and the resurgent hatred of Jews left 'nothing but catastrophe and problematic survival. We lived on borrowed time and knew it. To make long-term plans seemed senseless....' He notes that 'we knew about the October Revolution.... It proved that capitalism could and indeed must end, whether we liked it or not.' The experience of the war and the Russian Revolution, the Depression, political unrest and the rise of fascism – these, Hobsbawm writes, 'were the times in which I became political'. He describes the political formation and 'choices' of his generation as follows:

What could young Jewish intellectuals have become under such circumstances? Not liberals of any kind, since the world of liberalism (which included social democracy) was precisely what had collapsed. As Jews we were precluded by definition from supporting parties based on confessional allegiance, or on a nationalism which excluded Jews, and in both cases on anti-semitism. We became either communists or some equivalent form of revolutionary marxists, or if we chose our own version of blood-and-soil nationalism, Zionists. But even the great bulk of young intellectual Zionists saw themselves as some sort of revolutionary marxist nationalists. There was virtually no other choice. We did not make a commitment against bourgeois society and capitalism, since it patently seemed to be on its last legs. We simply chose *a* future rather than *no* future, which meant revolution. But it meant revolution not in a negative but in a positive sense: a new world rather than no world.[7]

Furthermore, he explains, 'Soviet Russia seemed to prove to us that a new world was possible.' In this regard, it should be recalled that when Hilton, Hill, and Thompson (along with so many others) left the Communist Party in 1956-7, Hobsbawm stayed in (as did Dobb). He did so, he states, because of his belief in the necessity of a 'strongly organized party'.[8]

What impact has Hobsbawm's continuing membership in the Party had on his work? First, as mentioned in Chapter 1, he and others had serious reservations about pursuing twentieth-century history, at least until 1956, and he acknowledges that he took up nineteenth-century history because when: 'I became a labour historian you couldn't really be an orthodox Communist and write publicly about, say, the period when the Communist Party was active because there was an orthodox belief that everything had changed in 1920 with the foundation of the C. P. Well I didn't believe it had, but it would have been impolite, as well as probably unwise, to say so in public.'[9] Second, we should note the comments by the American labour historian James Cronin that Hobsbawm's Party membership might explain 'the fact that many of his conclusions regarding matters of labor and socialist history are decidedly pessimistic in their implications for the present prospects of either movement'.[10] This is further illustrated in Hobsbawm's 1978 Marx Memorial Lecture, 'The Forward March of Labour Halted?' which was a critical and pessimistic, though perhaps realistic, look at the contemporary British labour movement in historical perspective.[11] Third, as Cronin also states, Hobsbawm's continued adherence to the base-superstructure model (which will be discussed) may have been related to his continued Party membership. Finally, in a much more positive sense, Hobsbawm's Party membership has provided him with a range of international contacts, experiences and research opportunities that have contributed to his decidedly international scholarship.[12]

The survey and examination of Hobsbawm's contributions to historical studies and to the British Marxist historians' theory of class determination which follows is divided into three parts, which represent the three fields in which Hobsbawm has been most active as a historian: labour history, peasant studies and world history.

Labour History

The active resistance of the English working class has its effect in holding the money-greed of the bourgeoisie within certain limits, and keeping alive the opposition of the workers to the social and political omnipotence of the bourgeoisie, while it compels the admission that something more is needed than Trades Unions and strikes to break the power of ruling class. Frederick Engels[13]

Hobsbawm began his scholarly career as a labour historian. His first major work, an edited collection of labour history documents entitled *Labour's Turning Point, 1880-1900* (1948),[14] appeared in 1948 as one of the volumes in the Communist Historians' Group's series, 'History in the Making'. At about the same time (1950), he completed his Cambridge doctoral dissertation, 'Fabianism and the Fabians, 1884-1914'.[15] (In 1960,

Hobsbawm was a founding member of the Society for the Study of Labour History.) Since *Labour's Turning Point,* Hobsbawm has written numerous articles and essays on British labour history. Many of these writings have been important either as contributions to or instigations of debates and further research, e.g. those on Methodism and the working class, the standard of living in the Industrial Revolution, and the labour aristocracy. Although he has never published a 'grand work' in the field (in fact, the only book-length study is *Captain Swing* (1969)[16] which he co-authored with George Rudé), his writings have clearly contributed to the transformation of the study of labour history. Not only has his work added to our knowledge of the British labour movement and working-class, it has also shaped the way we study it.

British labour history (as a subject of study) originated in the late nineteenth century, and its emergence and development in this century seems to have been due in great part to the scholarship of two outstanding intellectual partnerships – first, that of Beatrice and Sydney Webb and, second, that of John and Barbara Hammond.[17]

Beatrice and Sydney Webb were founders of the Fabian Society, the London School of Economics, the 'reconstructed' Labour Party, *The New Statesman,* and the *Political Quarterly.* As Royden Harrison writes, the Webbs in addition 'were the founders of British Labour historiography'. Beatrice Webb's interest in the co-operative movement and its uneasy and uneven relations with trade-unionism, combined with Sydney Webb's interest in trade-unionism and socialism, led them to seek to 'bring socialism and trade-unionism into new relationships with each other both in theory and practice... [Thus] the Webbs aspired to be the chroniclers... [and] advisers of working people whether they were *writing* their history or... trying to *make* it.'[18] Among their works are such books as *The History of Trade Unionism* (1894) and *Industrial Democracy* (1920).

The major criticism of their path-breaking labour history is that it was excessively institutional, narrowly political and elitist, focusing on legislation and trade union activities, especially the activities of the leaders. At the same time, though, it pioneered labour history as a political subject both in terms of its content and in its relationship to the labour movement.

John and Barbara Hammond are most noted for their trilogy *The Village Labourer* (1911), *The Town Labourer* (1917), and *The Skilled Labourer* (1919), which George Rudé describes in the following way: 'Each part of the trilogy had its own distinctive field of inquiry, yet each was part of a single common theme: the impact of the Industrial Revolution on the common people of England, on the craftsmen, domestic workers, the urban and village labourers who, in the process of industrialization were being moulded into a working class.' An important aspect of the Hammonds' histories, Rudé continues, is their argument that 'this process was not one of a gradual assimilation, still less of rising standards, opportunities and expectations. It was a "bleak age", an age of brutal exploitation, of misery and social degradation, in which "the test of success was the test of profits" and in which "the history of England. . . . reads like a history of civil war".'[19] Thus, the Hammonds became known as the leading exponents of the '"pessimist"' view of the English Industrial Revolution, with which both Hobsbawm and E. P. Thompson are now also identified.

The Hammonds' contribution to British labour historiography is not, however, limited to this view. At the same time as they exposed the harshness of the impact of industrialization on the labouring poor, they also documented the efforts of the working class to resist industrial capitalism. Although they tended to discount the political aspect of many of the struggles (e.g. food riots and Luddism) because such struggles did not appear to have made clear and direct contributions 'to the growth of a Labour Movement',[20] their histories are nevertheless not limited to the activities of trade unions. That is, as they themselves indicated, the Hammonds were interested in the experiences of the common people. In fact, they are seen as amongst the forerunners of the British Marxist historians in their efforts to develop the perspective of history from the bottom up. Hobsbawm, in a new introduction to *The Village Labourer,* states that their work, 'brought the discovery that poor men are just as much people as the rich and influential, though the history of the world had been mainly written by or in terms of the latter, and the vast bulk of the documentation on which historians worked left the lives and struggles of the poor in darkness'.[21]

The kind of labour history predominant when Hobsbawm began to write, so 'ably pioneered by the Webbs and G. D. H. Cole', was institutional and organizational history. As Hobsbawm observed in the early 1960s, 'there has been comparatively little work about the working classes as such (as distinct from labour organizations and movements) and about the economic and technical conditions which allowed labour movements to be effective.' His own efforts, influenced by the work of the Hammonds, were 'outside the borders of straightforward chronological or narrative history of labour movements'.[22] Rather, what he sought to develop was labour history as 'working-class' history; that is, a history not limited to the *organized* workers and their organizations and leaders, but one which looks at the *working class's* experiences. In *Labouring Men,* a collection of Hobsbawm's most important labour studies written between the late 1940s and early 1960s, we discover essays on such topics as Tom Paine, the radical democrat; Luddism (machine-breaking); working-class customs and traditions in Britain and France, and their impact on the respective labour movements; as well as several pieces on labour union subjects. Also, we find Hobsbawm's seminal contributions to the 'standard-of-living' debate (Did the English working class's living standards rise or decline during, and as a result of, the Industrial Revolution?); the debate over the relationship between Methodism and the potential for working-class revolution in early nineteenth-century Britain (both issues were also dealt with by E. P. Thompson, as we shall see in the next chapter); and the debate on the possible relations between a 'labour aristocracy' and social stability in the Victorian period.

In comparison to most of the work then being produced as labour history, Hobsbawm's studies are characterized by a concern for the 'totality' of working-class experience. Although he did not himself take up every aspect of working-class life, his writings in labour history contributed greatly to a broadening of that field. Moreover, his movement away from labour history as limited to the institutional or organizational, did not imply, in theory or practice, a movement towards a history with the 'politics' left out (as some would seem to have it),[23] though it did imply a reconceptualization of the *political* (as we also saw in the work of Christopher Hill). For Hobsbawm, to study the totality of working-class experience has meant not only to broaden the 'horizontal' perspective, but also the 'vertical'; that is, to situate the working class in the 'setting of the class struggle...and broader setting of national history, we cannot treat it as though it operated in isolation.[24]

A good example of the class-struggle approach, and also the perspective of history from the bottom up, is Hobsbawm's essay on Luddism, 'The Machine Breakers' (1952).[25] He begins by rejecting the standard interpretation which argues that the 'early labour movement did not know what it was doing, but merely reacted, blindly and gropingly, to the pressures of misery, as animals in the laboratory react to electric currents,' and which assumes that 'the triumph of mechanization was inevitable'. He does so, he says, because such views necessarily 'obscure a good deal of history . . . [and] make impossible any real study of the methods of working-class struggle in the preindustrial period'. Furthermore, he indicates that he does not see how it is possible to ignore the 'power of these early movements, at any rate in Britain'; and he insists that until we recognize that the 'basis of power lay in machine-wrecking, rioting and the destruction of property in general (or, in modern terms, sabotage and direct action)' we will be unable to fully appreciate their meaning and significance. He then proceeds to reconsider the actions of the machine-breakers in terms of a class-struggle analysis. There were, he points out, at least two kinds of machine-breaking. One expressed not so much enmity towards machinery but rather, in particular circumstances, it was a regular mode of 'putting pressure on employers or putters-out'. The other, however, can be viewed as the 'expression of working-class hostility to the new machines of the industrial revolution, especially labour-saving ones'. But even in the latter case, Hobsbawm notes, certain qualifications need to be made. First, machine-breaking was not so widespread as the mythology often implies. Second, it was not indiscriminate, but was most often directed at the introduction of machinery only when and where it meant increasing unemployment and threatened the 'customary standard of life, which included non-monetary factors such as freedom and dignity, as well as wages'. In this sense, the workers were not so much opposing the machinery but the 'threat' which it brought with it. They were reacting to the total transformation of productive relations, which endangered them. Moreover, Hobsbawm observes, on some occasions the breaking of machinery represented the workers' quite conscious opposition to the fact that the machinery was the property of the capitalist. Third, it appears that the machine-wreckers had the sympathy of not just fellow -fellow workers but also of the small masters, shopkeepers, and others who were not so eager as were the larger entrepreneurs for 'an economy of limitless expansion, accumulation, and technical revolution, the savage jungle pursuit which doomed the weak to bankruptcy and wage-earning status'. Yet a final historical point, which Hobsbawm makes in concluding the article, is that although machine-breaking was absolutely inadequate as a means of preventing the ultimate 'triumph' of industrialization, nevertheless it was not the completely 'ineffective weapon' that it has been portrayed as. He substantiates this by pointing to several cases where machine-breaking seems to have made a difference, including the 1830s English agricultural workers' movement known as 'Captain Swing' (which he and George Rudé were to write about later).[26]

Hobsbawm's contributions to the debate on Methodism and the potential for revolution in the nineteenth century ('Methodism and the Threat of Revolution in Britain')[27], and the debate on the working-class standard of living in the Industrial Revolution ('The British Standard of Living, 1790-1850', and 'History and 'The Dark Satanic Mills')[28] provide further evidence of his interest in shifting the field of labour history towards broader studies of working-class experience. They do so not only by way of the issues concerned, but also because of Hobsbawm's use of economic and sociological data.

His 'sociological' approach also provides the basis for his work on the issue of the labour aristocracy, which he presents in his essays, 'Trends in the British Labour Movement since 1850' and 'The Labour Aristocracy in Nineteenth-century Britain'.[29] In these essays Hobsbawm takes up the question which had first been raised in Marxist studies by Engels, but was more fully developed by Lenin as part of his discussion of imperialism and social reform[30]. Was there an elite stratum of the working class which, based on its differentiation from the rest of that class, contributed to the stability of the British capitalist social order of the Victorian period? (This stability was all the more remarkable in that it followed the radicalism of the 1830s and early 1840s.) Lenin argues that the labour aristocracy was an elite stratum of the British working class which had been bribed by the capitalists, who paid for the bribes out of the 'superprofits' they derived from imperialism.[31] This theory, John Field explains, became orthodox in Communist circles during the Stalinist years, and thus was rarely examined critically.[32]

What Hobsbawm seeks to do is to examine *sociologically* the basis for such a stratum. He indicates that there are several factors which need to be considered in identifying such a group. Those include the relations and conditions of work, relations of the group with strata above and below it, and the group's general conditions of life. However, the most important criterion, he insists, is the 'level and regularity of wages'. Thus, based on an analysis of wage patterns in particular, he argues that the zenith of the labour aristocracy – and its significance as a force for social stability – was in the period from the 1840s to the 1890s, with important changes occurring thereafter in the structure and character of the stratum.

Hobsbawm's writings on the labour aristocracy have become standard references on the subject. His propositions on the basis and significance of such a labour elite have instigated much additional research, giving rise in the 1970s to a lively debate involving a variety of theoretical perspectives. Of particular interest and importance are the studies by John Foster and Robert Gray.

Foster's book, *Class Struggle and the Industrial Revolution: Early Industrial Capitalism in Three English Towns*[33] (especially Oldham), which includes a foreword by Hobsbawm, represents an effort to test Leninist concepts of class analysis (i.e. false consciousness, labour or trade-union consciousness, class or revolutionary consciousness, and the proletarian vanguard) in order to explain the 'development and decline of a revolutionary class consciousness in the second quarter of the [nineteenth] century'. Foster follows Lenin and Hobsbawm in arguing that the labour aristocracy was a conservative force, inhibiting the emergence – or rather, persistence – of a class consciousness in favour of a trade-union consciousness. Unlike Hobsbawm, however, Foster does not attribute the development of the labour aristocracy to wage differentials but instead to its authority in the production process. This possession of authority came about as a result of deliberate actions by the industrialists and/or technological developments (Foster is not clear on this point). But, whatever the cause, it had the effect of divorcing the proletarian vanguard from its working-class base. The political consequence, Foster argues, was that the potential leadership of a revolutionary working class was neutralized.

The study by Robert Gray, *The Labour Aristocracy in Victorian Edinburgh*,[34] approaches the subject from a Gramscian perspective, as opposed to a Leninist one. Gray is interested in the development of bourgeois 'hegemony' and the relationship of the labour aristocracy to that process.[35] He acknowledges the contributions of Hobsbawm and Foster, but he is critical of Hobsbawm's (and Lenin's) economistic explanation, and Foster's argument regarding the degree to which the labour aristocracy actually 'collaborated' with the bourgeoisie. Gray argues that the labour aristocracy, though it did indeed come to accept the social order of industrial capitalism, did not do so in the way the ruling class would necessarily have liked. While the labour aristocracy, through its leadership role in the labour movement, inculcated 'accommodative responses to capitalism', and thereafter imparted them to the larger labour movement, the process of accommodation to industrial capitalism was at the same time, a 'negotiated one – and subject, moreover, to constant renegotiation'. This is important, Gray argues, if we are to make sense of the world-view of the 'manual workers, especially of the upper stratum'. For 'the process of negotiation presupposes strong and autonomous protective class institutions' and 'the defence of those institutions. . . . was a distinctive feature of the class-consciousness of the artisan.' Thus, although the labour aristocracy was partially responsible for the 'accommodationism' of the British labour movement to industrial capitalism, it also contributed a 'strong sense of class pride and an ethic of class solidarity'. These, Gray insists, were communicated to the working class as a whole and represent important legacies of the nineteenth-century labour aristocracy.[36]

It should be added that there have been other important contributions to the labour aristocracy debate. These range from historical studies offering variations on the theme to historico-sociological essays which reject altogether the labour aristocracy theory as an explanation for Victorian social stability.[37] The quantity and quality of the historical and theoretical contributions to the debate are a testament to Hobsbawm's own writing, though this has been limited to just a few articles.

Although Hobsbawm's sociological labour studies pioneered much of what is now referred to as the 'new social history', he has not written very much labour history since the 1960s.[38] In this regard it must be acknowledged that his labour history studies seem somewhat parochial in contrast to the work currently being done by many historians. Today the social history of the working class includes studies of women, the family, community, culture and ideology, in addition to studies of the labour movement and its various modes of struggle, and the technical and economic changes which have shaped working-class experience. But, of course, it was Hobsbawm (and later Thompson) who instigated the changes that laid the basis for the studies now being pursued by others.

One recent piece which Hobsbawm has written is the previously cited 1978 Marx Memorial Lecture, 'The Forward March of Labour Halted?' In it he describes the past thirty years of the British labour movement as a period of crisis. He states that his intention is to examine the crisis in the 'long-term perspective of the changing structure of British capitalism and the proletariat in it'. He does this by noting the recomposition of the proletariat and the changes which portended greater class cohesion in the century since Marx's death, and he then proceeds to examine the developments which represent new challenges to the solidarity of the working class. Hobsbawm closes his structural survey with the observation that there has, in fact, been an increase in 'sectionalism' in the 1970s, with each section 'pursuing its own economic interest irrespective of the rest.' Finally, he considers whether or not the renewed militancy of the unions in the 1970s represents greater 'class consciousness' on the part of British workers. His data are the size of trade union membership and the size of the Labour Party vote. In both instances, the numbers 'are troubling' and in the end he concludes that the labour and socialist movement 'seems to have got stuck' and that it is necessary to be 'realistic' about the nature of the crisis.[39]

Hobsbawm's assessment of the labour movement seems to have been confirmed by the 1979 and 1983 British general elections. His mode of analysis is similar to that of his earlier studies. In particular, he focuses on sociological and structural aspects of British capitalism and the labour movement. He did not, however, present the lecture in order to spread pessimism and gloom but to generate serious discussion about what is to be done in this critical period. In this sense, we should recall that Hobsbawm was not only carrying on a Marxist practice, but also a labour history practice in directing his arguments to socialist and labour activists. He once pointed out that 'labour history is by tradition a highly political subject, and one which was for long practised largely outside the universities.'[40] Once again, as with his work on labour history, his arguments instigated a very lively debate.

Peasants and Primitive Rebels

Villa was an outlaw for twenty-two years. When he was only a boy of sixteen, delivering milk in the streets of Chihuahua, he killed a government official and had to take to the mountains. The story is that the official had violated his sister, but it seems probable that Villa killed him on account of his insufferable insolence. That in itself would not have outlawed him long in Mexico, where human life is cheap; but once a refugee he committed the unpardonable crime of stealing cattle from the rich hacendados. And from that time to the outbreak of the Madero revolution the Mexican government had a price on his head. John Reed, Insurgent Mexico[41]

Hobsbawm's historical studies of class experience have not been limited to the British working class in the Industrial Revolution. He has also done much work of importance on pre-industrial urban and (especially) rural labouring classes' experiences. It is in this area that we really encounter Hobsbawm's international scholarship, for his writings on peasant and agrarian studies include British, European (especially Mediterranean) and Latin American studies. In fact, it might be said that a new subject in social history was actually opened up and given its name by Hobsbawm: the study of 'primitive rebellions'. It should also be noted that Hobsbawm was a founding member not only of the Society for the Study of Labour History but also, along with Rodney Hilton, of the editorial board of the *Journal of Peasant Studies,* providing the lead article, 'Peasants and Politics', for its opening issue.[42]

Hobsbawm's first work in this area, published in 1959, was the now-classic *Primitive Rebels* (1963).[43] Interestingly enough, his original scholarly interest was the agrarian problem in North Africa, but in the immediate post-war period he found it necessary to pursue labour history instead. During the 1950s, however, several things happened to renew his interest in peasant studies. He was making frequent trips to Mediterranean countries in this period and meeting and talking to a number of intellectuals in the Italian Communist Party, who knew a great deal about southern Italy. He was also reading the work of Antonio Gramsci, who has a lot to say about 'non-political protest movements' (what Hobsbawm was to call 'primitive rebellions'). At about the same time, he became involved in discussions with the social anthropologists Myer Fortes and Max Gluckman. They were studying the Mau Mau movement and were anxious to know if similar movements had occurred in Europe in earlier periods. It was these anthropologists who asked him to give a lecture 'out of which *Primitive Rebels* grew'.[44] (Thus, as in labour history studies, where Hobsbawm made links with sociology, in peasant studies he established links between history and anthropology, two decades before the 'interdisciplinary history' vogue.)

Yet another influence in the years during which Hobsbawm was writing *Primitive Rebels* was the Twentieth Congress of the Communist Party of the Soviet Union in 1956, and the process of de-Stalinization. He even refers to the work as a 'political as well as a historical one.'[45] He recalls that it had become necessary to reconsider the models of revolutionary activity which 'militant communists had accepted in the past'. In effect, he says, *PrimitiveRebels* can be viewed as an 'attempt to see whether we were right in believing in a strongly organized party'. Concerning this question he contends that the 'answer is yes'. He adds, however, that the book shows that such a path was not the only way forward.[46]

In *Primitive Rebels* Hobsbawm examines what he terms 'archaic' forms of social movements. Specifically, his studies are of: 'banditry of the Robin Hood type, rural secret societies, various peasant revolutionary movements of the millenarian sort, pre-industrial urban "mobs" and their riots, some labour religious sects and the use of ritual in early labour and revolutionary organization'. The importance of such studies, he explains, is that whereas historians have studied pre-capitalist 'ancient and medieval: slave revolts [and] peasant risings', and modern, i.e. industrial-capitalist, 'labour and socialist movements', little (or no) work has been done by historians on 'modern' (i.e. since the French Revolution) social movements of precapitalist groups in their confrontation with expanding capitalism. Focusing on Western and Southern Europe (especially Italy), Hobsbawm presents studies of rural and urban social movements which, though we should expect to find them in the Middle Ages, occurred in the nineteenth and twentieth centuries.

Primitive Rebels contains studies of people who were not born into a capitalist world, but who had to deal with the problem of adapting to it. Hobsbawm compares the experience these people confront with that of immigrants. But in this case it is the new social order which arrives 'from outside'. Sometimes it does so 'insidiously by the operation of economic forces' which the people do not comprehend and are incapable of mastering. At other times it arrives in a more specifically political fashion, that is, 'by conquest, revolutions, and fundamental changes of law whose consequences they may not understand, even when they have helped to bring them about'. *Primitive Rebels* treats the 'process of adaptation (or failure to adapt) as expressed in their archaic social movements'. He refers to these movements as 'primitive' and 'archaic' because they are social movements of 'pre-political people who have not yet found, or [have] only begun to find, a specific language in which to express their aspirations about the world'.[47]

Here, especially, we can see the usefulness of a class-struggle analysis from the perspective of the bottom up. Hobsbawm clearly acknowledges the historical specificity of "modern" politics. He does not view such movements as non- or apolitical, as historians and anthropologists have tended to do just because there were 'no committees, no agenda, no platform', or because they were not part of the "high politics" of the struggle for state power'.[48] Hobsbawm's analysis insists that we recognize the political dimension of these movements. Where others have seen *only* criminal activity in banditry or *Mafia,* and religious hysteria in millenarian movements, Hobsbawm uncovers the political. For example, in his presentation of banditry, which is further elaborated and refined in a fascinating little book, *Bandits,* Hobsbawm explains that not all banditry is primitive rebellion. That which is, he terms *social* banditry. Essentially, social bandits are distinguished from ordinary rural criminals by their relationship to the peasant society of which they are a part. While they are identified by the powers that be as 'criminals', to their fellow peasants these outlaws are 'heroes, champions, avengers, fighters for justice, perhaps even leaders of liberation, and in any case as men to be admired, helped and supported'.

Hobsbawm observes that, though social banditry is a global phenomenon, it does appear to be socio-historically limited. He argues that it seems to arise in those societies which 'lie between the evolutionary phase of tribal and kinship organization and modern capitalist and industrial society', yet including those moments when such societies are experiencing the process of transition to agrarian capitalism. Thus he comments that, whereas the high point of social banditry in 'most parts of Europe [was] the sixteenth to eighteenth century', the 'great age of socidal banditry in many parts of the world' has been since the early 1800s. But he adds that 'it is now largely extinct, except in a few areas'.[49]

Hobsbawm points out in the introduction to *Primitive Rebels* that the importance of primitive rebellions such as social banditry, millenarian movements, etc., is that though they may be struggles over the expansion of capitalism at its periphery, they are not marginal to history: 'Men and women such as those with whom this book deals form the large majority in many...countries even today, and their acquisition of political consciousness has made our century the most revolutionary in history.'[50] Almost twenty-five years have passed since this was written but events have further confirmed his argument.

Hobsbawm's work in this field has instigated, and inspired, many studies of rural outlawry. However, as he acknowledges in the postscript to the 1981 edition of *Bandits,* these new studies have led to criticisms of his thesis on the *social* character of banditry. From one position it has been asserted that Hobsbawm confuses the myth, or legendary character, of banditry with the reality of it. It is argued that bandits as heroes are inventions of the people, for in actuality bandits necessarily become servants of power – often against the peasantry – if they are to survive at all. Hobsbawm replies that, of course, it is essential to distinguish the 'good robber from the bad', adding that, in fact, peasants themselves have always done so. Yet another position argues that *all* banditry should be viewed as expressions of 'social protest or rebellion' and, thus, Hobsbawm is wrong to differentiate social bandits from criminal bandits. In response to this criticism, Hobsbawm states that while it may be true that even criminal bandits represent some form of social protest, nevertheless the differences between the social and the criminal bandits' relations with the peasantry make it necessary to distinguish between them as types. Moreover, he adds, there are serious political reasons for so doing.[51]

Hobsbawm's interests in agrarian primitive rebels and labour history (in particular, his essay on Luddism) came together in the work on *Captain Swing: A Social History of the Great English Agricultural Uprising of 1830,*[52] which he co-authored with George Rudé. It is a study of the subject originally treated by the Hammonds in *The Village Labourer.* Hobsbawm and Rudé wrote their own book, they said, not only because there was more to tell about the rising, but also because there were 'new *questions* to ask about the events; about their causes and motives, about their mode of social and political behaviour, the social composition of those who took part in them, their significance and consequences'.

They explain that, before 1830, the agricultural workers were no longer peasants but the social order in which they lived was still 'traditional, hierarchical, paternalist, and in many respects resistant to the full logic of the market'. This was not a static situation, however, and in the decades leading up to 1830 this rural society experienced major changes brought about by 'the extraordinary agricultural boom (and the subsequent, though temporary, recessions)'. The changes involved the alienation of the labourers' lands and transformation of their hiring contracts, that is, the actual or further proletarianization of the labour force. Moreover, the reduction of the relationship between farmer and labourer to the 'cash-nexus' stripped the labourer of 'those modest customary rights as a man (though a subordinate one) to which he felt himself to have a claim'. And yet, the agricultural workers were 'proletarian only in the most general economic sense', for the nature of their labour and the social order in which they 'lived and starved' inhibited the development of 'those ideas and methods of collective self-defence which the townsmen were able to discover'. Nevertheless, (finally) instigated by the economic crisis of 1828-30 and stimulated by the French and Belgian Revolutions of 1830 and the contemporary British crisis, the agricultural workers expressed their demands by a variety of means: 'arson, threatening letters, inflammatory handbills and posters. . . . and [most significantly] the destruction of different types of machinery'. These demands, 'to attain a minimum living wage and to end rural unemployment', appear merely economic or '(though not formally) trade unionist'. However, while the rising was never revolutionary (nor was there ever a call for land reform), Hobsbawm and Rudé's analysis shows that 'there was a wider objective: the defence of the customary rights of the rural poor as freeborn Englishmen, and the restoration of the stable social order which had – at least it seemed in retrospect – guaranteed them'.[53]

Captain Swing not only offered a re-interpretation of the

origins of the agricultural workers' movement, as well as its practices and its aims; it also offered a new view of its consequences. The widely held view of the rising was that it was a failure and that it merely succeeded in speeding up the reduction of the agricultural working class 'into that slow-moving, ox-like, passive and demoralized mass . . . which was all that so many of their Victorian superiors saw in the English villages'. But this (extreme) view is untenable. As Hobsbawm and Rudé reveal, contemporary observers were not so convinced that the rising was the concluding act of the labourers' struggle. Rather, they saw the rising as the first proof that a previously 'inert mass . . . was capable of large-scale co-ordinated or at least uniform movement over a great part of England'. Yet the urban bias of the historians of social movements produced a state of ignorance as to the forms of agrarian discontent between the rising (1830) and the growth of rural unionism (early 1870s), which was then translated into the assumption that there was no discontent. The assumptions, however, were wrong. Hobsbawm and Rudé say that even a superficial examination of the record reveals that 'agrarian unrest continued well into the 1850s, and *social* incendiarism can be traced down to about 1860.' Thus the important question which arises in this context, and to which they seek to provide an answer, is, 'Why did so long a period separate the revolt of 1830 from the first national explosion of rural unionism in the early 1870s?'

Nevertheless, as Hobsbawm and Rudé acknowledge, the rising *was* a failure in that it neither succeeded in restoring the old social order, nor – except for a brief period – did it do much to improve the workers' standard of living. And yet in one important respect the agricultural workers' movement succeeded: 'The threshing machines did not return on the old scale. Of all the machine-breaking movements of the nineteenth century that of the helpless and unorganized farm-labourers proved to be the most effective. The real name of King Ludd was Swing.'[54]

In addition to his European (and British) studies, Hobsbawm has also done work in Latin American peasant studies, which arose out of his travels to South America during the 1960s. He suggests in one article that certain regions of Latin America should be of particular interest to historians of the European past because they provide contemporary examples of a process Europe has already undergone, i.e. the transition to capitalism. Thus, keeping in mind the changes which have occurred in the process itself, historians can, in the Latin American context, study the complex (and sometimes seemingly contradictory) politico-economic changes of the transition to agrarian capitalism, and also the pre-political and political struggles which emerge from it. Following his own advice, Hobsbawm has written such essays as 'A Case of Neo-Feudalism: La Convencion, Peru', 'Peasant Movements in Colombia', 'Peasant Land Occupations'[55] (an excellent piece, focusing on Peru, which discusses these peasant movements both in terms of the peasants' understandings of their actions and their socio-political consequences at the national level), and 'Peasants and Rural Migrants in Politics'.[56]

Hobsbawm's studies of peasants and primitive rebels have forced him, like Dobb, Hilton, Hill and (as we shall see) Thompson, to confront the question: 'Do classes and class conflicts exist without class consciousness, or is class merely an analytical construct in such contexts?' His answer is that 'class *in the full sense* only comes into existence at the historical moment when classes begin to acquire consciousness of themselves as such,' and 'class consciousness is a phenomenon of the modern industrial era'.[57] However, he does not mean that class and class conflict – or for that matter, class consciousness – are unique to industrial capitalism, otherwise being of use only as an analytical construct. As indicated by the phrase 'in the full sense', class, according to Hobsbawm, exists in degrees, i.e. there are 'degrees of classness'. For example, Hobsbawm finds that 'peasants are usually a class of low classness' (to quote Teodor Shanin) and the 'industrial working class, a class of very high classness'.[58] Moreover, numerous references to peasants and class conflict show that 'the absence of class consciousness in the modern sense does not imply the absences of classes *and class conflict,'* (recognition of which, we shall see, E. P. Thompson has asserted in a radical and theoretically important fashion). 'But,' he adds, 'it is evident that in the modern economy this changes quite fundamentally.'[59]

Capitalism and World History

The bourgeoisie has played a most revolutionary role in history. Karl Marx, The Communist Manifesto

The editors of Hobsbawm's *Festschrift* have written that one thing which arguably remains most distinctively Marxist about his approach is a brilliantly illuminating but ultimately quite orthodox Marxist approach to the old problem of the relationship between 'base' and 'superstructure.'[60] If, as I have been arguing, one of the most important aspects of the collective work of the British Marxist historians is that it represents an effort to overcome the determinism (economic and/or technological) of the base-superstructure model, how then does Hobsbawm's supposedly quite orthodox Marxist approach fit in?

It is true that Hobsbawm continues to subscribe to the base-superstructure model, at least in theory. Unlike other Marxist historians who have either repudiated the model altogether – even as metaphor – or at least dropped it from their historical and theoretical vocabulary, Hobsbawm persists in presenting 'the Marxist approach' in terms of the model. Throughout his much-cited essay, 'Karl Marx's Contribution to Historiography', he argues that Marxism as a theory of society and history 'insists on a hierarchy of social phenomena (e.g. 'basis' and 'superstructure')'.[61] In fact, the essay seems to present Marxism as if it were merely a structural-functionalist theory which, as opposed to other such theories, also happens to provide for a way of understanding social change. We might also note his more than sympathetic review of G. A. Cohen's book, *Karl Marx's Theory of History – A Defence*,[62] a work which seems to revive an orthodox version of Marxism as a theory of technological determinism. And Hobsbawm's other writings of this sort also show his continued adherence to the base-superstructure model.[63]

Yet it is difficult to accuse Hobsbawm of holding a view of Marxism as a theory of economic or technological determinism. He regularly states that the 'base' refers not only to the merely economic and/or technological but to the 'totality of the relations of production, i.e. social organization in its broadest sense as applied to a given level of the material forces of production'.[64] Concerning this point we might look at his 1960 article, 'Custom, Wages and Work-load in Nineteenth-century Industry'. This essay is a good indication that Hobsbawm's conception of the social relations of production is not merely economic. He shows that the composition of the surplus extraction relations and patterns of 'labour productivity' in early nineteenth-century industry were as much determined by custom, tradition and political regulation as they were by existing technology and economic requirements (i.e. subsistence levels). Moreover, he also shows that the changes which occurred through the rest of the century were determined in great part by the changing attitudes and orientations of the workers (and their employers); their actions in relation to the state and their employers; and the employers' efforts to 'politically' reorganize the labour process through the implementation of 'scientific management'. Thus, even the seemingly specific 'economics' of surplus extraction relations are shown to be determined by the 'cultural' and the 'political'; that is, they are *social* relations of production.[65]

Hobsbawm is quite critical of both (vulgar) Marxist and 'bourgeois' historians who might seek to reduce the historical process to *economic* explanations, reminding them that 'history is the struggle of men for ideas, as well as a reflection of their material environments.'[66] Moreover, while he subscribes to the base-superstructure model in his theoretical writings, Hobsbawm's historical studies of the period since the seventeenth century have most often been pursued as class-struggle analyses, *starting* from the social relations of production in the broad sense. His theoretical writings, however, are (intentionally) more universal in their 'evolutionary' scope[67] and usually encompass those historical forms of society in which classes and class conflict do not exist but are, for example, primarily communal or kinship based. (This raises a serious issue regarding the historical limitations of the British Marxist historians' theory of class determination.) Finally, though there was a tendency to economism in Hobsbawm's earlier studies (especially, for example, in the labour aristocracy essays), he often reminds us in his theoretical writings, and shows us in his historical studies, that where classes do exist they develop in relation to each other and as *totalities:* 'class cannot be confined to any single aspect of that relationship, *not even the economic.* In short it implies the entire society.'[68]

At the same time, though it should be clear that Hobsbawm is not an economic determinist, he has never made the scholarly breakthroughs on 'class formation' that Thompson has, nor evidenced the critical sensitivity to 'popular' ideas found in Hill's seventeenth-century studies. While Hobsbawm's historical writings are characterized by class-struggle analysis, unlike Thompson, he has not presented a detailed study of the process whereby a class 'in the full sense' emerges out of class struggle – determined by both the development of capitalism and the customs, values, and practices of the working class itself. Nor has Hobsbawm's evident interest in cultural and ideological subjects provided the kinds of analyses of the ideas of the common people which are found in Hill's writings. Though this may be a function of the evidence with which they have been able to work, Hill does allow a greater autonomy to ideas in his class-struggle analysis. On this it should be noted that Hobsbawm's application of the concept of 'hegemony' has been the subject of criticism, because in his book *The Age of Capital, 1848-1875* (1975),[69] he equates hegemony much too easily with 'ideological predominance', and thus seems not to properly appreciate the complex and contradictory character of the process.[70] These 'shortcomings' of Hobsbawm's work may very well be due to his continued adherence to the base-superstructure model. It has even been suggested that they are derivative of Hobsbawm's continued membership in the Communist Party. Although he has done so much to force the reconsideration of modes of primitive rebellion, Hobsbawm has perhaps still been too committed to the necessity of the intellectual leadership of a strongly organized party and thus underestimates the significance of the 'inherent ideas' of the common people.[71]

I do not want to push these criticisms too far, for Hobsbawm has actively and effectively pursued cultural and ideological analyses.[72] Even if it were found that his argument about social bandits is actually more descriptive of the myth than the reality, he has done a magnificent job of detailing the existence of such 'ideas' among the peasantries of the world and of exploring what they mean. Also, it may well be argued that Hobsbawm has been *the* historian of the Group who has contributed most to the general study of social movements, and what may seem a shortcoming of his work from one perspective, may be a strength from another. He has never lost sight of what some view as the essential political question of the relation of a social movement to the problem of power and the state. Moreover, none of the other British Marxist historians has contributed directly to so many areas of study as has Hobsbawm. Thus we turn to consider yet another area in which he has contributed by way of a class-struggle analysis, i.e. world history.

A particularly important feature of Hobsbawm's labour history and peasant studies is that class relations and experiences are never viewed in isolation. He has always been interested in the totality of class experience, not just socially, but also in terms of the broader development of capitalism, which he rightly argues has been a world-historical phenomenon. At the same time, though he necessarily starts from the politico-economic essence of capitalism, he does not reduce the development of capitalism to its economic processes, as Wallerstein tends to do in his work on the modern world system. For example, to recall Hobsbawm's contribution to the transition debate, in his two-part essay 'The Crisis of the Seventeenth Century (1954)', he discusses the crisis of the European world economy in that century (in fact, as Christopher Hill notes, 'the idea was first put forward by Hobsbawm')[73] as the 'last phase of the general transition from a feudal to a capitalist economy',[74] and he examines the differential development which resulted in terms of the class structures and struggles of the European societies.

In *Industry and Empire* (1969),[75] a politico-economic history of Britain from 1750 to the 1960s, Hobsbawm treats the development of British industrial capitalism in a world-historical context. Not only does he necessarily consider the British economy in the context of its 'imperial' economy, but also with reference to the changes in the very process of industrial-capitalist development and their consequences for Britain's position in the capitalist world-economy. Whereas others, like W. W. Rostow,[76] present the development of British industrial capitalism as a model for newly industrializing countries, Hobsbawm retorts that British history is '*not a model* for the economic development of the world today'. Beyond a basic curiosity in history, Hobsbawm says that he can see only two really persuasive arguments for studying

Britain's economic history: (1) because the past two centuries still frame the present, any 'practical solution' to Britain's contemporary problems requires a historical perspective; and (2) 'more generally, the record of the earliest, the longest-lived industrial and capitalist power cannot but throw light on the development of industrialization as a phenomenon in the history of the world'.[77]

Hobsbawm's most important work in this field, however, is his long-term project of writing the world history of the nineteenth century. Examining, as he says, the development of the modern world, he divides that century into three distinct phases: *The Age of Revolution, 1789-1848* (1962), *The Age of Capital, 1848-1875* (1975), and *The Age of Empire, 1875-1914* (forthcoming).[78]

To properly appreciate his efforts and contribution to world-history studies, we should remember that the dominant paradigm when he began to write was modernization theory. (A noteworthy exception was the work of Barrington Moore.) In this theory, the very processes to be explained, 'e.g. population growth, the industrialization of the economy, and the modernization of the state', become the 'most obvious motors for change'[79]. Furthermore, as opposed to historically specific social structures, characterized by particular relations of exploitation and domination, and struggles against them, the modernization historians present us with processes of 'liberation' to which (truly) 'modem' and 'rational' groups adapt.[80]

Now Hobsbawm does not deny the 'liberating character' of the 'dual revolution' (as he calls the combination of the British Industrial and French Revolutions); but neither does he reduce the contradictions of the new modes of exploitation and domination of industrial capitalism to being merely social problems, to be overcome in the further course of modernization. Nor does he reduce the struggles between classes to a mere feature of the transitional process of adaptation to the seemingly inexorable forces of industrialization and progress. Rather, what Hobsbawm presents are studies which seek to explain the making of European societies and the European-dominated world of nineteenth-century industrial capitalism, in terms of the class-structured and 'determined' struggles of that century.

Thus, in *The Age of Revolution,* Hobsbawm 'traces the transformation of the world between 1789 and 1848 in so far as it was due to . . . . the "dual revolution".' Early in the work he identifies the class character of that revolution: 'The great revolution of 1789-1848 was then the triumph of *capitalist* industry: not of liberty and equality in general, but of middle class or *"bourgeois" liberal* society; not of the "modern economy" or the "modern state", but of the economies and states in a particular geographical region of the world.'[81] Similarly, in *The Age of Capital,* the theme of which is the 'global triumph of capitalism', he writes that, 'The history of our period is... primarily that of the massive advance of the world economy of industrial capitalism, of the social order it represented, and of the ideas and beliefs which seemed to legitimize and ratify it: reason, science, progress and liberalism. It is the era of the triumphant bourgeoisie.' He adds that the age of revolution was not completely over in one sense, the 'European bourgeoisie still hesitated to commit itself to public political rule.' This was due to the fact that workers and peasants continued to appear threatening to the middle classes of Europe: '"democracy" was still believed to be the certain and rapid prelude to "socialism".'[82]

These two books are particularly interesting examples of Hobsbawm's efforts to work through the problem of 'totality'. For, in spite of his adherence to the base-super-structure model, in neither book (as James Cronin points out, with particular reference to *The Age of Capital)* does Hobsbawm seek to establish simple causal relations between economics and politics or culture.[83] *The Age of Revolution* and *The Age of Capital* are studies of their respective historical periods as developing totalities, in which the political economy and class relations and struggles of industrial(izing) capitalism determine, structure or shape their development, including developments in the sciences, ideas, religion and the arts.

For example, regarding the origins of the Industrial Revolution in Britain, Hobsbawm is critical of those who would explain it in terms of Britain's supposed technological and scientific superiority. As he points out, France was much further advanced in those respects. Furthermore, he argues, the *necessary* technical advances were modest and were accomplishable by 'intelligent artisans'. As opposed to the standard explanation, then, Hobsbawm – in the tradition of Marx and Dobb – directs our historical attention to the English Revolution of the seventeenth century, which provided a state for which 'private profit and economic development . . . . became accepted as the supreme objects of government policy', and an agriculture which was: 'prepared to carry out its three fundamental functions in an era of industrialization: to increase production and productivity, so as to feed a rapidly rising non-agricultural population; to provide a large and rising surplus of potential recruits for the towns and industries; and to provide a mechanism for the accumulation of capital to be used in the more modern sectors of the economy.'[84] He *then* proceeds to discuss industry and the world market.

Later, in *The Age of Revolution,* Hobsbawm returns to consider the 'paradox' of French economic development. In spite of the French Revolution, which provided 'institutions ideally suited to capitalist development', and even though 'the ingenuity and inventiveness of [French] entrepreneurs was without parallel in Europe,' France's economic development was 'distinctly slower than that of other countries'. The explanation Hobsbawm provides is that the peasant structure of French agriculture (an outcome of the Revolution) inhibited industrial development because, in the absence of a 'sufficiently large and expanding market', French businessmen continued to produce luxury goods instead of goods for mass consumption, and French financiers invested in foreign rather than domestic industries.[85]

Among the political changes of the dual revolution, Hobsbawm points out that it was in this period that the experiences of the labouring poor led to the development of labour movements. It was not, of course, that collective action had not existed prior to this period, but what was original in these years was class consciousness and class ambition; that is, 'the "poor" no longer faced the "rich"'. A specific *class,* the labouring class, workers, or proletariat, faced another, the employers or capitalists. Moreover, while the French Revolution provided the European working classes with confidence, the Industrial Revolution convinced them of the need for permanent mobilization. Significantly, 'proletarian consciousness was powerfully combined with, and reinforced by, what may best be called Jacobin consciousness,' thus the labour movement established a symbiotic relationship with the democratic movement.[86]

Developments in science, ideas and the arts are also examined by Hobsbawm in relation to the class-structured dual revolution. For example, in perhaps one of the best chapter-length discussions of Romanticism available, Hobsbawm takes up the cultural movement which characterized the arts of the age, discussing both the historically unique experiences of the Romantic artists and the ways in which they articulated those experiences in their work. He writes that 'if a single misleading sentence is to sum up the relations of artist and society in this era, we might say that the French Revolution inspired him by its example, the Industrial Revolution by its horror, and the bourgeois society, which emerged from both, transformed his very existence and modes of creation.'[87]

Similarly, we might look at Hobsbawm's discussion of religion in *The Age of Revolution,* where he writes of the increasing secularization and (in Europe) religious indifference, of the period, but then turns to examine the contemporary 'revivals of religion in its most uncompromising, irrationalist, and emotionally compulsive forms'. In both instances he presents analyses which specify the class-differential character of the phenomena. For example, he notes the class-specific meanings of militant, literal, old-fashioned religion:

> *For the masses* it was, in the main, a method of coping with the increasingly bleak and inhuman oppressive society of middle-class liberalism: in Marx's phrase.... it was the 'heart of a heartless world, as it is the spirit of spiritless conditions.... the opium of the people'. More than this: it attempted to create social and sometimes educational and political institutions in an environment which provided none.... Its literalism, emotionalism and superstition protested both against the entire society in which rational calculation dominated and against the upper classes who deformed religion in their own image. *For the middle classes... religion* could be a powerful moral prop, a justification of their social existence against the united contempt and hatred of traditional society, and an engine of their expansion.... *For the monarchies and aristocracies...* it provided social stability. They had learned from the French Revolution that the Church was the strongest prop of the throne.[88]

In *The Age of Capital,* where Hobsbawm takes up the establishment of bourgeois hegemony in Europe and the extension of the capitalist economy to the entire world, we find similar discussions of the history of the nineteenth century in its totality, ranging from the politico-economic to the aesthetic. The book opens with a discussion of the revolutions of 1848 – 'the first potential global revolution' – which, in spite of their important differences, had in common the characteristic of being 'in fact or immediate anticipation, social revolutions of the labouring poor'. Thus, although the revolutions failed and Marx may have been exaggerating about 'the spectre haunting Europe' (except perhaps in Paris) the *presence* of the working classes as a potentially revolutionary force was made evident, and 'henceforth the forces of conservatism, privilege and wealth would have to defend themselves in new ways'. But not only Europe; Hobsbawm also discusses the uneven confrontation of expanding European capitalism with societies in Latin America, Africa and Asia, recognizing the centrality of those societies' own class structures and struggles in shaping their capacities to win, as in the case of Japan, or lose, as in the cases of the countries now referred to as the Third World.[89]

Hobsbawm's world histories are not intended to present new information about the nineteenth century, but neither do they represent mere summations or even syntheses of existing arguments. *The Age of Revolution* and *The Age of Capital* (and, assuredly, the forthcoming *Age of Empire*) offer a reinterpretation of the making of the modern world by way of a class-structure and struggle analysis.

Class Struggle and History

The British Marxist historians' theory of class determination posits the centrality of class struggle to the historical process. Eric Hobsbawm, as shown in this chapter, has clearly worked in terms of this theory and the results of his scholarship have been major contributions both to those fields in which he has been active and, thereby, to the development of the theory itself. Hobsbawm's early labour studies have been most important in shifting the focus of labour historiography from the study of organized labour to that of the working class, moving such studies beyond the merely institutional and organizational to working-class experience as a whole. Yet he has never lost sight of the political dimension of class experience. In peasant studies, Hobsbawm's reconsideration of several forms of peasant (and worker) collective behaviour as 'primitive rebellion' has contributed to our understanding of pre-political modes of class struggle. In fact, Hobsbawm must surely be recognized as the scholar who actually opened up, or established, 'primitive rebels' as a field of study. The combined effect of his labour and peasant studies has been to contribute to the reconceptualization of the political as not merely that which has been referred to traditionally as 'politics'. In world-history studies, Hobsbawm has extended and further developed the arguments made by Maurice Dobb on the transition from feudalism to capitalism. His essays on the seventeenth-century crisis and books on the making of the modem world in the nineteenth century examine the expansion and 'triumph' of capitalism as a class-structured, world-historical process in its totality. And, of course, it has been this concern – to comprehend the development of capitalism as a *totality* – that binds together Hobsbawm's labour, peasant and world-history studies.

There has been much talk of 'total history' and 'totality' in recent years, especially in discussions of the separate, but related, writings of Fernand Braudel and Immanuel Wallerstein. Yet, if there is to be an effort to construct a total history, I would offer Hobsbawm's work as a model. In Braudel's work, human experience is primarily materialist and the political dimension is minimized or rejected in a totality structured spatially by the environment and temporally by the *longue durée.* In Wallerstein's work, human experience is primarily economic and the political is reduced or negated in a totality determined by the specifically economic world system. But Hobsbawm's work, as class-struggle analyses, while acknowledging the determination of the social relations of production, does not reduce human experience to the economic or even the politico-economic.

Characteristic of Hobsbawm's career and interests, he remains a prolific scholar in several areas. He is not only completing the third volume of his nineteenth-century historical survey but is also involved in the editing of a multi-volume *History of Marxism*,[90] and he promises to continue his study of 'popular politics' which he began in *Primitive Rebels* and *Bandits*. In addition, he is a regular contributor to various non-Marxist magazines and to periodicals including *Marxism Today* (published by the Communist Party – Hobsbawm is on the editorial board).

These articles are particularly interesting, for in them he offers social and political commentary with a historical perspective. Often he makes what appear to be rather unorthodox recommendations, but he grounds them in both historical precedent and what he contends is contemporary reality. For example, in *Marxism Today* (January 1983) we find his essay 'Falklands Fallout' in which he analyses the patriotism and jingoism which characterized the British people during the confrontation with Argentina in the summer of 1982. Drawing on examples from the first half of the last century, he shows how the early history of the British labour movement was strongly imbued with patriotic fervour. But he observes that the Left in general and Marxists in particular have neglected – or been hostile towards – patriotism as a force. As a result, the Right has been able to harness and monopolize it for its own purposes. This is a 'dangerous' situation, he argues and he urges the Left to reconsider its notions about patriotism with a view to recapturing it for the labour and socialist movement. His two articles, 'The State of the Left in Western Europe' (October 1982) and 'Labour's Lost Millions' (October 1983), also appeared in *Marxism Today*. In both pieces he brings a historical perspective to bear upon the problems of current Left political strategy. In the latter essay he returns to the question of the 'Forward March of Labour Halted?' in light of the 1983 elections. He goes so far as to suggest that the possibility of a broad alliance of opposition parties be explored in order to confront and defeat the Conservatives in future elections.[91]

In other instances, his pieces are less specifically political. But here, as well, his historical imagination provides original perspectives on contemporary issues and concerns. Thus, in an essay entitled 'Are We on the Edge of a World War?', he argues that the resurgent Cold War should not be compared to the period before or immediately after the Second World War but rather to the years leading up to the First World War.[92] Of course, he notes, the ultimate consequences would be quite different this time. Hobsbawm himself sums up the intentions underlying these essays when he says: 'I am increasingly coming back to the old-fashioned opinion that it is useful in politics to have a historical perspective if you want to know what is new in a situation.[93]

Chapter 6

E. P. Thompson on the Making of the English Working Class

Social history can therefore not be limited to describing the external aspects of antagonistic classes. It must also come to understand the mental outlook of each class. Georges Lefebvre[1]

Historian, essayist and political activist E. P. Thompson is probably the most widely known and controversial of the British Marxist historians. Most noted as a historian for his book The *Making of the English Working Class* (1963),[2] he is also the author of a series of seminal articles and a book, *Whigs and Hunters* (1975),[3] on eighteenth-century English history and society, and a major biographical study, *William Morris: Romantic to Revolutionary* (1955).[4] In a collection of extended essays he has taken up such topics as modern English historical experience and the 'defence' of history, specifically historical materialism, against ahistorical social sciences and philosophies. (The most significant of these have been published together as *The Poverty of Theory* [1978].)[5] As a political essayist, his writings include critical pieces on the political culture of the Cold War, on what he sees as a crisis of British civil liberties (several of the best appear in his book *Writing by Candlelight* [1980]),[6] and articles on the threat of nuclear holocaust and the need to organize in order to bring about British and European nuclear disarmament (the most important of which are published in *Zero Option* (1982),[7] or in his co-edited work *Protest and Survive* [1980]).[8] In recent years Thompson has devoted almost all of his energies to the cause of nuclear disarmament, participating in the resurgence of the Campaign for Nuclear Disarmament (CND) and the founding of END (European Nuclear Disarmament).

In this study I will focus on Thompson's historical writings: *The Making,* the eighteenth-century studies and the historiographical and theoretical essays. Clearly written in terms of the British Marxist historians' theory of class determination, Thompson's histories have made major contributions to British historical studies in particular, and social history in general. *The Making,* for example, has been important in effecting a reconstruction of the social history of the Industrial Revolution and, along with Eric Hobsbawm's work, has transformed the writing of labour history. Thompson's eighteenth-century studies, in which he has begun to offer a new interpretation of English history and society in that period, have contributed to a reconsideration of the 'stability and order' which followed the seventeenth-century revolution and preceded the Industrial Revolution. But Thompson has not only made important contributions to historical studies, but also, directly confronted the historical and theoretical problems of class, its formation, class struggle and consciousness and, in such terms, consciously pursued an alternative to the base-superstructure model in Marxist thought.

There has been an understandable tendency to discuss Thompson's work separately from that of the other British Marxist historians.[9] But I would argue that his writings must also be viewed in terms of their historical and theoretical tradition or, as he himself has referred to it, 'collective'.[10] It in no way reduces his accomplishments to say that what he has often done in his more theoretical writings is to articulate the ideas of the British Marxist historians as a theoretical tradition. That is, as will be shown, he has developed and presented in a more explicitly theoretical fashion the theory of class determination itself.

E.P. Thompson

Edward Palmer Thompson was born in 1924. His father, Edward John, was English; his mother, by origin, American. Both were liberals (with a small 'l') and critics of British imperialism.

Edward John, a writer, had been an educational missionary in India and became known as a friend of the cause of Indian nationalism (and personally a friend of Nehru and other Congress figures).[11] 'E. P.' (as he came to be known, in order to distinguish him from his father) grew up near Oxford and was educated at Kingswood (a Methodist public school). He entered Cambridge University, where he started in literature but then switched to read history. Like most of his contemporaries, his studies were interrupted by the war. He was commissioned an officer in the army and fought in Italy and France.

At university, before his military service, Thompson joined the Communist Party.[12] In the immediate post-war years, he returned to Cambridge to finish his degree, but also spent some time in Yugoslavia and Bulgaria serving as a volunteer building railroads and doing basic reconstruction work. He acknowledged this experience as important in shaping his understanding of what popular collective struggle was about.[13]

It was at Cambridge, following the war, that Thompson met his wife, Dorothy, who is also a historian and a lecturer in modern history at the University of Birmingham. (In fact, Dorothy was much more active in the Communist Party Historians' Group than was Edward.)[14] In 1948, the Thompsons moved to Halifax, Yorkshire, where he took up an extra-mural lectureship with Leeds University and the Workers' Educational Association. (It was during the early 1950s that Thompson wrote his book on William Morris, which he says grew out of his teaching activities.)[15]

During the late 1940s and early 1950s, Thompson remained very active in the Communist Party. But, as he has written, referring to his separation from the Party in 1956, 'I commenced to reason in my thirty-third year, and, despite my best efforts, I have never been able to shake the habit off.'[16] It was in that year that he and John Saville began to publish *The Reasoner*.[17] Thompson's departure from the Party, like Hilton's and Hill's, did not represent a rejection of socialism or Marxism. It did, however, indicate a rejection of Marxism-Leninism. Thus, in the years since he left the Party, Thompson has come to define his socialism as socialist humanism, and his Marxism as Morrisian-Marxism, that is, a Marxism transformed by the concerns and values represented in the work of William Morris.[18] In fact, his departure from the Party did not even mean for Thompson a repudiation of communism (with a small 'c') as a movement, though he now identifies himself as a 'democratic, libertarian communist'.[19]

The Making was published in 1963. In 1965, Thompson joined the faculty of the then new Warwick University as a Reader in the Centre for the Study of Social History, and pursued his work there on the eighteenth century. He was not, however, inactive politically. In 1966-7, he and other socialists (in particular, Raymond Williams and Stuart Hall) joined together to issue what came to be entitled the *May Day Manifesto 1968*,[20] which was intended to be a socialist challenge to the rightward drift of Harold Wilson's Labour government. Also, in 1970, Thompson became involved in campus political battles at Warwick, which revealed activities by the University's administration that he viewed as threatening to academic freedom and civil liberties.[21]

In the mid-1970s, Thompson left Warwick in order to write full-time. (He has since held visiting professorships at several United States universities, such as Rutgers and Brown, where he has taught history and literature.) Though he has written a few historical articles, and an extended critique of structuralist-Marxism (i.e. 'The Poverty of Theory'), Thompson has devoted most of his energies to the CND/END. Awaiting his attention are two promised works: *Customs in Common,* a collection of his writings on eighteenth-century England; and a study of Blake and the Romantic poets.

Like the previous biographical sketches, this one has been brief. Fortunately, in Thompson's case, much has already been written (and, no doubt, will continue to be written) on him and his work. For example, there are Perry Anderson's *Arguments Within English Marxism,* and the Canadian historian Bryan Palmer's *The Making of E. P. Thompson.*[22] Of particular interest among such writings is a short, but perceptive, review essay of *The Poverty of Theory* by Henry Abelove, an American historian.[23] Abelove argues that a fundamental aspect of Thompson's life and work has been his interest in poetry. (In fact, Thompson's original intention was to be a poet, not a historian. Both his father and brother were poets.) He shows that even as a historian Thompson has remained involved with poetry. Most of his life as a teacher has been in adult education which, given the structure of such coursework, has meant that he has been able to integrate literature/poetry and history in his lecturing and tutoring.[24] Moreover, Thompson's historical studies are often framed by references to historically contemporary poets and poetry. The best example is in *The Making,* which opens and closes with references to Blake. Here Thompson argues that much was lost when the double resistance to capitalism of the Romantic poets and Radical craftsmen failed to become a single effort.[25] Another example is in *Whigs and Hunters,* which ends with a discussion of the poets Pope and Swift.[26] Finally, Abelove points out:

> When Thompson titles his major book *The Making of the English Working Class,* he draws attention to that paralleling of art and popular struggle which is in effect the plot of all his work as a historian. For the word 'making' is ambiguous. Maker is the old English term for poet, and making means poetry writing as well as building, achieving. *The Making of the English Working Class* names both what Thompson has done as a writer and what the English working people have in struggle achieved for themselves. In that title, the parallels converge.[27]

The Making of the English Working Class

I know the heroic struggles the English working class has gone through since the middle of the last century; struggles not the less glorious because they are shrouded in obscurity and burked by middle-class historians. Karl Marx[28]

In his historical studies and critical essays, Thompson has persistently pursued an intellectual struggle against those varieties of Marxism and social science which are characterized by economic determinism and the denial of human agency. Moreover, he has insisted that Marxism is best conceived as a theory of history, *not* laws of history in which human beings merely live out pre-determined patterns of development, and that class is a historical concept not just a sociological category or construct. Thus, in the first issue of *The New Reasoner,* Thompson states his objections to the base-superstructure model. He notes that, in spite of Marx and Engels always having 'kept in view [the] dialectical interaction between social consciousness . . . . and social being', the base-superstructure metaphor 'reduced [their] concept of process to a clumsy static model'. Moreover, it is a *'bad and dangerous* model, since Stalin used it not as an image of men changing in society, but as a mechanical model, operating semi-automatically and independently of conscious human agency.'[29]

In 1961, in a review essay of Raymond Williams' book *The Long Revolution,*[30] Thompson voices concern about the need to develop alternatives to the base-superstructure and other similar models. He proposes that Williams give up his vocabulary of 'systems' and 'elements', that Marxists abandon the metaphor of base and superstructure and the determinist notion of 'law', and that both reconsider the concept of 'mode of production'. Quoting Alisdair MacIntyre, he writes that 'what . . . . the mode of production does is to provide . . . . a kernel of human relationship from which all else grows.'[31]

Offering an organic conception of the social whole as an alternative to the mechanical one does not necessarily resolve the problem (which he himself realizes, as we shall see later in this chapter), but Thompson's intentions are clear. He has sought, through class-struggle analysis, to reconceptualize the materialistic dialectic of social being and social consciousness as much as possible away from a static model to a dynamic one. Although it was never an easy task, since the static character of the base-superstructure model, and its tendency to economic determinism, has also affected the Marxist concept of class. This was the central intellectual problem Thompson confronted in the writing of *The Making,* as he has also indicated in several of the articles he wrote around 1960.[32]

The Making is a study of the *formation* of the working class in England from 1790 through to the early 1830s and the coming to consciousness of that class, culminating in Chartism – the first working-class political party. It is probably the most important work of social history written since the Second World War. Moreover, as Thompson intended, it has been important both in terms of historiography and social theory. He writes: 'I hope this book will be seen as a contribution to the understanding of class.'[33] And, in a now-classic statement, he makes very clear what he sees his task as a historian to be (p. 12):

I am seeking to rescue the poor stockinger, the Luddite cropper, the 'obsolete' hand-loom weaver, the 'utopian' artisan, and even the deluded follower of Joanna Southcott, from the enormous condescension of posterity. Their crafts and traditions may have been backward-looking. Their communitarian ideals may have been fantasies. Their insurrectionary conspiracies may have been foolhardy. But they lived through these times of acute social disturbance, and we did not. Their aspirations were valid in terms of their own experience; and if they were casualties of history, they remain, condemned in their own lives, as casualties.

At the same time, he makes known what he opposes. As a study of *class formation, The Making* is written to counter the practice by sociologists in 'stratification studies' of defining class as a static structure or category.[34] Thompson writes that class is a 'historical phenomenon, unifying a number of disparate and seemingly unconnected events, both in the raw material of experience and in consciousness'. Moreover, he insists, class is 'something which in fact happens (and can be shown to have happened) in human relationships' (p. 8).

The term 'experience' appears over and over again in the pages of *The Making* and in Thompson's other historical writings, and is crucial to an understanding of his conception of class. For experience denotes *time,* the stuff of history and, again, above all else, classes are *historical* phenomena: 'If we stop history at a given point, then there are no classes but simply a multitude of experiences. But as we watch these men over an adequate period of social change, we observe patterns in their relationships, their ideas and their institutions.' Furthermore, class as a historical phenomenon, not as an analytical category or structure, involves agency and consciousness. He entitles the book *The Making* 'because it is a study in an active process, which owes as much to agency as to conditioning' (p. 8). In fact, he later adds, 'class is defined by men as they live their own history, and in the end this is its only definition' (p. 10).

Thompson is, of course, directing his arguments not only at sociologists, but also at economic and social historians working on the Industrial Revolution. He feels that economic historians view working people 'as a labour force, migrants, or as the data for statistical series' and, thereby, illustrate an extremely reduced conception of human experience and the process of social change. Social historians and historical sociologists, who work from the perspective of modernization theory and structural-functionalism, he sees as reducing class conflict to an 'unjustified disturbance-symptom', tending to 'obscure the agency of working people, [and] the degree to which they contributed by conscious efforts, to the making of history' (pp. 11-12).[35] This has not been limited to 'bourgeois' historians and social scientists. Marxist historians themselves have often written as if the working class was merely the *creation* of the new instruments of production associated with the Industrial Revolution. Such ideas can even be found in Marx and Engels' own writings (e.g. in Engels' *The Condition of the Working Class in England).* They persisted, no doubt, due to the continuing use of the base-superstructure model, and were still being reproduced in the 1960s, as in such otherwise interesting works as Jurgen Kuczynski's international labour history *The Rise of the Working Class.*[36]

Thompson does not offer an idealism or a simple voluntarism in place of economic and/or technological determinism. He writes: 'class experience is largely determined by the productive relations into which men are born – or enter involuntarily . . . . class consciousness is the way in which these experiences are handled in cultural terms: embodied in traditions, value-systems, ideas and institutional forms.' However, 'If the experience appears as determined, class-consciousness does not. We can see a *logic* in the responses of similar occupational groups undergoing similar experiences, but we cannot predicate any law. Consciousness of class arises in the same way in different times and places, but never in just the same way' (p. 9).

Nor should we forget that class, as a historical phenomenon, is also a historical *relationship:* 'we cannot have two distinct classes, each with an independent being, and then bring them *into* relationship with each other. We cannot have love without lovers, nor deference without squires and labourers. And class happens when some men as a result of common experience . .

. . feel and articulate the identity of their interests as between themselves, and as against other men whose interests are different from (and usually opposed to) theirs.' (p. 8). Here again, Thompson's argument is to be read as a criticism of sociologists who pursue social stratification studies as if classes were merely layered masses of rock.

There is yet another dimension to *The Making* which should be emphasized. It is not only intended as a work of history *and* theory, it is also intended as a political work (a shared characteristic of the work of the British Marxist historians). Thompson is not only writing against the practices of historians and social scientists, but also against a particular intellectual practice (and its political consequences) of the Left, specifically *elitism* – a characteristic of both the 'Old' and the 'New' Left. Regarding the Old Left, he is opposed to the assumption that the working class has a real existence – objectively defined – from which one can 'deduce the class-consciousness which 'it' ought to have (but seldom does) if 'it' was properly aware of its own position and interests', and the proposition which follows, that a 'party, sect, or theorist', is needed who can furnish the consciousness 'not as it is, but as it ought to be' (p. 9). Concerning the New Left, Thompson is opposed to the view of the working class as 'irretrievably co-opted, economically and/or ideologically, by capital' (as presented in both the embourgeoisment thesis of sociologists, and the one-dimensional man thesis of Herbert Marcuse and the Frankfurt School theorists), which produces its own variation of substitutionism, i.e. intellectuals and/or students standing in for class-conscious workers. In both cases, Thompson argues, what is lacking is a sense of history and a proper understanding of class struggle.[37]

Thompson claims, in his preface to *The Making,* that the book is more a series of related studies than a consecutive narrative, but it is now generally agreed that the work, as a whole, is a narrative – a story. The book is divided into three parts. In part one, 'The Liberty Tree', Thompson examines three popular traditions which significantly influenced the English Jacobin agitation of the 1790s. First, he looks at the tradition of Dissent and the changes which it underwent in its Methodist form. Then he considers the collection of popular assumptions and expectations which together made up what was understood to be an 'Englishman's birthright'. Finally, he discusses the political organizations of the English Jacobins, the Corresponding Societies. By taking up the subjective influences which contributed to 'the making' at the outset of the work, Thompson intends to overcome the standard approach to the economic and social, especially labour, history of the Industrial Revolution, which starts with the economic and technological changes and then views the political and cultural developments of the age as pre-determined by them. Again, Thompson is not seeking to eschew materialism. Rather, he starts with popular traditions – religious, sub-political and political – and political organizations in order to show us, before we are presented with 'political economy', that 'the making of the working class is a fact of political and cultural, as much as of economic, history' (p. 213).

Thus, in relation to the tradition of Dissent, Thompson discusses the religious transition of the seventeenth to eighteenth century, which he encapsulates as 'the positive energy of Puritanism, the self-preserving retreat of Dissent', and considers the ambivalences and tensions in the ideas and practices of the dissenting sects. They combined, he says, 'political quietism with a kind of slumbering Radicalism – preserved in the imagery of sermons and tracts and in democratic forms of organization' (p. 33). The literary embodiment of these tensions was Bunyan's *Pilgrim's Progress*, which he calls, along with Tom Paine's *Rights of Man*, 'one of the foundation texts of the English working-class movement' (p. 34).

There were two other features of the dissenting tradition

which were important according to Thompson: its continuing 'communitarian ideas and experiments . . . . sometimes found in association with millenarianism', and its emphasis on the 'liberty of conscience – the one great value which the common people had preserved from the Commonwealth' (pp. 51-3, 56-7). Also, he points out, there were elements of the tradition of Dissent which were to be inherited, though transformed, by Methodism, thereby persisting as experiences in the formation of the working class. (As we shall see, he discusses Methodism quite critically and at length in the second part of the book.)

On the popular tradition of the 'mob', Thompson begins by briefly discussing eighteenth-century social crime (a theme to which he and his colleagues at Warwick were to return later), and proceeds to explain, following George Rudé's approach,[38] the two different forms of riotous action observable in that period. On the one hand, there were actions which arose spontaneously. These occurred when the popular sense of what was fair was piqued or provoked. On the other hand, there were crowd actions which were instigated and manipulated by those who stood above or apart from the 'people'. In particular, he looks at food riots, which, he argues, were efforts by the people to maintain and, later, 're-impose the older moral economy as against the economy of the free market' (pp. 68-73). He also discusses the 'London mob', whose actions in this period might best be characterized as a 'mixture of mob and revolutionary crowd' and whose politics might be viewed as *transitional*.[39]

The third tradition, that of the 'free-born Englishman', involved, in spite of the continuing limitations placed on 'freedom of the press, of public meeting, of trade union . . . . [and] political organization, and of election', a birth right of liberties: 'Freedom from absolutism . . . . freedom from arbitrary arrest, trial by jury, equality before the law, the freedom of the home from arbitrary entrance and search, some limited liberty of thought, of speech, and of conscience' (p. 86). As a result of their being persistently asserted, contested, and re-asserted, they became part of a moral consensus which, Thompson says, should not be underestimated. He discusses this moral consensus as if it were a map of a liberated territory. Its boundaries denote the area in which the English people were unwilling to tolerate interference or transgression by the authorities. He states that the world-view of the common people was not necessarily democratic, in any positive sense, but it was 'anti-absolutist'. They saw themselves as individualists, with few affirmative rights, yet nevertheless secured by the laws against the intrusion of arbitrary power.

It was Tom Paine who best articulated this tradition, and he did so in a new and radically significant fashion. In his extremely popular *Rights of Man* (his reply to Edmund Burke's *Reflections on the Revolution in France)*, Paine provided 'a new rhetoric of radical egalitarianism, which touched the deepest responses of the 'free-born Englishman' and which penetrated the sub-political attitudes of the urban working people' (p. 103). The arguments of *Rights of Man* broke through the categories and conventions of constitutionalism which had structured the moral consensus and set forth far wider democratic claims that were so necessary for the emergence of a labour movement.

Together, the traditions of Dissent and liberty shaped the English Jacobin agitation of the 1790s, which had been precipitated by the French Revolution. *But*, Thompson emphasizes, however much they were instigated and excited by what was transpiring across the Channel, the English agitations were for an *English* democracy. Moreover, the Corresponding Societies, the English Jacobin organizations, represent a 'junction-point'. He describes the London Corresponding Society as extending out in one direction 'to the coffee-houses, taverns and dissenting churches off Piccadilly, Fleet Street and the Strand, where the self-educated journeyman might rub shoulders with the printer, the shopkeeper, the engraver or the young attorney'. But at the same time it extended out in the other direction, making contact with the older working-class communities – the waterside workers of Wapping, the silk-weavers of Spitalfields, the old dissenting stronghold of Southwark. The Corresponding Societies of the North as, for example, that of Sheffield, were also predominantly artisans' organizations, though less diverse in their occupational composition than the London Society.

Furthermore, Thompson argues, the years of the Jacobin agitation were not just a social but also a *historical* junction-point. Although the Corresponding Societies were effectively repressed and the possible alliance between the radically minded middle class and the embryonic working class was inhibited by the example of the French Revolution, nevertheless, he insists, we are mistaken in viewing this as a termination point. It was also a starting point. That is, in these years there were developments which can be comprehended as an English revolution for the powerful way in which they moulded the consciousness of the post-war working class. The results of these years were not immediately evident. But in the years which followed the Jacobin experience of the 1790s, when the radical mechanics, artisans and labourers were politically cut off from the middle-class radicals, they made use of their experiences to promote and sustain traditions and forms of organization of their own. In fact, Thompson says, it was in these years of repression that a specific working-class consciousness began to mature – imbued with a strong democratic impulse.

In part two of *The Making,* entitled 'The Curse of Adam', Thompson turns to examine the changing production and social relations of the period 1790-1830, which were determinant in the formation of the working class. In 'Exploitation', the first chapter of this section, he indicates that he intends to confront directly the assumption that 'steam power and the cotton mill = new working class'. He points out that the factory hands, far from being the 'eldest children of the industrial revolution', were late arrivals. Thompson proceeds to argue that the formation of the working class was actually to be found in the seemingly quite diverse experiences and struggles of field labourers, domestic workers, artisans and others. He observes, however, that to present this argument is to confront, as well, those historians who assert that the terms 'working *classes*' or 'lower *classes*' are more appropriate than the singular 'working *class*' on account of the very diversity of experience.

Thompson's task, then, is to show that what seems to have been diversity of experience was, in fact, a shared, common experience. He is able to accomplish such a task because, unlike those historians who study the Industrial Revolution as a technological and/or economic process, Thompson focuses in particular on the social relations of production and class relations. The common experience of the Industrial Revolution which he reveals was the intensification of two intolerable forms of relationship: those of economic exploitation and political oppression. Moreover, he adds, the intensification of exploitation and oppression became ever more transparent. On exploitation he writes (p. 217):

In agriculture the years between 1760 and 1820 are the years of wholesale enclosure, in which, in village after village, common rights are lost, and the landless and – in the south – pauperized labourer is left to support the tenant-farmer, the landowner, and the tithes of the Church. In the domestic industries, from 1800 onwards, the tendency is widespread for small masters to give way to larger employers (whether manufacturers or middlemen) and for the majority of weavers, stockingers, or nail-makers to become wage-earning outworkers with more or less precarious employment. In the mills and in many mining areas these are the years of the employment of children (and of women underground); and the large-scale enterprise, the factory-system with its new discipline, the mill communities – where the manufacturer not only made riches out of the labour of the 'hands' but could be *seen* to make riches in one generation – all contributed to the transparency of the process of exploitation and to the social and cultural cohesion of the exploited.

On political oppression, Thompson discusses how the development of capitalism involved the reduction of the relationship between employer and labourer to the cash-nexus. This allowed a greater degree of possible freedom to the worker, but it also meant that he felt his lack of freedom more, and these feelings were confirmed each time that he attempted to resist exploitation, for he was met by the forces of employer, of state, and commonly of both.

What Thompson highlights in this early phase of the Industrial Revolution are the changes in, and intensification of, the process of capital accumulation as a human and social experience. Though he himself would not describe it in such terms, he is in effect presenting us with the process which Marx defines in *Capital* as the 'formal' as opposed to the 'real' subsumption of labour by capital. The formal subsumption of labour is the process in which the capitalist relations of production are established. This provides the basis, or premise, upon which the real subsumption of labour, or industrialization, can occur. Marx states that the formal subsumption may involve an intensification of the work being done, an extension of the amount of time being worked, or the work may become more continuous or orderly under the eye of the interested capitalist. But it *does not necessarily* involve significant changes in the labour process itself; that is, it is not necessarily accompanied by changes in the division or technology of labour.'[40] While Marx seems to discuss it as a universal process in capitalist development, and it does have contemporary applications in the Third World, in Britain this can be seen as having occurred after the primitive accumulation of capital in the early enclosure movement, and before the capitalist industrialization of the nineteenth century, though bound up with both. Its social significance is that 'it acts as a determinative force upon various kinds of workers, and as a unifying experience among them, even before the process of "real subjection" incorporates them all and "assembles" them in factories'.[41]

This is a very important point, particularly in light of some recent criticisms of Thompson's work. As an example, we might recall Richard Johnson's argument that Thompson's work is 'culturalism' – especially *The Making* - and represents a break with Dobb's problematic in *Studies in the Development of Capitalism.* It would appear, on the contrary, that Thompson is, in fact, working very much within the problematic laid out by Dobb, though clearly he develops the transition question further, both temporally and socially.[42] We should also mention Perry Anderson's criticism in *Arguments Within English Marxism,* that Thompson fails to consider the 'whole historical process whereby heterogeneous groups of artisans, smallholders, agricultural labourers, domestic workers, and casual poor were gradually assembled, distributed, and reduced to the condition of labour subsumed to capital'[43] and that he focuses on cultural continuities instead. But Anderson is surely somewhat mistaken, for although Thompson does not pursue the Industrial Revolution *through* the 'real' subjection of labour in the factories, which occurred beyond 1830 (nor, unfortunately, does he examine cotton, iron and coal workers), he does examine the very 'objective' historical process of the formal subjection of labour by capital – in fact, it was central to this part of *The Making.*

More persuasive is the criticism made by Keith McClelland, which he offers in response to Richard Johnson's assertions. McClelland suggests that while it is true that Thompson treats economic relations inadequately in *The Making,* this is not because he fails to acknowledge them as 'objective' and 'determining'. Rather, it seems to be the result of the fact that in several sections of the book Thompson keeps economic relations at a distance from political and cultural developments such that they appear to 'determine (but not dictate) political and cultural activity'. By so doing he occasionally inhibits the comprehension of the 'economic' as involving both objective and subjective moments. McClelland acknowledges that this problem does not characterize all sections of the work.[44]

An important feature of *The Making* is Thompson's narrative skill. He effectively establishes the *collective* character of the English workers' experiences of exploitation and oppression. But he regularly does so by drawing on and highlighting the actions and experiences of *individual* artisans and labourers. That is, he makes use of individual experience to express and represent the common experience. In this way, we see what C. Wright Mills refers to as the 'intersection of biography and history'. At the same time, Thompson avoids literary, or sociological, reification in which collectivities are treated as possessing individual identities or are made into objects and paraded through history.

To indicate the experience of the formal subsumption of labour by capital, Thompson quotes from an address by a journeyman cotton spinner on the occasion of a strike in Manchester in 1818. Then he himself proceeds to itemize the grievances felt by working people regarding the changes in the social relations of production (pp. 221-2):

the rise of a master-class without traditional authority or obligations; the growing distance between master and man; the transparency of the exploitation at the source of their new wealth and power; the loss of status and above all of independence for the worker, his reduction to total dependence on the master's instruments of production; the partiality of the law; the disruption of the traditional family economy; the discipline, monotony, hours and conditions of work; loss of leisure and amenities; the reduction of the man to the status of an 'instrument'.

In the three chapters which follow, entitled 'The Field Labourers', 'Artisans and Others' and 'The Weavers', Thompson presents the changes involved and how they were experienced by those groups of workers.

Not surprisingly, on the historical controversy of the standard of living in the Industrial Revolution, Thompson aligns himself with the Hammonds and Eric Hobsbawm, i.e. the 'pessimistic view'. While he does attempt to take up the subject of quantitative measurement of living standards in the period 1780-1850,[45] his major contribution to the debate must surely be his challenge of the assumption that there exists some simple correlation between standard of living, as indicated by statistical indices, and the quality of life, either 'objectively' or as it was perceived. For example, he cites 'those trades, such as coal-mining, in which real wages advanced between 1790 and 1840, but at the cost of longer hours and greater intensity of labour, so that the breadwinner was "worn out" before the age of forty. In statistical terms, this reveals an upward curve. To the families concerned it might feel like an immiseration' (p. 231). It should be pointed out that it is this kind of statement by Thompson which is too readily viewed as culturalist or subjective. But it is no more culturalist than it is economistic. What Thompson is illustrating is that those economic historians who are fixated on particular standard-of-living indices fail to acknowledge the equally 'objective' intensification of exploitation. At the same time, Thompson is showing that exploitation, even in the limited sense of economic relations, involves both objective and subjective moments. In this way, he is making it quite clear that exploitation is not merely a concept invented by politico-economically minded Marxists with moralistic intentions, but was in fact *felt* by those who actually experienced it. Moreover, he is calling attention to the fact that the changes in the social relations of production not only involved the intensification of exploitation but also greater insecurity. Thus he is able to conclude that 'by 1840 most people were "better off" than their forerunners had been fifty years before, but they had suffered and continued to suffer this slight improvement as a catastrophic experience' (p. 231).

In the second part of the book, Thompson takes up a critical examination of Methodism: 'Puritanism – Dissent – Noncomformity: the decline collapses into a surrender. *Dissent* still carries the sound of resistance to Apollyon and the Whore of Babylon, *Nonconformity* is self-effacing and apologetic: it asks to be left alone' (p. 385). Essentially, Thompson presents Methodism as an important force in the development of an industrial work-discipline. But the real issue, he states, is why so many working people were willing to submit to this form of psychic exploitation. He offers three reasons: 'direct indoctrination, the Methodist community-sense, and the psychic consequences of the counter-revolution' (p. 411). Direct indoctrination refers to what took place in the Sunday schools, which he calls 'psychological atrocities'. The Methodist sense of community (the 'heart of a heartless world') was important because the tension between the authoritarian and democratic tendencies of Old Dissent persisted in it, however much the Methodist leadership sought to break with both the intellectual and democratic traditions of Dissent (pp. 411-17).

Regarding the psychic consequences of the counterrevolutionary years, Thompson at this point enters the debate over whether or not Methodism inhibited revolution in England. His argument, which differs somewhat from Hobsbawm's (i.e. that Methodism and Radicalism advanced together), is that 'religious revivalism took over at the point where 'political' or temporal aspirations met with defeat.'[46] He then discusses the millenarian movement of Joanna Southcott and the Southcottians.

In the last chapter of part two, 'Community', Thompson examines the confrontation between the old and newer modes of production, 'each support[ing] distinct kinds of community with characteristic ways of life'. Industrial capitalism won but, he argues, at the same time – and in opposition to it – there was also developed in the working-class communities an 'ethos of mutuality' and 'working-class consciousness'.

In part three, 'The Working Class Presence', Thompson returns to the subject of plebeian radicalism and follows its development from Luddism to the end of the Napoleonic Wars. He starts with the political capture of the Westminster Parliamentary constituency by Radicalism, observing that, in the capital, communication had never ceased between the middle-class and working-class reformers. The Radical movement took a markedly different form in the Midlands and industrial north, however. There the repression against Jacobinism and trade unionism (i.e. the Combination Acts) drove those struggles underground. In the course of the chapter, 'An Army of Redressers', Thompson furthers Hobsbawm's argument that machine-breaking was rational and organized, and extends it by showing that Luddism was not only industrial action in an illegal and underground form but, in fact, was the junction of the 'secret *industrial* tradition' *and* the 'secret *political* tradition'. He insists that Luddism was a quasi-insurrectionary movement and argues (controversially) that there was a continuous underground tradition, of which Luddism was an essential part, linking the Jacobins of the 1790s to the movements of 1816-20.[47]

In the following chapter, 'Demagogues and Martyrs', Thompson analyzes the 'heroic years of plebeian Radicalism' (1816-20). He discusses the problems of leadership, the Hampden Clubs, the Pentridge rising, Peterloo – 'a one-sided class war, waged by the ruling class', and the Cato Street conspiracy. In the final chapter, 'Class Consciousness', Thompson explains how the 1820s, which appear to have been so calm and peaceful, were, in fact, 'the years of Richard Carlile's contest for the liberty of the press; of growing trade union strength and the repeal of the Combination Acts; of the growth of free thought, cooperative experiment, and Owenite theory'; that is: 'they are years in which individuals and groups sought to render into theory the twin experiences... of the Industrial Revolution, and .... popular Radicalism insurgent and in defeat' (p. 781). He writes of the Radical, and highly literate, artisan culture and how, in the struggles over such issues as the unstamped press, artisans and workers made the tradition of liberty and the free-born Englishman very much their own. He also discusses the developments in political thought made by William Cobbett, then Carlile, Wade and Cast, and Robert Owen. Finally, he concludes, the working class came to be formed or, better, *made,* in the early 1830s – influenced once again by a French Revolution (1830) and reinforced politically by the drawing of class lines by the middle class in the passage of the Reform Bill of 1832.

Thompson argues that the suggestion that for the 1830s 'working *classes'* is a more accurate description than 'working *class',* is grossly mistaken. There was, he insists, the growth of class consciousness and the growth of corresponding forms of political and industrial organization: 'By 1832 there were strongly based and self-conscious working-class institutions – trade unions, friendly societies, educational and religious movements, political organizations, periodicals – working-class intellectual traditions, working-class community-patterns, and a working-class structure of feeling' (pp. 212-13).

Of course, there have been criticisms of *The Making* from non-Marxist historians.[48] But there have also been criticisms from Marxists. I have already mentioned two related criticisms offered by Richard Johnson and Perry Anderson. There is another of Anderson's criticisms which ought to be acknowledged at this point, for it is directed at the central historical argument of the book. Following up a criticism of *The Making* offered in 1964 by his colleague at *New Left Review,* Tom Nairn,[49] Anderson asks to what extent the working class can be understood to have been made if *industrialization* had not yet actually taken place.[50] Thompson's reply would surely be two-fold. First, as we have already seen, he shows that the formation of the English working class was not the product of industrialization, as traditionally conceived, but rather was determined in the prior experience of capitalist exploitation and accumulation which itself gave rise to and structured the specific process of industrialization. Nevertheless, to return to the criticism made by Keith McClelland, Thompson occasionally presents the economic as overly objective and, thus, what is missing from *The Making* is the way in which the formation of the working class actually determines the further course of capitalist industrialization. *The Making* points the way towards work on this issue but it does not itself treat the question. Second, regarding the dramatic changes and discontinuities of working-class experience of the period 1850-80, which Anderson offers as a challenge to the idea of the working class having been made in the 1830s, Thompson has always insisted on seeing working-class experience in historically specific terms and as a process. Thus, as Anderson recognizes, Thompson himself calls for study of the changes and discontinuities in working-class experience and consciousness during that period,[51] as for example, the work being carried on by the historian Gareth Stedman Jones,[52] which he strongly praises.

Eighteenth-Century Studies: Hegemony and Class Struggle

Sworn to remedy a capital fault
And bring down the exorbitant price of the malt.
From Dudley to Walsall they trip it along And Hampton was truly

alarmed at the throng.
Women and children, wherever they go Shouting out, 'Oh, the
brave Dudley boys. O';
Nailers and spinners the cavalcade join,
The markets to lower their flattering design.
John Freeth, The Colliers' March (1780s)[53]

Instead of moving ahead to the 1840s and 'later chapters' in the history of the English working class, Thompson moved back in time, after *The Making,* to the eighteenth century. He did so, he reports, partly because his wife, Dorothy, was involved in work on Chartism and, thus, he 'didn't want to move forward into that'. However, he also considered that there were 'a lot of unfinished problems which remained from the beginning of *The Making'*. Finally, he was drawn further into eighteenth-century subjects as a result of his history teaching and curriculum development at Warwick University.[54] This 'turning back' to the eighteenth century led him to confront – as in his work on *The Making* – both historical and theoretical issues, and in the process to make new contributions to both areas. It also enabled him to develop points which he had begun to make in that book, especially regarding class, class struggle and class consciousness.

Though not specifically a part of what are being called the eighteenth-century studies, we should attend here to Thompson's essay, 'The Peculiarities of the English', which appeared in 1965.[55] It represents his response to the efforts by Perry Anderson[56] and Tom Nairn[57] to offer a Marxist historical interpretation of the contemporary crisis of Britain. In particular, 'Peculiarities' was written in reply to Anderson's essay, 'Origins of the Present Crisis', in which Anderson seeks to sketch out a framework for a 'totalizing history . . . . of modern British society', focusing on 'the global evolution of the class structure'.[58] (There was a personal/political dimension to the exchange in that Thompson was a founder and original member of the editorial board of *New Left Review* which, not long after publication began, invited Anderson to take over editorial directorship. He accepted, and soon after the board was reorganized, Thompson was excluded and the journal's orientation changed, placing more emphasis on Continental Marxism.)[59]

Essentially, Anderson argues that the crisis in Britain and of the British labour movement can be traced back to the English Revolution of the seventeenth century which, according to him, transformed the economic structure but not the social structure or superstructure and which, due to its religious and 'pre-Enlightenment' character, left no significant ideological legacy. Furthermore, Anderson argues, the intact social structure meant the continued domination of the (feudal) landed aristocracy which, for a variety of historical reasons, was later able to merge, as the senior partner, with the rising industrial bourgeoisie, and thus continue to shape British life. Because the proletariat's most heroic struggles against capitalism occurred before the adequate development of socialist (i.e. Marxist) theory, 'it evolved separately but subordinate, within the apparently unshakeable structure of British capitalism'. Thus, 'a supine bourgeoisie produced a supine proletariat'.[60]

Thompson's reply is both historical and theoretical in form. Regarding Anderson's argument that the seventeenth-century revolution had provided for the persistence of a (feudal) landed aristocracy which was later able to incorporate the industrial bourgeoisie, he responds that the aristocracy was already a highly successful agrarian bourgeoisie in the eighteenth century, whose origins antedated the Revolution. Moreover, at a methodological level, Thompson argues that a major fault of Anderson's in 'Origins' was his ahistorical use of models. In particular, Thompson objects to Anderson's construction of a model of historical development which focuses on a single 'dramatic episode – the Revolution – to which all that goes before and after must be related'. He further objects to the fact that Anderson proffers an ideal type of revolution, derived in most part from the French Revolution, 'against which all others may be judged'. With reference to the supposed absence of an ideological legacy of the English Revolution and bourgeoisie, Thompson asks how it is possible, for example, to disregard the significance of the 'Protestant and bourgeois-democratic inheritance', to miss the importance of capitalist political economy as 'authentic, articulated ideology', and to fail to consider the contribution, over more than three centuries, of British natural scientists.[61]

Thompson offers a series of historical hypotheses, questions and criticisms of Anderson's and Nairn's work on the premature working-class movement and criticizes their schematic handling of the concept of *class*. He writes: 'In their extraordinarily intellectualized presentation of history, class is clothed throughout in anthropomorphic imagery. Classes have the attributes of personal identity, with volition, conscious goals, and moral qualities. Even when overt conflict is quiescent we are to suppose a class with an unbroken ideal identity, which is slumbering or has instincts and the rest.'[62] Later in the essay he restates his own conception of class, in words very reminiscent of the preface to *The Making*.[63] Also, though he does so inadequately, Thompson criticizes Anderson's use of the Gramscian concept of hegemony, anticipating his own later use of the concept in his analysis of eighteenth-century English society (which will be discussed below).

Another point which Thompson makes in 'Peculiarities' regards the base-superstructure model. He again rejects it as inadequately representing the 'dialectical intercourse between social being and social consciousness – or between 'culture' and *'not* culture' – [which] is at the heart of any comprehension of the historical process within the Marxist tradition'. Derived from 'constructional engineering (similar to the boxes and building terms beloved by some sociologists)', it is quite incapable of describing the 'flux of conflict, the dialectic of a changing social process'. At the same time, indicating his dissatisfaction with his own formulation of the social totality, he says that while organic metaphors are better, in the end they too are inadequate because they also expel the *human* dimension. The problem, then, is that such metaphors (mechanical and organic) necessarily tend to reductionism and fail to capture the 'interaction of being-consciousness'. Thompson makes it clear that if the dialectic between social being and social consciousness is displaced from our analysis then we have completely abandoned the Marxist tradition.[64]

The task remains, therefore, 'to find a model for the social process which allows an autonomy to social consciousness within a context which, in the final analysis, has always been determined by social being'. These words should be read carefully, for a similar – but quite different – proposition is regularly presented in Marxist studies. Thompson is not advocating the model offered by Marxist-structuralists, derived from some comments by Engels, in which the 'base, or economic level, is determinant *in the last instance'*, because 'if the "economic movement" is thrust back to an area of ultimate causation, then like Bacon's first cause, it can be forgotten in its empyrean. If we relegate it to in-the-last-analysis epochal determination . . . . then it may be asked how far – except at moments of transition between historical epochs – this model has any relevance?' Nor is Thompson seeking a new model to describe the old relationship between economics and culture. Challenging the assumed equation of 'social being' with 'economics', he writes: 'Even if "base" were not a bad metaphor we would have to add that whatever it is, it is not just economic but human – a characteristic human relationship entered into involuntarily in the productive process . . . . social and cultural phenomena do not trail after the economic at some remote remove; they are, at their source, immersed in the same nexus of relationship.' This argument is consequential for historical, social, and political analysis, since it draws attention to the fact that modes of exploitation are not just 'economic' but rather historically specific configurations of *social* relations. At the same time, it points to the fact that the very assumption that there is a particular dimension of human life – the economic – which can be isolated and treated separately from non-economic social relations is itself the consequence of a particular phase of capitalist evolution. Furthermore, he adds, the struggle against capitalism has involved, in at least one of its forms, opposition to the propensity of capitalism to 'reduce all human relationships to economic definitions'.[65]

The 'importance of the real history', Thompson says, is that 'it not only tests theory, it reconstructs theory'.[66] As we shall see, out of his work on the eighteenth century, Thompson further articulates his conception of class – and the British Marxist historians' theory of class determination – and begins to offer an alternative model to the base-superstructure one to describe the social totality.

The first two of his essays on the eighteenth century deal with subjects derived directly from *The Making*. In 'Time, Work-Discipline, and Industrial Capitalism',[67] Thompson takes up an issue which Weber had raised in *The Protestant Ethic and the Spirit of Capitalism*,[68] and which he himself had discussed in regard to Methodism;[69] that is, the transformation in the work-ethic and orientation to labour entailed in the development of industrial capitalism. He shows that this involved the imposition and eventual internalization of a 'time orientation' to labour and life, in contrast to – and displacing – a 'task orientation'. Moreover, in opposition to modernization theorists, he argues that the changes must not be viewed as a 'supposedly-neutral, technologically-determined, process known as "industrialization"'. Although it is true that such 'changes in manufacturing technique...demand greater synchronization of labour and a greater exactitude in time-routines in *any* society,' it must be realized that the way in which such changes transpire may vary. He points out that since the 'transition' is not limited to merely the specifics of the labour process, but affects the whole culture, it is necessary to consider the changes in terms of the structures 'of power, property-relations, religious institutions, etc.' What he is stressing is the fact that the process of change 'is not to "industrialism" *tout court* but to industrial capitalism or (in the twentieth century) to alternative systems whose features are still indistinct'. Thus it is necessary to consider both 'time-sense in its technological conditioning and time measurement as a means of labour exploitation'.[70]

The second essay which arose out of *The Making,* 'The Moral Economy of the English Crowd in the Eighteenth Century (1971)',[71] expands Thompson's previous analysis of a specific form of crowd action, the food riots. He points out that they were 'a highly complex form of direct popular action, disciplined and with clear objectives.' They were the common people's way of asserting the traditional moral economy against the newer political economy of the market place and of reminding the authorities and the rich of their responsibilities in the changing paternalist model of social order, and of indicating to them that the working people and the poor were capable of upsetting that social order if obligations were not met. The food riots were '*threats* of class war' and should, then, be viewed as *political* actions.

His next major study, *Whigs and Hunters,* grew out of Thompson's work at Warwick, where he and his colleagues were pursuing the social history of eighteenth-century England, in particular 'the law, both as ideology and actuality . . . . and that century's definition of crime'.[72]

Whigs and Hunters is a study of the Black Act of 1723 and what its passage tells us about eighteenth-century English society. The Act itself was passed in response to a number of disturbances around the forests of Windsor and east and south-east Hampshire. These included deer-hunting, poaching, the cutting down of young trees, harassment of forest officials and sending of anonymous threatening letters. It was so-named because the perpetrators of the disturbances were armed and disguised with blackened faces. (This was actually a practice of poachers dating back to the medieval period, which continued into the nineteenth century in some areas.) What the Act did was to make these and related activities (fifty in all) capital offences.

Thompson describes the Black Act as 'legislative overkill' but his task is to elucidate how such a draconian measure came to be law. He shows that 'blacking' arose as the mode of resistance by the foresters to the re-assertion and extension of forest authority by the state and large property holders. He states that the Blacks were 'armed foresters, enforcing the definition of rights to which the "country people" had become habituated, and also resisting the private emparkments which encroached upon their tillage, their firing and their grazing'. Thinking of Hobsbawm's work, he states that they 'are not quite social bandits [or] agrarian rebels, but they share something of both'.[73] To those of property and authority the disturbances were viewed as an emergency, although as Thompson points out there was little 'blood shed... No gentleman or magistrate was harmed. This was no Jacquerie.' Nevertheless, the fear on the part of the propertied as expressed by the Act resulted in the hanging, imprisonment, or transportation of those convicted of the offences set forth in it. But, Thompson argues, the propertied did not see the specific actions of the Blacks as threatening. Rather, what made the situation an emergency, 'was the repeated public humiliation of the authorities; the simultaneous attacks upon royal and private property; the sense of a confederate movement which was enlarging its social demands . . . . the symptoms of something close to class warfare, with the loyalist gentry in the disturbed areas objects of attack and pitifully isolated in their attempts to enforce order.[74]

Yet, he acknowledges, even this is insufficient to explain the extreme character of the repression provided for by the Black Act. So he explores the passage of the Act in terms of both the socio-historical development of capitalism and the immediate needs of the political elite, especially Walpole and his fellow Whigs. Thompson discusses the way in which the increasing depersonalization of class relations necessitated the imposition of new methods of class control and discipline. He writes that 'economists advocated the discipline of low wages and starvation, and lawyers the sanction of death'. This, he says, also shows the changing conception of crime itself, as defined by the propertied. What was now the object of punishment was not 'an offence between men . . . . but an offence against property'. In this fashion, he observes, law is projected as impartial or indifferent to status in the social hierarchy: 'it was neutral as between every degree of man, and defended only the inviolability of the ownership of things.'[75] He also investigates the 'high politics' of Parliament and the Crown and argues that the Act, as a means of restoring order to a particular region, served the interests of Walpole and his supporters in their ascendance to power in the state. That is, it was used by Walpole and the Whigs as proof that he was an 'able and vigilant minister' in a period when the Government was in crisis due to the events surrounding the South Sea Bubble (1720-21). Thompson describes English political life in these years as similar to that in a 'banana republic' and those who sought power as 'parasites'.[76] Though there is much more which can be said of this book, one further point which must be made is that Thompson asserts that, in spite of the repression, the efforts of the Blacks were not without effect. He shows that the foresters were able through the rest of the century to hold onto and perhaps even extend their common rights in the area around Windsor Forest, though of course they were ultimately doomed.[77]

In *Whigs and Hunters* and the related volume, *Albion's Fatal Tree* (1975), Thompson and his colleagues began to offer a reinterpretation of eighteenth-century England's 'political stability and social order'. In one of his contributions to *Albion's Fatal Tree,* 'Property, Authority and the Criminal Law', Douglas Hay shows that religion was displaced by law as the central legitimizing ideology in eighteenth-century England (and was itself displaced by the 'ideology of the freemarket and of political liberalism in the nineteenth').[78] From a related, though different, perspective, their studies, in Thompson's words, 'remind us that stability, no less than revolution, may have its own kind of Terror'.[79]

In two other articles, 'Patrician Society, Plebeian Culture' (1974), and 'Eighteenth-century English Society: class struggle without class?' (1978),[80] Thompson develops further the efforts to provide a re-interpretation of the eighteenth century and comes to present his analysis in terms of Gramsci's concept of hegemony. By hegemony (and this is important) Thompson does *not* mean consensus. At least in the eighteenth century, he says 'hegemony does not entail any acceptance by the poor of the gentry's paternalism upon the gentry's own terms or in their approved self-image.' Rather, it refers to an *order of struggle* that is constantly being disputed and negotiated, but does not become revolutionary conflict, nor entail the continuous use of physical force or coercion by the state (or similar authority) to maintain the social order. This understanding of hegemony is arguably the one which Gramsci intended when he offered it, and one which is shared by Eugene Genovese, particularly in his book *Roll, Jordan, Roll: The World the Slaves Made.*[81] In reply to those critics who had not properly grasped the argument of his work regarding the hegemonic relationship between masters and slaves, Genovese writes: 'Hegemony implies class struggles and has no meaning apart from them.... It has nothing in common with consensus history and represents its antithesis – a way of defining the historical content of class struggle during times of apparent social quiescence.'[82] In eighteenth-century England, Thompson asserts, there was a robust plebeian culture greatly distanced from the patrician culture and its conception of social order – sometimes resisting or even opposing it, sometimes accommodated to it but, nevertheless, operating within its limits. The maintenance of the hegemonic order, then, was no simple process, especially following the upheavals and changes of the seventeenth century.

In 'Patrician Society, Plebeian Culture', Thompson discusses the ongoing changes in the social order and relations between the gentry and labouring poor or, as he calls them, 'patricians and plebeians'. He starts his analysis by pointing out that this was a transitional period in which the old 'paternalist control over the whole life of the labourer was . . . . being eroded.' That is, there were qualitative changes taking place in the social relations of production: 'the erosion of half-free forms of labour, the decline of living-in, the final extinction of labour services, and the advance of free, mobile, wage labour'. These changes meant that labourers were experiencing greater freedom in their working lives at every level, from the selection of employers down to the daily routine of work. In general there were fewer immediate restrictions on their activities both during and outside their working time. The ruling gentry, who saw these changes as leading to the 'indiscipline of working people, their irregularity of employment, their lack of economic dependency, and their social insubordination', were increasingly distanced from the process of production and immediate relations of exploitation. They removed themselves from direct contact with the labouring poor and ensconced themselves in the confines of their landscaped estates. They continued to appropriate surplus value produced by the labouring poor but they did so through their tenants and by commerce or taxation. Yet, in spite of what appeared to contemporaries to be 'old paternalism at the point of crisis', the transition process of the eighteenth century was relatively stable: 'The insubordination of the poor was an inconvenience; it was not a menace. The styles of politics and of architecture, the rhetoric of the gentry and their decorative arts, all seem to proclaim stability, self-confidence, a habit of managing all threats to their hegemony.'[83]

It was in the immense distance between the lives and activities of working people and the gentry that the plebeian culture developed. It was a culture epitomized, Thompson says, by 'Defoe's fictional cloth worker [who] called before the magistrate to account for default, [declared]; "not *my Master,* and't please your Worship, I hope I am *my own Master".*' That is, the worker was anxious to liberate himself 'from the immediate, daily humiliations of dependency'. Yet at the same time, the broader structures of power and authority, and his relation to it, are comprehended as being as 'inevitable and irreversible as the earth and sky'. This understanding of the world, Thompson argues, is the consequence of the process of hegemony; it 'does not preclude resentment or even surreptitious acts of protest or revenge, [but] it does preclude affirmative rebellion.'

To describe the process and relationship of hegemony in this period, Thompson adopts the metaphor of public theatre. He allows that a great part of politics and law is always theatre, but what is remarkable about the eighteenth century, he says, is the 'style and the self-consciousness with which it was deployed' by the gentry. Their performance did not depend upon regular, daily activities, 'but upon occasional dramatic interventions: the roasted ox, the prizes offered for some race or sport, the liberal donation to charity in time of dearth.'[84] Yet there was one regularized public activity which they did make fully their own: the administration of the law.

While the plebeian culture was not a revolutionary, nor even a proto-revolutionary, culture, neither was it deferential: 'It bred riots, but not rebellions, direct actions but not democratic organizations.' In particular, Thompson discusses three characteristics of eighteenth-century action; 'the anonymous tradition', e.g. the sending (or publishing) of anonymous threatening letters; the 'counter-theatre of threat and sedition' evidenced in the 'language of crowd symbolism...effigy burning; the hanging of a boot from the gallows; the illumination of windows'; and the 'crowd's capacity for swift direct action, as in destruction of machinery and intimidation of employers or dealers...before troops came on the scene'. Yet as he adds, they refrained from taking life.[85]

At one point in 'Patrician Society, Plebeian Culture', Thompson writes of relations between the gentry and common people: 'There is some mutuality of relationship here which it is difficult not to analyze at the level of class relationship.'[86] In 'Eighteenth-century English Society', he focuses on 'theoretical implications of this particular historical formation for the study of class', and it is here that Thompson provides the clearest articulation yet of the British Marxist historians' theory of class determination.

In *The Making* Thompson insists that class is a historical phenomenon and he follows Hobsbawm (in effect) in arguing that class in the 'full sense' only exists when there is class consciousness, which is why *The Making* is to be considered a study in *class formation*. But then what about eighteenth-century English society – is it a society of classes if the 'classes' are not conscious of themselves as such? Thompson uses the terms 'gentry' and 'common people', 'patricians' and 'plebeians' (which are not specifically class terminologies) because he feels that class in the full sense is not present in the evidence. Referring directly to Hobsbawm's article, 'Class Consciousness in History',[87] Thompson remarks that class as a historical phenomenon can imply two modes of analysis: '(a) with reference to real, empirically observable correspondent historical content [i.e. class in the full sense]; (b) as a heuristic or analytic category to organize historical evidence which has a very much less direct correspondence' but makes sense of a complex of otherwise inexplicable facts. He explains that, as much as he is drawn towards use of the concept of class in sense (b), as a tool for analysis, he is wary of doing so because of the danger of reading too much class into the evidence. All this leads him to declare:

> class, in its heuristic usage, is inseparable from the notion of 'class struggle'. In my view, far too much theoretical attention (much of it plainly ahistorical) has been paid to 'class', and far too little to 'class-struggle'. Indeed, class struggle is the prior, as well as the more universal, concept. To put it bluntly: classes do not exist as separate entities, look around, find an enemy class, and then start to struggle. On the contrary, people find themselves in a society structured in determined ways (crucially, but not exclusively, in productive relations), they experience exploitation (or the need to maintain power over those whom they exploit), they identify points of antagonistic interest, they commence to struggle around these issues and in the process of struggling they discover themselves as classes, they come to know this discovery as class-consciousness. Class and class-consciousness are always the last, not the first, stage in the historical process.[88]

Thompson thus reformulates class analysis as class-struggle analysis.

Let us be clear what Thompson is and is not saying, especially since his critics often fail to understand his work and persist in seeing it as 'culturalist'. He is *not* claiming that the formation of class is independent of objective determinations or that classes can be defined simply as a cultural formation. In fact, he insists that 'these objective determinations require the most scrupulous examination.' However, he does argue – reminding us that class is both a relationship and a process – that 'no examination of objective determinations (and certainly no model theorized from it) can give one class and class-consciousness in a simple equation . . . . Class eventuates as men and women *live* their productive relations, and as they *experience* their determinate situations, within 'the *ensemble* of the social relations', with inherited culture and expectations and as they handle these experiences in cultural ways.'[89] As Ellen Wood states in her defence of Thompson's work, insistence on *'the* concept of class as *relationship* and *process* stresses that objective relations to the means of production are significant insofar as they establish antagonisms and generate conflicts and struggles; that these conflicts and struggles shape social experience in "class ways", even when they do not express themselves in class consciousness and clearly visible formations; and that over time we can discern how these relationships impose their logic, their pattern on social processes.' All of this is in contrast to 'purely "structural" conceptions of class [which] do not require us to look for the ways in which class actually imposes its logic, since classes are simply there by definition.'[90]

Contrary, then, to the assertions of critics such as Perry Anderson and G. A. Cohen,[91] Thompson does not deny the presence of class in the absence of class consciousness. In fact, his formulation of class formation insists that class determinants structure life and the historical process even without the presence of classes in the full sense. In this way, class struggle is anterior to class because classes in the full sense *'presuppose* an experience of conflict and struggle' issuing from social relations of production in the form of relations of exploitation; and also because 'there are conflicts and struggles structured in "class ways",' even in those societies where there have not (yet) emerged class-conscious class formations.[92] Moreover, Thompson is thus able to confront those 'bourgeois' historians and social scientists who deny the historical significance, even existence, of class experience where class does not present itself directly.

So, to sum up, Thompson states that while there was class struggle there was not class in its nineteenth-century form. The point is that 'class is a historical formation, and it does not occur only in ways prescribed as theoretically proper. Because in other places and periods we can observe "mature" (i.e. self-conscious and historically-developed) class formations, with ideological and institutional expression, this does not mean that whatever happens less decisively is not class.'[93] He presents the metaphor of a 'societal field-of-force' to describe eighteenth-century relations between the gentry and common people: 'The crowd at one pole, the aristocracy and gentry at the other, and until late in the century, the professional and merchant groups bound down by lives of magnetic dependency on the rulers, or on occasion hiding their faces in common action with the crowd.' He acknowledges that by 'employing the terminology of class conflict while resisting the attribution of identity to *a* class' he might be seen as heretical but he is confident that the field-of-force metaphor can co-exist fruitfully with his own alternative to the base-superstructure model which, as we shall see in the next section, is based on a statement by Marx.

History vs. Theory

As if the task were the dialectic balancing of concepts, and not the grasping of real relations! Karl Marx, *Grundrisse*[94]

Thompson closes his book, *Whigs and Hunters,* with a discussion of the rule of law in English historical experience, and what he sees as its inadequate treatment by historians and social scientists. He is critical of those historians, influenced by a conservative reading of the *Annales* tradition, who reject political and/or legal questions in favour of the *'longue durée*

[of] demographic, material, almost geological formations of history'.[95] He is equally critical of Marxists who diminish the significance of law either by treating it as merely a tool of the ruling class or by relegating it to being part of the superstructure. In his essay, 'The Poverty of Theory', Thompson makes clear that he found that:

> law did not keep politely to a 'level' but was at *every* bloody level; it was imbricated within the mode of production and productive relations themselves (as property-rights, definitions of agrarian practice) and it was simultaneously present in the philosophy of Locke; it intruded brusquely within alien categories, reappearing bewigged and gowned in the guise of ideology; it danced a cotillion with religion, moralizing over the theatre of Tyburn; it was an arm of politics and politics was one of its arms; it was an academic discipline, subjected to the rigour of its own autonomous logic; it contributed to the definition of the self-identity both of rulers and ruled; above all, it afforded an arena for class struggle, within which alternative notions of law were fought out.[96]

Thompson does not deny the relationship between class power and the law in the eighteenth century. As he himself shows, 'the law did mediate existent class relations to the advantage of the rulers.' In fact, the law became an instrument of the ruling classes on too many occasions. Yet, he adds, 'the law mediated these class relations through legal forms, which imposed, again and again, inhibitions upon the actions of rulers.' (Actually, the law itself was not merely imposed, it was struggled over and contested, for, in the eighteenth century, there were two definitions of property-rights confronting each other.)[97]

The point Thompson is making is that the law must be examined as a complex and contradictory practice and ideology.

Moreover, he argues that the 'inhibitions upon power imposed by law seem . . . . a legacy as substantial as any handed down from the struggles of the seventeenth century to the eighteenth, and a true and important cultural achievement.'[98] This is not just a crucial issue in historical and theoretical terms but remains a critical political question and one that has not been adequately addressed by socialists. Thompson himself claims that 'no serious socialist thinker can suppose that a rule of some kind of law – albeit, socialist law and not capitalist law – is a profound human good.'[99] The difficulty in this area, which Thompson would acknowledge, is indicated by Perry Anderson in his critique of Thompson's work. He observes that the rule of law is most problematic, for 'even the most despotic states have typically had comprehensive legal codes and [been] ruled by laws.'[100] The issue of the rule of law and with it the entire subject of rights in the state must be placed high on the agenda of social history, social thought, and socialist debate.

It is in the course of his eighteenth-century studies that Thompson finally begins to offer an alternative to the base-superstructure model. He takes it directly from Marx, in the *Grundrisse:* 'In all forms of society it is a determinate production and its relations which assign every other production and its relations their rank and influence. It is a general illumination in which all other colours are plunged and which modifies their specific tonalities. It is a special ether which defines the specific gravity of everything found in it.'[101]

In his essay, 'Folklore, Anthropology, and Social History' (1977),[102] Thompson repeats this quotation from Marx and further explains its advantage as an alternative materialist conception of the social totality. He recalls his earlier criticism of the assumption that social being is the economic base and social consciousness the superstructure, and contends that this quote from the *Grundrisse* emphasizes 'the simultaneity of expression of characteristic productive relations in all systems and areas of social life rather than any notion of the primacy (more "real") of the "economic", with the norms and culture seen as some secondary "reflection" of the primary'. He then asks if it is still possible to maintain that social being determines social consciousness, to which he replies in the affirmative. But he stipulates that if we are to be able to do so we must throw away the narrow conception of 'economic' and go back to the full sense of 'mode of production'. This reconceptualization of the mode of production away from the narrowly economic is important because the mode of production furnishes the 'attendant relations of production (which are also relations of domination and subordination) into which men and women are born or involuntarily enter', and 'this provides the "general illumination in which all other colours are plunged and which modifies their specific tonalities".' Moreover, 'relations of production, of modern societies, find expression in the formation and struggle (on occasion, equilibrium) of classes'.

Thus, we are again at class, *a historical category* – describing *people in relationship over time* – and the crucial concept of *experience* (and also agency):

> class is an 'economic' and it is also a 'cultural' formation: it is impossible to give any theoretical priority to one aspect over the other. And it follows that 'in the last instance' determination may equally work its way out through cultural and through economic forms. What changes, as the mode of production and productive relations change is the *experience* of living men and women. And this experience is sorted out in class ways, in social life and in consciousness, in the assent, the resistance, and the choices of men and women.

In other words, experience mediates between social being and social consciousness, not as a simple dialectic, or point of interaction, but as the experience of the pressures, limits, and possibilities of social being upon social consciousness. Thus Thompson states that the influence of being upon consciousness presents itself not in the form of a base-superstructure relationship but by way of '(a) *congruities,* (b) *contradiction,* and (c) *involuntary change'*. He elaborates upon this. 'Congruities' refer to the '"necessary" rules, expectations, and values as people *live* their productive relations'. People cannot rebel incessantly. To some extent, they must accommodate themselves to that which exists, if they are to survive. 'Contradiction' refers to both the oppositions and antagonisms between the culture of 'the local and occupational community and the dominant outer society', and the 'ways in which the essentially exploitative character of productive relations are experienced and give rise to the expression of antagonistic values and to a general criticism of the "commonsense" of power'. Finally, 'involuntary change' refers to changes of a technological, demographic or other material sort (e.g. new crops, new trade routes, etc.) which modify the mode of production itself and discernibly affect the equilibrium of the relations of production. But even in this last case, which he feels might be seen as 'change in the basis', no such change has reorganized a mode of production, though it may have 'brought new forces onto the scene, [or] altered the balance of power and wealth as between different social classes.' Nevertheless, 'the consequent restructuring of *relations* of power, forms of domination and of social organization, has always been the outcome of struggle'.[103]

The importance of experience as a historical concept in *The Making* has already been discussed. Its broader theoretical significance in Thompson's understanding of class is explained by Ellen Wood. She points out that Thompson's insistence that relations of production are not co-equal with relations of class is quite logical, since obviously the persons who come to form a class are not all brought together directly by either the process of production or the process of appropriation. On the one hand, production relations do not reckon for all those who are capable of being members of historical classes. On the other hand, all the potential members of specific historical classes are never in reality gathered together in a single production operation or in confrontation with a common exploiter in a single operation of appropriation. Thus, whereas people are never in fact assembled into classes, the ways in which a mode of production determines the formation of classes (to whatever degree) cannot be readily comprehended without reference to 'something like a *common experience* – a lived experience of production relations, the divisions between producers and appropriators, and more particularly, of the conflicts and struggles inherent in relations of exploitation'. The determination of social consciousness by social being transpires in the course of this experience and concomitantly the inclination, or propensity, to act as a class. Moreover, as Wood states: 'Once the medium of "experience" is introduced into the equation between production relations and class, so too are the historical and cultural particularities of this medium.' In response to the accusations of culturalism, she adds that Thompson's insistence on the centrality of experience definitely complicates matters. But to recognize the intricacy of the process by which relations of production generate class relations 'is not to deny their determining pressure'.[104]

It is the centrality of the concept of experience – and, within experience, agency – in Thompson's thought that leads him to confront directly the work of Louis Althusser, the French philosopher and Communist Party member.[105] Throughout 'The Poverty of Theory', Thompson points out that the major absence in Althusserian thought is a way of handling *experience.* For this and other reasons, Thompson accuses 'Althusserianism' of being idealism, a 'structuralism of *stasis',* and 'Stalinism'.

Althusser's project is to reconstruct Marxism as science. He separates out those of Marx's works which he feels are characterized by empiricism, historicism and humanism (specifically, the earlier writings), from those which are 'scientific' or from which scientific elements can be salvaged (that is, the later writings, in particular *Capital* – but not all of it). He believes that scientific thought and concepts can then be derived from a careful, 'symptomatic reading' of the latter ('mature') works and can be theoretically elaborated upon. In other words, he believes that knowledge is the product of 'theoretical practice'. In the course of his theorizing and in an effort to overcome economic determinism Althusser offers a revised version of the base-superstructure model (previously mentioned in Chapter 2 in relation to Perry Anderson's histories). In it the mode of production is understood as constituted by three *relatively autonomous levels* – the economic, political and ideological – in which the economic level is only determining *in the last instance.*

'The Poverty of Theory'[106] is more than a defence of Marxist historical materialism presented in the form of a critique of Althusser; it is also intended as a direct attack on the development of Marxism as structuralism.[107] And it represents an extension of arguments which Thompson has been making since at least 1956. It is essential to recall the historical context in which Thompson wrote the essay. Though it now seems that Althusserianism was merely an intellectual fashion, in the 1970s it appeared to be firmly rooting itself in Marxist social and cultural studies in Britain. In the vanguard of Marxist-structuralist thought was the iconoclastic work of Barry Hindess and Paul Hirst, represented by such books as *Pre-Capitalist Modes of Production*.[108] Also important were the Centre for Contemporary Cultural Studies at the University of Birmingham and the journal *New Left Review*. (The book division of *New Left Review* was the major English-language publisher of Althusser's work.) Though some have argued that Thompson over-reacted to the Althusserian 'menace', such comments may be based on hindsight. However, Eric Hobsbawm's response was much more reserved than Thompson's. He felt that 'Althusser...has practically nothing to say to historians.'[109]

Thompson argues that Althusser's 'epistemological stance prevents him from understanding the two "dialogues" out of which our knowledge is formed: the dialogue between social being and social consciousness, which gives rise to experience; and that between the theoretical organization (in all its complexity) of evidence, on the one hand, and the determinate character of its object on the other' ('Poverty', pp. 32-3). That is, Thompson explains, Althusser starts with the just assumption that real objects do not present themselves directly in experience or evidence, but he then proceeds to the unreasonable assumption that experience or evidence cannot be the sources of knowledge of the real objects. Because Althusser is incapable of distinguishing between empiricism and the empirical mode of investigation, he then ends up rejecting both and establishing a procedure for knowledge production, that provides for 'theoretical practice' to both 'elaborate and verify its own facts' as opposed to providing for a 'dialogue between concept and evidence'. In this way, Althusserian theoretical practice is 'wholly self-confirming. It moves within the circle not only of its own problematic but of its own self-perpetuating and self-elaboratory procedures.' This is idealism, not in the sense of denying the primacy of an ulterior material world (which Althusser does not, of course), but because it is a 'self-generating conceptual universe which imposes its own reality upon the phenomena of material and social existence, rather than engaging in continual dialogue with these' ('Poverty', p. 13).[110]

Thompson then offers his own conception of the process and practice of knowledge production. Experience, he argues, is not merely a producer of the 'grossest "common sense", ideologically contaminated "raw material",' adding that such an assumption is a 'very characteristic delusion of intellectuals, who suppose that ordinary mortals are stupid'. His own view is that 'experience is valid and effective but within determined limits: the farmer 'knows' his seasons, the sailor 'knows' his seas, but both may remain mystified about kingship and cosmology' ('Poverty', p. 7). On the relationship between social being and social consciousness, Thompson asserts, as a historical materialist, that experience changes with changes in social being and is 'determining, in the sense that it exerts pressures upon existent social consciousness, proposes new questions, and affords much of the material which the more elaborated intellectual exercises are about' ('Poverty', p. 8). He feels that it must then, surely, to some extent, be determinate of the intellectual practices themselves. Furthermore, he reminds us of the 'thrusting-forth of the 'real world', spontaneously and not at all decorously, proposing hitherto unarticulated questions to philosophers.' That is: 'Experience walks in without knocking at the door, and announces deaths, crises of subsistence, trench warfare, unemployment, inflation, genocide . . . . In the face of such general experiences old conceptual systems may crumble and new problematics insist upon their presence.' Thompson explains that it is necessary to stress the determination of consciousness by being in the process of experience because so many Western Marxists have over-emphasized ideological domination and, furthermore, because Althusser himself seems to have practically nothing to tell us on it ('Poverty', p. 9).

On the dialogue between the theoretical organization of evidence and the determinate character of its object, Thompson also rejects empiricism but not the empirical mode of investigation. Just because the object of study is epistemologically inert, he observes, 'does not mean that it is inert in other ways; it need by no means be sociologically or ideologically inert'. In other words, the dialogue can occur 'not on any terms which thought prescribes but in ways which are determined by the properties of the real object: the properties of reality determine both the appropriate procedures of thought (that is, their "adequacy or inadequacy") and its product' ('Poverty', p. 17). Moving from this to historical knowledge, he insists that: 'a historian is entitled in his practice to make a provisional assumption of an epistemological character: that the evidence which he handles has a 'real' (determinant) existence independent of its existence within the forms of thought, that this evidence is witness to a real historical process and that this process (or some approximate understanding of it) is the object of historical knowledge. Without making such assumptions he cannot proceed: he must sit in a waiting-room outside the philosophy department all his life.' This is not to assume, however, that facts spontaneously divulge their own meanings. On the contrary, the evidence available to historians must be 'interrogated by minds trained in a discipline of attentive disbelief' ('Poverty', pp. 28-9).[111]

Thompson then proceeds to present the ways in which historians interrogate evidence. He contends that in the long course of its development, the historical discipline has developed its own discourse of the proof – a historical logic quite different from the philosopher's 'analytic' logic. It is not that historians are less logical but that the materials with which they work are different. By historical logic Thompson means 'a logical method of enquiry appropriate to historical materials, designed as far as possible to test hypotheses as to structure, causation, etc., and to eliminate self-confirming procedures ("instances", "illustrations")'. This involves a dialogue between concept and evidence ('Poverty', pp. 38-9).

In elaborating upon the historical discourse of the proof, Thompson asserts that the uniqueness of historical materialism is not 'in any epistemological premises, but in its categories, its characteristic hypotheses and attendant procedures, and in the avowed conceptual kinship between these and the concepts elaborated by Marxist practitioners in other disciplines'

('Poverty', p. 44). In contrast to Althusser, Thompson does not see Marxist theory as standing separate, independent and dominant over these but developing out of historical materialism which, he argues, is the common ground for all Marxist practices. He insists, moreover, that 'history is not a factory for the manufacture of Grand Theory'. Its task is to 'recover, explain, and understand its object: real history'. The strength of historical materialism, then, is *not* that its concepts (e.g. exploitation, hegemony, class struggle, feudalism and capitalism) are '"derived from" a true theory outside this discipline' but rather that they 'stand up better to the test of historical logic'. Finally, as *historical* concepts they are to be treated more as expectations than as models ('Poverty', p. 46).

Thompson argues that Althusserian thought is basically no different than Parsons' and Smelser's structural-functionalism (or Stalin's orthodox Marxism) in that it treats history as a process without a subject; that is, it 'evicts human agency from history'. Since Althusser is anxious to rid Marxism of historicism (and he cannot accept that history is propelled by some extra-human compulsion) he constructs a model of the totality in which process as well is evicted ('Poverty', pp. 75, 79-84, 89-94). Not surprisingly, Thompson is scornful of Althusser's totality. He repeats his criticism from 'Peculiarities' of 'last instance determination by the economic' and he adds that the 'three relatively autonomous levels – the economic, the political, and the ideological' – represent an arbitrary selection of categories which merely reproduce the standard (bourgeois) categories of the academy. Moreover, the 'notion of 'levels' motoring around in history at different speeds and on different schedules is an academic fiction' which splinters, or disintegrates, the totality of historical process and thus class experience ('Poverty', pp. 94-8). But, of course, Thompson's major argument is that Althusserian thought has no way of handling experience – wherein 'structure is transmuted into process, and the subject re-enters history'

('Poverty', pp. 164-5).

Thompson does acknowledge that Althusser posits the 'class struggle as the motor of history'. Yet, noting that this is a revision of the original proposition offered by Marx and Engels in the *Communist Manifesto* that 'the history of all hitherto existing society is the history of class struggles', he points out that Althusser defines classes quite statically as functions of the process of production. Moreover, Thompson shows that the analogy of class struggle as the motor of history is completely inadequate for it 'supposes two distinct entities: "history", which is inert, an intricate composite of parts; and a "motor" (class struggle) which is brought *to* it, and which drives the parts or sets them in motion'. Rather, Thompson writes: 'class struggle *is* the process of history . . . . ..history is its own motor.' It should be added that Thompson does not reject the notion of structure, but he insists that it actually be understood as 'structural actuation (limits and pressures) within a social formation which remains protean in its forms' ('Poverty', pp. 103-10).[112]

It seems that Thompson does not hold Althusser completely responsible for having constructed Marxism as structuralism for he points out that structuralism is the illusion of the epoch and that among Marx's own writings there is the basis for such a development. He also presents a historical explanation for this. Whereas 'evolutionism' (i.e. progress) was dominant in the earliest part of the twentieth century, and 'voluntarism' emerged in the struggles of 1936-46 against fascism, surviving for a while in the anti-colonial and liberation struggles of the Third World, Thompson points out that 'structuralism' is the product of the Cold War. He elaborates on this by referring to the suppression of democratic struggles by the two superpowers in Hungary (1956), Czechoslovakia (1968) and Chile (1973), and the little room there has apparently been for movement in the contemporary world structure. The emergence of Althusserian and other types of structuralism out of a particular historical moment does not, however, excuse them, for they remain ideological and ideologically conservative ('Poverty', pp. 71-4).

Thompson acknowledges that Marx made several philosophical breakthroughs, and in his writing of *The German Ideology, The Poverty of Philosophy* and *The Communist Manifesto* presented the essential hypotheses of historical materialism. But he feels that, in turning to confront and overthrow bourgeois political economy, Marx became partially entrapped within it, and ended up in some degree producing another 'political economy'. This is most evident, Thompson asserts, in the *Grundrisse,* the notebooks kept in the 1850s in preparation for writing *Capital,* for there we find Marx's thought 'locked inside a *static, anti-historical structure'* ('Poverty', pp. 162-3). However Marx never completely distanced himself from historical thinking. Thus, *Capital,* written in the 1860s, represents the zenith of political economy, but at the same time 'signals the need for its supersession by historical materialism'. In other words, while *Capital* 'does not *produce* historical materialism,' nevertheless 'it provides the pre-conditions for its production' ('Poverty', pp. 58-67). The problem, according to Thompson, is that Althusser and his followers are eager to re-imprison historical materialism in the categories of political economy.

Finally, regarding his accusation that Althusserian thought is Stalinism, Thompson again returns to the missing element, experience. He writes that it is not only a 'junction between structure and process' it is also a 'point of dis-junction between alternative and incompatible traditions.' Whereas in 1973 Thompson wrote of Marxism as a common tradition,[113] he now says that he has been forced to acknowledge that there are two distinct traditions – the one with which he identifies and the one in which Althusserian thought resides. The latter is not just political economy (as opposed to historical materialism), it is Stalinism. In fact, 'Althusserianism *is* Stalinism reduced to the paradigm of Theory,' because it presents Marxist thought as Marxism, (to repeat) an 'idealist dogma', a 'static structuralism which evicts agency as process'. As such, it is also Stalinism because it is a system of closure, which, again, has no way of handling experience, nor culture and values which are, Thompson insists, as central to class struggle as political economy. Furthermore, Althusserian thought is Stalinism because it *actively* seeks to repress historical materialism, moralism and socialist humanism. Thus Thompson views his 'declaration of intellectual war' against Althusserianism as continuing the task begun in 1956 ('Poverty', pp. 165-92).[114]

Thompson does not oppose history, or experience, to theory, as critics such as Richard Johnson assert.[115] He does not elevate theory to self-sufficiency as does Althusser, but nor does he assert the self-sufficiency of history or the historical discipline. He feels that historical knowledge is produced by historians establishing a dialogue between concepts and evidence (i.e. historical theory and the historical past). Furthermore, though Thompson views history as the 'Queen of the humanities', he has always been open to the idea of dialogue with the social sciences, but not just on any terms. In the same way that the historical discipline is characterized by competing, though qualitatively different, 'interpretive orderings', so too, as we know, are the social sciences.[116]

The Contemporary Crisis

In spite of all his criticisms of Thompson's history, theory and political strategy, Perry Anderson nonetheless writes that, 'Edward Thompson is our finest socialist writer today.'[117] *The Making of the English Working Class* has reshaped the writing of the social history of the Industrial Revolution, and while its influence can be seen in particular among labour historians,[118] it has by no means been limited to labour studies, nor for that matter, nineteenth-century history. Thompson's eighteenth-century studies have also been important, not least for having forced a reconsideration of that century's apparent political stability and social order.

There is, however, yet another group of Thompson's writings of a historical nature – those specifically political writings in which, like Hobsbawm, he concentrates his historical imagination directly upon contemporary issues. In fact, more than any of the British Marxist historians (perhaps more than any British historian in recent years), Thompson has spoken out and influenced thought on crucial topics in British political life and culture. His most recent and important writings of this sort fall under two headings: the crisis of civil liberties and the threat of nuclear war. The author of *The Making* is clearly visible in the writings on the crisis of civil liberties[119] In both, the tradition of the free-born Englishman is central to Thompson's arguments. However, whereas the subject of *The Making* is the united struggle of middle-class and artisan Radicals to assert and extend the rights and liberties of the free-born Englishman, the subject of the essays is the ever-increasing power and authority of the British state and its encroachment on the rights of the free-born Briton. Among the things he calls attention to in the essays are the government's tampering with the jury system, the persistent and growing surveillance and harassment of radicals by the security services, and the management of public information and the news, which is essentially 'licensed' by the Official Secrets Act and by appeals to the 'national interest'. These practices clearly worry Thompson, but what seems to concern him as much is the cynicism and apathy which he feels characterize the British people. He is particularly distressed by the apathy of the Left. He sees this to be in part the consequence of Marxist thought. He says Marxists too often treat the capitalist state in terms of a model in which civil rights and democratic practices are comprehended as ideologies which camouflage the state's real character.

Thompson is anxious that the Left, and the British people in general, 'regain its libertarian memory'.'memory'. Thus, in his political essays he writes to arouse their historical and political consciousness, by reminding his readers of the struggles and precedents which secured their now-threatened rights. As he asserts; 'The Chartist, Radical Liberal, Irish Nationalist, and formative labour movements were distinguished by their sensitivity to libertarian issues, and their suspicion of the polity of statism.'[120] One especially interesting argument which Thompson makes by way of historical perspective is with regard to the jury system. Against attacks on it by both the Right and the Left, he contends that the jury system is a 'democratic *practice* which has been asserted and defended as an Englishman's birth right for seven centuries'. The qualifications for jury service have, of course, changed over the centuries but those changes, he observes, were themselves the products of struggles for the expansion of democratic practices. He insists that if democracy is to be understood as active self-rule, in contrast to being ruled by others, then surely the 'rotation among all ordinary citizens of public responsibilities and roles' is an exceptionally democratic practice.[121] While Thompson identifies his major English intellectual influences as Blake and Morris, anyone who has read Paine and Cobbett (and Thompson's discussion of them in *The Making*) would agree that Thompson writes in their radical-democratic tradition as well.

Thompson's writings on the threat of nuclear war are closely bound up with his discussions of the crisis of civil liberties. For many years he has been arguing that the range of political discourse and practice in Britain and elsewhere has been narrowly structured by the ever-present threat of nuclear confrontation between NATO and the Warsaw Pact, more specifically, the United States and the Soviet Union. He has himself been subject to the constraints on political discussion, as for example in 1981, when his invitation from the BBC to give the Dimbleby Lecture was withdrawn. The talk, which he presented elsewhere, was entitled 'Beyond the Cold War'. In it, as in his many other such talks and essays, he calls for British and European nuclear disarmament with the goal of destructuring the world of the Cold War and thereby reconnecting 'the cause of freedom and the cause of peace'.[122] (A year later, he was invited by television's new Channel Four to inaugurate their programme, *'Opinion'*. In his talk Thompson spoke of the 'prejudicial handling of particular political issues' and the limited definition of 'politics' which frames the broadcast media's handling of ongoing debates and struggles. In particular, he cited the distorted presentation of the Campaign for Nuclear Disarmament and its coverage of the Falklands War.)[123]

The two most significant pieces among the disarmament writings are his pamphlet *Protest and Survive*[124] and his essay 'Notes on Exterminism, the Last Stage of Civilisation' (1980).[125] *Protest and Survive* was written in 1980 in reaction to the leaking of a Government document which recommended the steps to be taken in the event of nuclear attack. His pamphlet has been referred to as the rallying cry of the British peace movement for it has been read and responded to by many thousands of Britons (as well as Europeans and Americans). Here the parallel between Thompson and Paine seems most clear.

'Notes on Exterminism' is a different kind of essay. In this case Thompson seeks to analyse the dynamic of the contemporary structure of the world in terms of the threat of nuclear holocaust and to offer a theoretical and class analysis of the present crisis. He argues that imperialism is a concept which is incapable of adequately comprehending more than a part of this situation of global contradiction and collision. Thus, he says, it is necessary to develop a new category to analyse its internal dynamic and reciprocal logic. Thompson does not deny the respective histories and dynamics of the social orders of the two superpowers. But he contends that the separate dynamics of those states have become mutually determining and, moreover, have given way to a new and autonomous dynamic – exterminism. The institutional base of this new self-generating condition is the weapons-system and its entire economic, scientific, political and ideological support-system, i.e. the social system which 'researches it, "chooses" it, produces it, polices it, justifies it, and maintains it in being'. He compares exterminism to the process of imperialism but he says that at a crucial point the analogy breaks down. Whereas the dialectic of imperialism involves its negation in the struggles for self-determination, exterminism 'confronts itself. It does not exploit a victim: it confronts an equal.' But he adds that exterminism is characterized by internal contradictions (which he discusses). In the end he calls for organization, resistance, and internationalism, unmediated by the states of either East or West.[126]

Thompson's arguments and analysis in 'Notes on Exterminism' have been the subject of much discussion and criticism, and the criticisms have come not only from the political right and centre. Raymond Williams responded in a sympathetic but critical article in *New Left Review,* 'The Politics of Nuclear Disarmament'.[127] He questions Thompson's formulation of exterminism and is especially concerned that the concept may actually inhibit adequate analysis and thus stunt efforts to create a socialist strategy on disarmament. He observes that Thompson's conception of exterminism seems to involve 'technological determinism' which he says can too readily foreclose intellectual examination of the complexities of social process. Whereas Thompson concludes in his essay that class analysis is limited in its appropriateness to the problem, Williams proceeds to offer an outline for such an analysis and what it implies for socialists. To what extent Thompson eschews a class-struggle analysis because of his central involvement in trying to build an international broad-based people's movement is difficult to assess.

Finally, I should reiterate, as this and the preceding chapters have tried to make clear, that there is no break between Dobb and Thompson, or the other historians. Admittedly, there is a change of emphasis from the political economy of historical development to a broader social analysis often focusing on culture, but a change in emphasis is not necessarily a break in a problematic. The relationship between Dobb and his younger colleagues – Thompson as much as Hilton, Hill, and Hobsbawm – in their concern to develop a class-struggle analysis of historical change and development, is continuous. This can be seen by recalling the following previously quoted proposition, which sounds so much like Thompson:

> *Historical experience* is a moving process in which man himself is an active agent. The 'reality' of history, if it has a meaning, can only mean the *totality* of history itself: and precisely in activity – in making history – does man establish his relation to the objective world and learn what history is.

But the words are Dobb's.[128]

Chapter 7

The Collective Contribution

It is then not easy to say which sense of 'history' is currently dominant. 'Historian' remains precise, in its earlier meaning. 'Historical' relates mainly but not exclusively to this sense of the past, but 'historic' is most often used to include a sense of process or destiny. 'History' itself retains its whole range, and still, in different hands, teaches or shows us most kinds of knowable past and almost every kind of imaginable future.
Raymond Williams, *Keywords*[1]

As we have seen in the preceding chapters, Dobb, Hilton, Hill, Hobsbawm and Thompson have each made outstanding contributions to their respective areas of historical study. Yet beyond this there is also their collective contribution. I have argued that their work, viewed as a whole, represents a theoretical tradition which seeks to reconstruct historical studies and theory by way of what I term 'class-struggle analysis' and the perspective of 'history from the bottom up'. Also, with particular reference to Marxist thought, their work represents an effort to transcend the base-superstructure model of the social totality and its inherent tendency to economic determinism by developing Marxism, or historical materialism, as a theory of class determination.

This concluding chapter will focus on their collective contribution. I will discuss their perspective of history from the bottom up, and then the theory of class determination. Finally, the chapter will close with a look at the issue of history, historical consciousness, and politics, and the contribution of the British Marxist historians to it.

History from the Bottom Up

I think you must like history, as I liked it when I was your age, because it deals with living men, and everything that concerns men, as many men as possible, all the men in the world in so far as they unite together in society, and work and struggle and make a bid for a better life, all that can't fail to please you more than anything else. Isn't that right? Antonio Gramsci in a letter to his son[2]

To properly appreciate the British Marxist historians' perspective we should consider it in relation to other modes of critical history writing and, in particular, to other approaches to history from below. First, it is necessary to make clear what I mean by the term *critical* history writing. Barrington Moore Jr has written that all too often historians and social scientists confuse objectivity and neutrality. That is, they fail to distinguish between the research activity, wherein objectivity (i.e. the willingness to find oneself wrong) is essential to honest intellectual enquiry, and the impact of the research, where neutrality (i.e. impartiality) must necessarily be an illusion for any significant study. Neutrality is an impossibility, he states, because, given the structures of historical and contemporary societies, any simple straightforward truth about political institutions or events is bound to have some political consequences and to damage some group interests. Moreover, since 'in any society the dominant groups are the ones with the most to hide about the way society works... .... truthful analyses are bound to have a critical ring, to seem like exposures rather than objective statements, as the term is conventionally used'. Therefore, to maximize objectivity, *and* to write critical history, he makes the following recommendation: 'For all students of human society, sympathy with the victims of historical processes and skepticism about the victors' claims provide essential safeguards against being taken in by the dominant mythology. A scholar who tries to be objective needs those feelings as part of his ordinary equipment.'[3]

Moore's recommendation is, of course, a necessary habit of mind for the historian or social scientist anxious to pursue studies from the bottom up, but it has not been limited to such scholars. For example, another mode of critical history and social studies writing, which is characterized by sympathy with the victims and skepticism about the victors' claims, is what might be termed 'power-structure studies'. Particularly American in character, such studies are carried out by both historians and social scientists, and are important in calling attention to or unveiling historical and contemporary practices of domination and exploitation. Broadly speaking, American power-structure studies include such works as C. Wright Mills' *The Power Elite,* Stuart Ewen's *Captains of Consciousness,* and Harry Braverman's *Labor and Monopoly Capital.*[4] An outstanding British example is Ralph Miliband's *The State in Capitalist Society.*[5] The problem is that too often power-structure studies are merely the radical version of the classic elite-mass model of social structure, order and change, in which the elites are viewed as active and the masses inert. That is, such studies tend to reproduce the conception of the historical process characteristic of history from above, wherein history is viewed as the product of the actions of the elites or ruling classes, though in this case the actions of the elites are understood as carried out 'over' or 'against' the interests of the masses or lower classes.

History from below represents an alternative to some extent in that it shifts attention away from the elites or ruling classes, by focusing on the lives, activities and experiences of the masses, or the people. However, history from below is actually a generic term for a variety of approaches, of which the British Marxist historians' is just one. Significant among the others are those which have developed as part of the French *Annales* tradition. We should mention in particular the history of 'mentalities' which originated in the writings of Marc Bloch and Lucien Febvre (themselves influenced by work in French sociology[6]), and the 'materialist' history which has its origins, especially, in the work of Fernand Braudel.[7]

In their efforts to develop an alternative to a narrow political history, which they call the 'history of events' (*histoire evenementielle*), Bloch and Febvre provide for the possible development of a history from below (though they themselves did not pursue it) by way of the concept of 'mentality' (*mentalité*) which is variably defined as a 'vision of the world' or a 'mode of thought'. That is, they allow for such a development by supplying a concept which can be applied to the experiences and thoughts of those outside the elites or ruling classes. There have been problems, however. From the outset there has been a tendency among *Annales* historians to conceive of the history of mentalities as psychological history, or historical psychology, and thus to focus on the 'inert, obscure, and unconscious elements in a given world view'.[8] This is due in great part, no doubt, to their emphasis on the *longue durée* (in opposition to events) and their structuralist analysis (in opposition to agency and volition). As Peter Burke notes: 'Historians of mentalities are concerned with change over the long term, for societies do not change their modes of thought in a hurry.'[9] The problem is that such a conception of mentality not only (wrongly) eschews events, it also neglects, or eliminates, consciousness, action and the political dimension of human relations – which is hardly an adequate basis for a history from below.

Another, related, problem is that mentalities, regularly referred to as 'collective mentalities', are quite often treated without adequate reference to social, and specifically class, structures. They are too often presented as if they were shared by, or common to, all the people of their given social orders *and* as if they were classless in character. This is indicated by the *Annales* term, 'civilizations,'[10] which, in 1946, was added to the original (1929) title of the journal, though it has not been true of all *Annales* historians. Furthermore, and traceable to Febvre himself, there is a derived tendency when dealing with the (less 'total') concept of culture, to equate the 'culture imposed on the popular classes' (i.e. common people) with 'popular culture', and thus to ignore the 'culture produced by the popular classes themselves.'[11]

In Braudel's work the experiences of peasants and other labouring groups are often the central human activities. As the Genoveses comment, in appreciation of his masterpiece, *The Mediterranean and the Mediterranean World in the Age of Philip II*:[12] 'The smell of lavender, the glistening of olives, the laborious motion of the oxen, the stooping, sowing, scything gestures of the men and women bound to that soil blend in his evocation of a total environment.' The problem is that in the space of the 'total environment' and in the time of the *longue durée,* human experience and agency are greatly reduced. Thus, as the Genoveses go on to argue:

Braudel's great and anti-Marxist work, with its structural interpretation and its anthropological, ecological, and archaeological predilections, implicitly negates the historical process itself and distorts the temporal dimension. The traditional preoccupation of historians, that outmoded political narrative, figures in his work almost as accident or afterthought. This treatment not only minimizes the human or political dimension of change over time, it also – and more perniciously for social history – negates the centrality of relations of production, of authority and exploitation, within the given historical moment.[13]

From such an approach to history there is little distance to travel to the position of another *Annales* historian, François Furet, who insists that the 're-integration of the subordinate classes into general history can only be accomplished through 'number and anonymity', by means of demography and sociology, 'the quantitative study of past societies'. All of this leads the Italian historian Carlo Ginzburg (himself influenced by the traditions of both Annales and the British Marxist historians) to comment: 'Although the lower classes are no longer ignored by historians, they seem condemned, nevertheless, to remain 'silent'.[14]

These criticisms should not be misinterpreted, for there is no denying the contributions of the *Annales* historians to historical studies and the development of history from below. The history of mentalities has provided one of the alternatives in the history of thought to the elitist version of the history of ideas, and Braudel's geographical and environmental determinism ought to be seriously considered by social theorists who have been not only ahistorical, but also 'aspatial' in their thinking,[15] and reconsidered by Marxists and others who have too often over-distanced their histories from the natural and physical world.[16] Also, though not without problems, demographic and quantitative histories have definitely contributed to our knowledge of the everyday lives of the masses.[17] Moreover, as Raphael Samuel notes, 'in the wake of the student revolt of 1968', there has been 'a shift in the *Annales* school from 'a history without people' – a history built on the impersonal determinants of climate, soil, and centuries-long cycles of change – to [a] kind of ethnohistory, dealing with individual experience at a particular time and place.'[18] In particular, he has in mind the work of Emmanuel Le Roy Ladurie. This is because, whereas Le Roy Ladurie's first book, *The Peasants of* Languedoc,[19] emphasized environment, climate, demography, and quantitative analysis[20] (though not without interest in social and political struggles), his more recent work, i.e. *Montaillou* and *Carnival in Romans*,[21] actually focuses on social and political events.

On the subject of French historians, we cannot help but mention the two great scholars who wrote on the French

Revolution, Georges Lefebvre and Albert Soboul (the former, Marxist-influenced, the latter, a Marxist). Working apart from the *Annales* tradition, they wrote exceptional histories from the perspective of the bottom up: Lefebvre authored such works as *Les paysans du Nord* and *The Great Fear of 1789,*[22] and Soboul *The Parisian Sans – Culottes and the French Revolution 1793-4* and *The French Revolution, 1787-1799.*[23] Moreover, Lefevre directly influenced the British Marxist historians by way of George Rudé's 'revolutionary crowd' studies (in fact, it was Lefebvre who originally coined the term 'history from below').

There are two other approaches worth mentioning for the contrasts they provide to that of the British Marxist historians. The first is characteristic of modernization historians, whom I have previously discussed in relation to Hobsbawm's work. It should be noted again that, in their attention to the everyday lives and experiences of people in the past, the modernization historians have contributed to the broadening of historical studies beyond the actions of the elites. Nevertheless, their conception of the historical process ignores the political dimension. That is, modernization theory – in a manner similar to the *Annales* tradition – emphasizes the long term and although it focuses on processes of change (e.g. urbanization), it reduces the actions and experiences of labouring people to the process of adaptation, or the failure to adapt, to the inexorable transformations involved in 'modernization'. The result, as Tony Judt comments, is that modernization historiography 'denies to people of the past their political and ideological identity'.[24] Thus modernization historians, though they do concern themselves with the 'lower classes', actually fail to write 'critical history' (as we have defined it following Barrington Moore).

The other approach worth mentioning here is called 'radical' by some (and 'left-liberal' by the Genoveses) but might best be termed 'radical-populist'. In this case, historians present the lives, experiences *and* struggles of the lower classes and oppressed as if they have regularly been able not only to endure oppression, but also to miraculously create an 'autonomous culture' and resist successfully the values and aspirations of their oppressors. Such historians tend to see *only* resistance and struggle and, thus, inadequately attend to the harsh realities of accommodation and incorporation in lower-class experience and cultural practices. The Genoveses argue that this provides (in studies of slavery and labour history) for the persistence of a 'paternalist ethos. . . . however much clothed in radical rhetoric'. This happens, they contend, because these historians focus on the private experiences of the subordinate classes, i.e. 'those not claimed by the ruling classes', to the neglect of the 'public experiences'. Thus, while they do recognize the political dimension of cultural practices, it is a one-sided understanding of the political.[25] Often, this version of history becomes history *of* the bottom, as opposed to history from the bottom *up*. Among the historians whom they have in mind is the American Herbert Gutman. The contributions of Gutman's studies of Afro-American slaves and black and white American workers, which have been so important in the development of a new labour and social history in the United States, have, nevertheless, been limited by his seeming adherence to modernization theory and a decided tendency to discount the 'dialectic' of class confrontation.[26]

Then what of the British Marxist historians' own approach to history? As we have seen, they do not study peasant and working-class experience in isolation but, rather, consistently pursue their historical studies in the context of historically specific class relations and confrontations, that is, as history from the perspective of the bottom *up*. In this way, at the same time that they broaden the conception of class experience in historical studies, the British Marxist historians never lose sight of the essential political dimension of that experience. That is, class relations are 'political' in that they always involve domination and subordination, struggle and accommodation. Thus, here again the ascription of 'culturalism' to the work of the British Marxist historians seems inappropriate and inadequate. Moreover, their approach does not preclude serious attention being given to elites and ruling classes, as evidenced, for example, by Hilton's *A Medieval Society*,[27] Hill's *Economic Problems of the Church*,[28] Hobsbawm's *The Age of Capital*,[29] and Thompson's *Whigs and Hunters*.[30] In fact, Hobsbawm states: 'What I would like to do is not simply . . . . to save the stockinger and the peasant, but also the nobleman and the king of the past, from the condescension of modern historians who think they know better.'[31] (But it should be remembered that this statement comes after years of effort to 'rescue' the peasant and worker in historical studies!) Therefore, the British Marxist historians would not necessarily disagree with Perry Anderson's call for a 'history from above' – as the study of the 'intricate machinery of class domination' – but such a history would have to grant due weight to the continuous class struggles and moments of upheaval forged by the lower classes themselves, and the way in which such struggles, in turn, shape or affect the machinery of domination.

Not only do the British Marxist historians stress the importance to historical studies of studying the experiences of the lower classes; they also insist that the lower classes themselves have been active participants in the making of history, rather than merely its passive victims. Moreover, they show that such struggles and movements have been significant to the *totality* of historical development, i.e. to values and ideas as much as to political economy, and that they have, therefore, also contributed to the experiences and struggles of later generations. Hobsbawm describes his and his fellow historians' intentions well when he says: 'I would like to restore to men of the past and especially the poor of the past, the gift of theory. Like the hero of Moliere, they have been talking prose all the time. Only whereas the man in Moliere didn't know it himself, I think they have always known it, but we have not. And I think we ought to.'[32] It is with the intention of 'restoring the gift of theory to people of the past', and also of understanding class struggle as a whole, that the British Marxist historians have selectively appropriated some of the methods and 'sensibilities' of sociologists and, especially, of anthropologists.

A final point to consider regarding the perspective of the British Marxist historians is in regard to their decided emphasis on resistance and rebellion. Admittedly, they do not deal adequately with the more conservative and 'reactionary' practices and social and political actions of the lower classes.[33] However, it must be remembered that they began to write in opposition to the prevailing paradigm in historical and social studies, which assumed not only that social order meant the absence of social conflict, both in the form of rebellion *and* resistance, but as well that it indicated normative acceptance,[34] whether achieved by a process of consensus or one of total domination. At the same time, although they emphasize lower-class struggles in their writings, they are not oblivious to, or unrealistic about, the (often inherent) limitations of these struggles, nor to the limitations of lower-class modes of accommodation and incorporation. Yet they do not reduce the resistance of peasants and workers of the past (and the present) to being merely apolitical hysteria, criminal activity or deviance.

As I have pointed out before, the British Marxist historians were not the first to write what Raphael Samuel has called 'people's history' nor, as we have just seen, the only historians who have sought to develop history from below. However, as I have tried to show, they surely represent best what Walter Benjamin had in mind when he wrote: 'Only that historian will have the gift of fanning the spark of hope in the past who is firmly convinced that *even the dead* will not be safe from the enemy [the ruling class] if he wins. And the enemy has not ceased to be victorious.'[35]

The British Marxist historians' perspective of history has shaped a whole generation of younger historians' writings. While there is not space to review all the evidence for this, I should mention, first, the journal – and the movement of which it is a part – *History Workshop* (its subtitle states that it is a 'journal of socialist and feminist historians'). Originating in the 1960s at Ruskin College,[36] this movement seeks to integrate the tradition and perspective of the British Marxist historians with the tradition of worker-historians in the labour movement.[37] Raphael Samuel, the leading figure in *History Workshop,* writes of the influence of the British Marxist historians: 'We grew up in the shadow of respected seniors – Hill, Hobsbawm and Thompson in particular.'[38] Samuel was one of the youngest members of the Communist Party Historians' Group in the pre-1956 period and thus the link between Dobb et al. and the History Workshop movement is a direct one.[39]

The influence of the British Marxist historians can be seen especially in the movement's emphasis on popular resistance, which is being developed further as a result of its commitment to socialist *and* feminist history. Two other historians connected with the History Workshop who are carrying on the efforts begun by Hilton et al. are Sheila Rowbotham[40] and Gareth Stedman Jones.[41]

In the United States, the influence of the British Marxist historians can be seen, as in Britain, throughout social history writing, but especially in the efforts of those historians who work with and/or contribute to the journal *Radical History Review.* In particular, one might mention such historians as Alan Dawley,[42] Sean Wilentz,[43] William Sewell Jr[44] and Steven Stern.[45] Of course, there are also the previously mentioned, and more senior, historians, Eugene Genovese and Herbert Gutman, and David Montgomery, who pursues the study of the American working class from the nineteenth *into* the twentieth century.[46]

The collective contribution of the British Marxist historians has not only influenced the *writing* of history, as a corrective to history written from the perspective of the elites or ruling classes, it also has challenged the *conception* of the historical process which accompanies history from above. As Stuart Hall comments, it has crucial political consequences: 'It can restore a sense of agency, a sense of activity, a sense of the capacity of the working class and the repressed.[47] Of course, to discuss the conception of the historical process is to discuss historical theory, and though E. P. Thompson insists that their historical studies have not led them to find a 'better Theory (historical materialism as a new closed ism),'[48] nevertheless, their historical studies are theoretically consequential. Perhaps it would be an exaggeration to assert that their theoretical contribution is to 'provide a theory' but, at the least, their work develops Marxism, or historical materialism, as a theory of class determination.

The Theory of Class Determination

In addition to their collective contribution, the British Marxist historians, as we have seen, have also made an important contribution to the concept of class. E. P. Thompson has said of what he believes to be their accomplishment: 'We greatly enlarged the concept of class, which historians in the Marxist tradition commonly employ – deliberately and not out of some theoretical "innocence" – with a flexibility and indeterminacy disallowed both by Marxism and by orthodox sociology.'[49]

Let us consider their 'enlargement'. They have shifted the study of class experience from class analysis to class-struggle analysis, largely as a result of their recognition of lower-class experience as an active, though structured, process. This has been in contrast to existing sociological practice. Social stratification studies were characterized for a long time by static and ahistorical analyses of class. Sociologists, until recently, did not pursue historical studies (i.e. studies of the past). Moreover, their treatment of classes as 'simple [or complex] statistical and hierarchically arranged strata',[50] ignored *time* and *social relations*. In recent years this has become a significant issue in social theory but it was 1965 when, in 'Peculiarities of the English', Thompson wrote (as he had done previously in the preface to The Making of the English Working Class):

> Class is a social and cultural formation (often finding institutional expression) which cannot be defined abstractly or in isolation, but only in terms of relationship with other classes; and ultimately the definition can only be made in the medium of time – that is, action and reaction, change and conflict.... class itself is not a thing, it is a happening.[51]

Nor, as Thompson also clearly acknowledges, has the construction of static and ahistorical versions of class been uncommon in Marxist studies. Quite often, Marxists have been 'more interested in abstractly defined class *locations* than in the qualitative social breaks expressed in the dynamics of class relations and conflicts'.[52] This is especially true, as David Stark states, among structuralist–Marxists who pursue class analysis at the level of a mode of production and view their task as the rigorous formulation of more sophisticated schemes of classification. Thus, what often happens is that 'the debate about class becomes a battle of classification – in many cases a survey of the topography of class boundaries rather than a study of the processes of class formation and the real historical battles which produce the evershifting lines of demarcation.'[53]

The British Marxist historians examine classes as historical relationships *and* processes. Implicit in their work, and occasionally explicitly stated, most strongly perhaps in Thompson's essay, 'Eighteenth-century English Society: class struggle without class?',[54] is the analytical and historical priority given to class struggle, out of which, in specific historical circumstances, class – in the full sense – has emerged or been 'made'. They do not, however, deny the existence of class in the absence of class consciousness. In fact, as we have seen, their writings are most important in showing evidence of the effect of class relations and struggles even in the absence of class consciousness (i.e. class *in the full sense*). However, there exists a historically different reality when class formation develops out of class struggle, involving an elaborated class consciousness. (This is surely a proposition no Marxist could reject.) Thompson has described this as a historical situation in which *class* is 'present in the evidence itself, as opposed to those situations in which class is used as an 'analytical category to organize historical evidence which has a very much less direct correspondence'.[55] At the same time, as Raymond Williams comments, it becomes ever more necessary to distinguish between those moments, or modes of class struggle, which are characterized by class consciousness, and those involving lesser degrees of class consciousness (e.g. distinguishing between class conflict, class struggle, and class war).[56]

Of course, the British Marxist historians have constantly made clear that it has been their intention to distance their class-struggle approach from economic determinism, which brings us to another aspect of their 'enlargement' of the concept of class, and also to their efforts to overcome the base-superstructure model. In the course of shifting from class analysis to class-struggle analysis, and broadening the concept of class, they have developed Marxism, or historical materialism, as a theory of class determination, the core proposition of which is that class struggle is central to the historical process. As Thompson has put it, 'class struggle *is* the process'. This proposition, we know, is derived from Marx but, as we also know, it is not the only direction in which Marx's thought has been developed – or been taken. I have sought to show in this book that while it is not a proposition unique to the work of the British Marxist historians (and their tradition), they have been uniquely effective in developing historical materialism in this manner.

It might well be asked to what extent their stress on class, and the 'prior' and more universal class struggle, represents a break with the equally central Marxist proposition that social being determines social consciousness and the related master category of the mode of production? This is not an unimportant question, for both Hobsbawm and Thompson acknowledge that to reject that proposition is to abandon Marx's line of analysis.[57] It is also the basis upon which structuralists such as Richard Johnson make their criticism that the British Marxist historians, except Dobb and to some extent Hilton, are culturalists.[58] The problem, I would argue, is that the critics fail to comprehend what the British Marxist historians have been seeking to accomplish. In their efforts to overcome the base-superstructure model and its inherent tendency to economic determinism, the British Marxist historians do not reject determination in favour of voluntarism. Nor do they reject the proposition that social being determines social consciousness or the formulation of social being as mode of production. They do not reject structural determination in favour of voluntarism, though they do reject determinism and emphasize the importance of agency. Rather, they take determination, as Raymond Williams has recently presented it, to be a duality – as both the 'setting of limits *and* the exertion of pressures'. As previously stated, they view the historical process as an 'active, though structured, process'. We should note that the work of the British Marxist historians was recognized by the late Philip Abrams as particularly relevant to the development of the problematic of structuring. In more formal terms, Anthony Giddens calls this the 'theory of structuration': a theory built round the idea of the 'fundamentally recursive character of social life' and designed precisely to express 'the mutual dependence of structure and agency' in terms of 'process in time.'[59]

As opposed to the structuralist formulation of the proposition that social being determines social consciousness, wherein the economic level, or base, is only determining in the last instance, and also the (well-intentioned) counter-formulation wherein the economic level, or base, is treated as a starting-point, i.e. as a matter of the first instance,[60] the British Marxist historians seek to elucidate the 'ever-present' pressure of social being upon social consciousness. They do so not by way of a simple identity or reflection but through *experience* in which, as Thompson puts it, 'structure is transmuted into process and the subject re-enters into history.' Admittedly, this concept is not without problems, but 'experience' situates material determination in *time,* as part of the *historical process.* Furthermore, 'men and women also return as subjects within this term – not as autonomous subjects, "free individuals", but as persons experiencing their determinate productive situations and relationships, as needs and interests and antagonisms..."handling" this experience within their *consciousness* and their *culture....* .in the most complex.... ways, and then (often but not always through the ensuing structures of class) acting upon their determinate situation in their turn.[61]

Finally, in their concern for class, the British Marxist historians do not eschew the master category of mode of production, though they do seek to recompose and historicize it. From Dobb to Thompson, they have been attempting, with varying degrees of success, to reformulate the assumed equation of social being as mode of production = economy and/or technology as the base. For example, we saw that Dobb – even if he did not himself follow it consistently – insisted on a politico-economic conception of mode of production. And Thompson insists on a still 'fuller' conception, for the mode of production 'gives us also the attendant relations of production (which are also relations of domination and subordination)', and 'provides the "general illumination in which all other colours are plunged and which modifies their specific tonalities"'.[62] That is, *social* relations of production are simultaneously economic, political, cultural and moral. This recomposition of the concept of mode of production is, perhaps, particularly well-evidenced in such historical studies as Thompson's 'Time, Work-Discipline, and Industrial Capitalism', Hill's 'Pottage for Freeborn Englishmen', and Hobsbawm's 'Customs, Wages, and Work-load', as well as in several of Hilton's writings on lord-peasant seigneurial relations in medieval England.[63] An example of the historicization of the concept is Thompson's discussion in *The Making of the English Working Class* of the historically specific separation of the economic and the political in the development of the capitalist mode of production in terms of the dual, but separate, moments of 'economic exploitation' and 'political oppression.'[64]

We should be careful at this point, for the British Marxist historians have not only been misread by their structuralist critics, but also, to some extent, by their humanist defenders. While they insist, Thompson most strongly, on the total character of the social relations of production, they do not, as I have discussed previously, conflate the social relations of production with class relations. This is, however, what Simon Clarke does in his defence of Hilton, Hill, Hobsbawm and (especially) Thompson. As noted at the end of Chapter 1, it is this which actually leads Clarke as well to (mistakenly) assert that there was a break between Dobb and his younger colleagues.[65]

We should also recall Robert Brenner's contributions to the debate about the transition from feudalism to capitalism, in which he extends Dobb's approach. Brenner's work provides the immediate basis upon which Ellen Wood has begun the theoretical elaboration of a political Marxism, that is, one in which relations of production are presented in their '*political* aspect, that aspect in which they are actually *contested:* as relations of domination, as rights of property, as the power to organize and govern production and appropriation'. At the same time., Wood explains, political Marxism is as persuaded as economistic

Marxisms of the primacy of production. It neither specifies production in such a way as to omit it from consideration, nor inflates it so as to encompass the totality of social activity or even class 'experiences'. Rather, it is committed to the proposition that a mode of production is a *social* phenomenon. Furthermore, political Marxism is effectively distanced from the base-superstructure model, for it does not present the social totality as 'an opposition, a 'regional' separation between a basic 'objective' economic structure, on the one hand, and social, juridical, and political forms on the other, but rather as a continuous structure of social relations and forms with varying degrees of distance from the immediate process of production and appropriation, beginning with relations and forms that constitute the system of production itself.' Thus, Wood repeats that production relations assume the 'form of particular juridical and political relations – modes of domination and coercion, forms of property and social organization – which are not mere secondary reflexes but constituents of the productive relations themselves'. She refers directly to Brenner's argument that the juridical-political sphere can be seen as involved in the productive base in at least two ways. First, 'a system of production always exists in the shape of specific social determinations, the particular modes of organization and domination and the forms of property in which relations of production are embodied – what might be called, the "basic" as distinct from "superstructural" juridical-political attributes of the productive system.' Second, considered from a historical perspective, even political institutions like village and state are among the determinants of relations of production and can be viewed as anterior to them. This is so not only where these institutions are the direct instruments of surplus-appropriation but more generally insofar as production relations 'are historically constituted by the configuration of political power that determines the outcome of class conflict.'[66]

Political Marxism can be viewed, then, as an extension of

the British Marxist historians' theory of class determination. In fact, Wood's discussion can be read as an elaboration of what Thompson is pointing to in his quotation from the *Grundrisse*[67] which he offers as an alternative conception of the social totality – without rejecting the proposition that social being determines social consciousness.

Then what are we to make of Perry Anderson's structuralist argument regarding the problem of social order? He intends this argument as a criticism of Thompson's theory and it is, therefore, in effect, a critique of the British Marxist historians' conception of the historical process. He writes:

> It is, and must be, the dominant mode of production that confers fundamental unity on a social formation, allocating their objective positions to the classes within it, and distributing the agents within each class. The result is, typically, an objective process of class struggle. But class struggle itself is not a causal prius in the sustentation of order, for *classes are constituted by modes of production, and not vice versa.* The one mode of production of which this will not be true is communism – which, precisely, will abolish classes.[68]

At first sight, the British Marxist historians would probably not reject Anderson's propositions. However, on further consideration they would most likely find them inadequate, both in terms of historical and political theory. They would grant that there is a certain logic in viewing a mode of production as prior to the classes which are specified by it, in that relations of production – in the form of relations of exploitation – are the basis of class antagonism and struggle. Nevertheless, they would argue that in historical terms it is, at the same time, *class relations which structure modes of production.* As Thompson puts it, 'Class struggle *is* the historical process,' and ultimately the reproduction – *or not* – of a mode of production is determined in the outcomes of class struggles. But that is not all, for it is not just the epochal question of the persistence or demise of a mode of production which is determined in the course of class struggle, but the specific historical course of development of the mode of production itself.

Anderson himself seems to realize the problematic nature of his statements (which may have been due to his emphasis on 'epochal' order), yet he continues to give priority to the mode of production when he adds that 'in both reproduction and transformation – maintenance and subversion – of social order, mode of production and class struggle are always at work. But the second must be activated by the first.' Thus the problem remains. This can, perhaps, be seen more clearly when we consider what he seems to offer as the 'exception which proves the rule', i.e. that the 'one mode of production of which this will not be true is communism – which, precisely, will abolish classes'. In fact, rather than showing that *classes are constituted by modes of production and not vice versa*, the example of the historically hypothesized communist mode of production would actually seem to support the British Marxist historians' theory of class determination and the priority given to class struggle, as it is precisely the development of the communist mode of production, according to Marx, which will be most dependent on the outcome of a particular class struggle – specifically that waged by a class-conscious and revolutionary working class. Even if we find it increasingly difficult to conceive of such a mode of production, it should, nevertheless, be more than apparent to those of us who are anxious to establish a truly democratic, free and equal social order that such an alternative can only be accomplished through the *active* agency of working people themselves.

Moreover, if, as has been argued, production relations are the basis for, but not co-equal with, class relations, then Anderson's propositions are inadequate not only because they fail to pose the crucial issue of *class structuration* of modes of production, but also because they fail to pose the related issue of *class formation.* We are not necessarily asked to consider the process by which classes as historical actors in the full sense emerge out of class struggles. This, of course, has been central to the work of the British Marxist historians. I am not saying that Anderson intends this to happen. However, the proposition that classes are constituted by modes of production can too readily lead to the practice of identifying a class as an objective structure in itself. The consciousness which it 'ought' to have, but seldom does, is thus deduced and it is found to be characterized by 'false consciousness'. Then it is a short route to the assertion that a particular party, sect, or theorist is needed to disclose the class's 'true consciousness' and 'real interests' to it. This practice is most likely to persist where classes are identified by, and equated with, their objective determinants – as in structuralist-Marxism. For example, we can recognize the potential, or basis, for such a practice in the following definition of class interests offered by Erik Olin Wright in his structuralist class-analysis: 'Class interests in capitalist society are those potential objectives which become actual objectives of struggle in the absence of the mystification and distortions of capitalist relations. Class interests . . . . are hypotheses about the objectives of struggles which would occur if the actors in the struggle had a scientifically correct understanding of their situations.'[69] This, we should note, is in spite of Wright's efforts to overcome the theoreticism of Althusser and Poulantzas and to theorize relationship and process.

Finally, we might consider the words of Eugene Genovese, whose work owes so much to the influence of the British Marxist historians:

If historical materialism is not a theory of class determinism it is nothing.... The relationship of [the] classes from this point of view determines the contours of the historical epoch. It follows, then, that changes in the political relationship of classes constitute the essence of social transformations; but this notion comes close to tautology, for social transformations are defined precisely by changes in class relationships. What rescues the notion from tautology is the expectation that these changes in class relationships determine – at least in outline – the major psychological, ideological, and political patterns, as well as economic and technological possibilities, that changes in class structure constitute the most meaningful of all changes. To argue that they constitute the only meaningful changes is to reduce historical materialism to nonsense and to surrender its dialectical essence.[70]

History, Historical Consciousness and Politics

The work of the British Marxist historians, then, has forced a reconsideration of the way we think about class. We can no longer continue to view it simply in terms of the class in itself/ class for itself (objective/subjective) dichotomy, and the derived false/true consciousness dichotomy. We are now asked to see class in terms of people's experiences and activities, structured especially but not exclusively by their productive relations, with those experiences and activities expressed in class, sometimes 'fully' class-conscious ways. But to pursue such class-struggle analysis we must understand the class-struggle experience in its totality and in its many forms of articulation. As William Sewell Jr writes in introducing his method of studying nineteenth-century French workers: 'The "language of labour" in the broadest sense [is] not only... workers' utterances or... theoretical discourse on labour, but... the whole range of institutional arrangements, ritual gestures, work practices, methods of struggle, customs and actions.'[71] (Sewell clearly acknowledges the influence of the British Marxist historians in his work.) Or, as E. P. Thompson states, when insisting on the necessity of considering values as much as interests and ideas in materialist analysis: 'A materialist examination of values must situate itself, not by idealist propositions, but in the face of culture's material abode: the people's way of life, and, above all, their productive and familial relationships.' At the same time, we should note his 'preface' to this statement:

> This is not to say that values are independent of the colouration of ideology: manifestly this is not the case, nor how, when experience itself is structured in class ways, could this be so? But to suppose from this that they are 'imposed'.... as 'ideology' is to mistake the whole social and cultural process. This imposition will always be attempted, with greater or lesser success, but it cannot succeed at all unless there is some *congruence* between the imposed rules and view of life and the necessary business of living a given mode of production. Moreover, values no less than material needs will always be a locus of *contradiction* of struggle between alternative values and views-of-life.[72]

This is filled with possibilities, for we can see in this, first, a means of 'rescuing' the study of values from the disrepute which it has suffered as a result of its association with Parsonian structural-functionalism and, second, the basis for both a broadening of the history of ideas[73] and the (re-)introduction of the political into the history of mentalities. Moreover, it is potentially politically consequential. We might consider, for example, individualism. This has been presented in historical and social scientists' accounts as originating in the Renaissance and/or Reformation with the bourgeoisie and as constituting their dominant value and/or ideology. Of course, there is abundant historical (and contemporary) evidence to support this argument. As a result of this supposed identity between capitalism and individualism, the socialist alternative has all too often been represented as a statist-collectivist model of social order; a model which has, apparently, been regularly rejected by working people in the liberal-democratic, capitalist West (especially in Britain and North America). This is not surprising given the real historical examples of the Soviet Union and other so-called socialist states. Now, whereas the Parsonian common-culture explanation would likely be that such an alternative is antithetical to the culture's dominant value of individualism, the (simple) Marxist response would likely be that the Western working classes have suffered from bourgeois-individualist ideology.[74] But, in both cases it is assumed that individualism is necessarily antithetical to socialism, based on the dichotomous model of individualism *vs.* collectivism.

Of course, the history of individualism has been intimately connected to the rise and predominance of the bourgeoisie, and as such, it has developed and often been expressed as a significant element of capitalist ideology. At the same time, individualism has not been *merely* bourgeois ideology or the dominant value of capitalist culture. That is, as practice, value, and/or idea, the history of individualism has not been so one-dimensional as either the dominant ideology or dominant value theories assume. Moreover, within that history there has existed the basis for an alternative conception of individualism, which is by no means antithetical to socialism.

In *Individualism,* Steven Lukes surveys the intellectual history of the term and pursues a conceptual analysis of it. He contends that the 'four unit ideas of individualism' are respect for human dignity, which represents the core of 'equality'; and autonomy, privacy, and self-development, which represent the three faces of 'liberty, or freedom'. Then, based on his conceptual analysis, he proposes that the 'only way to realize the values of individualism is through a humane form of socialism.'[75]

To Lukes's work we must juxtapose that of the Canadian political theorist C. B. Macpherson. His writings represent a long and persistent effort to examine historically and conceptually the theoretical foundations of liberal democracy, in order to provide a theoretical basis for the making of a liberal-democratic social order shorn of its connection to capitalism.[76] An important part of Macpherson's work has been the study of individualism, in the course of which he has come to argue that there have been two competing, though not necessarily contradictory, conceptions in liberal-democratic thought: one in which 'man is viewed as an infinite consumer or appropriator,' and another in which 'man is viewed as an infinite developer of his human attributes'. The former emphasizes the making of a social order which maximizes utilities and the latter, one which maximizes individual human powers.[77] What Macpherson offers for the fulfilment of the latter is participatory democracy, which might be viewed as a form of democratic socialism.

The discussions by Lukes and Macpherson are significant in that they show the existence and possibility of developing further a conception of individualism compatible with, if not dependent upon, the making of a democratic socialism. Nevertheless, such discussions are inadequate, for they fail to comprehend the history, development, and making of individualism – even as a complex and contradictory idea – in more than a merely idealist, 'philosophical' or theoretical, and (possibly) elitist fashion.[78]

Yet in the work of the British Marxist historians, especially the writings of Hilton, Hill, and Thompson, there is the basis for an alternative social history of (English) individualism (though they would probably use the term most reservedly – if at all – due to its associations with bourgeois ideology, preferring the couplet libertarianism/egalitarianism).[79] In their respective studies of the Peasant Rising of 1381, Puritanism and the radical religious sects of the common people of the seventeenth century, and the making of the English working class, we find a history of individual and collective struggles for liberty and equality. In their own historically specific ways, these struggles have contributed not merely to individualism as the dominant ideology or value in capitalist society, but to individualism as a class-differentially lived and experienced set of relations, practices, values and ideas. From this perspective individualism is viewed as characterized by the tensions and contradictions one might expect of ruling and, occasionally, hegemonic processes which have 'continually to be renewed, recreated, defended, and modified', because they have been 'continually resisted, limited, altered, [and] challenged by pressures not all [their] own'.[80]

In this way we are able to see that individualism has been meaningful to people not only because it has been propagated in one form as bourgeois ideology (or as a dominant value in socialization), but also because, historically and contemporarily, people have lived relations which have structured their lives (however collectively) in a variety of 'individualistic' forms. And, at the same time, because they themselves struggled, individually and collectively, to assert their historically specific and class-differential interpretations of individualism, often involving 'fuller' conceptions of liberty, or freedom, equality *and* community. Therefore, the making of a democratic socialism which would further the development of individualism – conceived of as involving libertarian, egalitarian, and communitarian-collective relations, practices, values, and ideas – would represent not merely the actualization of the thought of philosophers and theorists but, at least equally so, the realization of historical struggles of the lower classes themselves.[81] Thus the British Marxist historians would seem to have elucidated in historical fashion what Gramsci intended when he wrote that the working class develops in embryonic form its own conception of the world which manifests itself in action, and what Marx meant when he stated in the *Communist Manifesto* that 'the theoretical conclusions of the Communists are in no way based on ideas or principles that have been invented, or discovered, by this or that would-be universal reformer. They merely express, in general terms, actual relations springing from an existing class struggle, from a historical movement going on under our very eyes.'[82]

It is, perhaps, unfortunate that the British Marxist historians have not pursued social histories of the twentieth century, but we can see the beginning of such work in, for example, the recent studies of the American labour historian David Montgomery, especially in *Workers' Control in America*. His work is particularly interesting since he was previously a factory worker and labour organizer.[83] Based on his own experience and research, he states that, 'my study of both shop floor struggles and the Reconstruction period [i.e. the years following the United States Civil War] has underscored for me the fact that the working class has always formulated alternatives to bourgeois society in this country, particularly on the job.'[84] And thus, he argues that:

Socialism grows from the work and living patterns of working people. Its tap root is the mutualism spurred by their daily struggle for control of the circumstances of their lives. But that mutualism is manifested in values, loyalties, and thoughts, as well as in actions, and it can triumph only by becoming increasingly self-conscious and articulate. The struggle for workers' control advances only as it moves from the spontaneous to the deliberate, as workers consciously and jointly decide what they want and how they want to get it.[85]

Though I would not suggest that the British Marxist historians have been strategists of socialist politics, nevertheless, in their pursuit of class-struggle analysis of history from the bottom up they have been, in effect, pursuing a political strategy, which might be described as a 'political *aesthetic*'. By this I am not referring just to the fact that they have each shown so much interest in the arts, though this is not unrelated. Rather, I am referring to the making of a democratic and socialist historical consciousness. Historical consciousness might be defined, following John Berger, as 'the essential historical experience of our relation to the past: that is to say the experience of seeking to give meaning to our lives, of trying to understand the history of which we can become the active agents.'[86]

It is not that historical knowledge can inform us as to what to do *now, specifically* – for, at best, knowledge of the past is a counsel, not a scientific proof; but it shapes our understanding of historical experience, of which the present is as much a part as is the past. Gramsci recognized this when he wrote of the French Revolution that it 'has abolished many privileges, has raised up many oppressed; but it has only replaced one class in power with another. Yet, it has left a great teaching: that privileges and social differences, as products of society and not of nature [a la Vico], can be overcome.'[87] Or, as Rodney Hilton indicates in his conclusion to *Bond Men Made Free*:

> What could the fate of peasant societies in the present world of almost world-wide commercial and industrial monopoly capitalism have in common with that of the peasant societies of the late medieval world? Clearly, the tasks of leadership in contemporary peasant society have nothing in common with the tasks of the past, except in the recognition that conflict is part of existence and that nothing is gained without struggle.[88]

Yet, as we know, for Hilton and his fellow historians there has been more to it than the proposition that the history of all hitherto existing societies has been the history of class struggles. As Christopher Hill puts it, 'all knowledge of the past should help to humanize us,'[89] or as E. P. Thompson says even more explicitly: 'Historical consciousness ought to assist one to understand the possibilities of transformation and the possibilities within people.'[90] Marx himself would surely have subscribed to such a strategy, and yet this is also the point at which the British historians seem to break with him, at least, that is, with the Marx who wrote that, 'the social revolution of the nineteenth century can only create its poetry from the future, not from the past.'[91] For, while the British Marxist historians have realized, like Marx, that 'the past is not for living in,' nevertheless, they have also realized, more than Marx, that, 'it is a well of conclusions from which we draw in order to act,' and a 'people or a class which is cut off from its own past is far less free to choose and to act as a people or class than one that has been able to situate itself in history.'[92]

In other words, they have accepted that the making of a truly democratic socialism – or libertarian communism, requires more than 'necessity' – the determined struggle against exploitation and oppression – and more than organization. It also requires the desire to create an alternative social order. And yet, even that is not enough. There must be a 'prior *education of desire*' for, as William Morris has warned: 'If the present state of society merely breaks up without a conscious effort at transformation, the end, the fall of Europe, may be long in coming, but when it does, it will be far more terrible, far more confused and full of suffering than the period of the fall of Rome.'[93]

The strategy, or aesthetic, of the British Marxist historians – and of those who would work in their tradition – is, then, the *historical* 'education of desire' in order to provide 'a historical, dialectical conception of the world, which understands movement and change, which appreciates the sum of effort and sacrifice which the present has cost the past and which the future is costing the present, and which conceives the contemporary world as a synthesis of the past, of all past generations, which projects itself into the future.'[94] In other words, we must educate those for whom struggle is a determined necessity today with the historical experiences of those for whom struggle was a determined necessity yesterday. At the same time, we should be fully aware that such an educational process must be dialectical and that the educators, too, must be educated.

Endnotes

Chapter 1: Introduction

1. E.H. Carr, *What is History?* (Harmondsworth: Penguin, 1964), p. 84. Originally 1961.
2. P. Burke, *Sociology and History,* (London: George Allen and Unwin, 1980); C. Tilly, *As Sociology Meets History,* (New York; Academic Press, 1981); and P. Abrams, *Historical Sociology,* (Somerset: Open Books, 1982).
3. C. Wright Mills, *The Sociological Imagination,* (Oxford: Oxford University Press, 1959), p. 146.
4. G. Stedman Jones, 'From Historical Sociology to Theoretic History', *British Journal of Sociology, 27* (September 1976), pp. 295-305.
5. P. Abrams, *Historical Sociology,* and A. Giddens, *Central Problems in Social Theory,* (London: Macmillan, 1979).
6. Particularly as a result of work done by scholars at the Centre for Contemporary Cultural Studies, to be discussed in the course of this study, the relationship between history and theory has become a major issue in British Marxist discussions since the late 1970s.
7. P. Anderson, *Considerations on Western Marxism,* (London: New Left Books, 1976).
8. Ibid., pp. 111-12. Also, Anderson does note the 'high calibre of British Marxist historiography' (p. 102).
9. E. Genovese, *The World the Slaveholders Made,* (New York: Vintage Books, 1971), p. vii.
10. In Karl Marx, *Early Writings,* (Harmondsworth: Penguin Books, 1975), p. 425.
11. R. Williams, *Marxism and Literature,* (Oxford: Oxford University Press, 1977), p. 83. The two lines are reversed from the text but the meaning is the same.
12. M. Dobb, *Studies in the Development of Capitalism,* (London:

Routledge and Kegan Paul, 1946, 1963 rev. edition).

13. The contributions to the debate, to be considered with Dobb's work in chapter 2, are published together in Rodney Hilton (ed.). *The Transition from Feudalism to Capitalism,* (London: New Left Books, 1976).

14. C. Hill, *Society and Puritanism in Pre-Revolutionary England,* (London: Seeker and Warburg, 1964).

15. E.P. Thompson, *The Making of the English Working Class,* (Harmondsworth: Penguin, 1963, 1968 rev. edition, new postscript 1980).

16. E. Hobsbawm, *Primitive Rebels,* (Manchester: Manchester University Press, 1959, 1963 rev. edition, new preface 1971).

17. Eugene Genovese has referred to a 'theory of class determinism', but I prefer the word 'determination'. See Genovese, *In Red and Black: Marxian Explorations in Southern and Afro-American History,* (New York: Vintage Books, 1972), p. 40. On 'Determine' and 'Determination', see Raymond Williams, *Keywords: A Vocabulary of Culture and Society,* (New York: Oxford University Press, 1976), pp. 86-91, and *Marxism and Literature,* pp. 83-8, respectively. As he writes: 'Determination is never only the setting of limits, it is also the exertion of pressures.'

18. *E. Genovese, The World the Slaveholders Made,* p. viii.

19. Barrington Moore Jr, *Injustice,* (London: Macmillan, 1978), p. 474.

20. E.P. Thompson, 'An Open Letter to Leszek Kolakowski', reprinted in *The Poverty of Theory,* (London: Merlin Press, 1978, 4th impression), p. 333; originally in *The Socialist Register 1973,* (London: Merlin Press, 1973).

21. R. Samuel, 'The British Marxist Historians' T, *New Left Review,* 120 (March-April 1980), pp. 21-96.

22. E. Hobsbawm, 'The Historians' Group of the Communist Party', in M. Cornforth (ed.). *Rebels and Their Causes,* (London: Lawrence and Wishart, 1978), pp. 21-8.

23. R. Johnson, 'Culture and the Historians', in J. Clarke, C. Critcher, and R. Johnson (eds), *Working-Class Culture: Studies in History and Theory,* (London: Hutchinson, 1979), pp. 41-71.

24. On this, see R. Samuel, 'People's History', in R. Samuel (ed.). *People's History and Socialist Theory,* (London: Routledge and Kegan Paul, 1981), pp. xiv-xxxix. It should be noted that GDH Cole was one of Britain's most important socialist and labour historians, and co-authored, among the many works he wrote, a classic of 'people's history': GDH Cole and R. Postgate, *The Common People, 1746-1946,* (London: Methuen, 1938, 1946 rev. edition).

25. E. Hobsbawm, 'The Historians' Group', p. 22.

26. Ibid., p. 21.

27. A.L. Morton, *A People's History,* (London: Lawrence and Wishart, 1979 rev. edition).

28. E. Hobsbawm, 'The Historians' Group', pp. 25-6.

29. Ibid., pp. 28, 30.

30. All published by Lawrence and Wishart. The volumes edited by Hill (with Dell) and Hobsbawm have been republished with revisions and are noted in the chapters on their respective works.

31. J. Saville et al. (eds). *Democracy and the Labour Movement,* (London: Lawrence and Wishart, 1954).

32. Hobsbawm's words, though he himself was not very close to her ('The Historians' Group', p. 46.)

33. These biographical notes were provided by Christopher Hill in a letter to the author in September 1983. He noted that she was a very private person and, thus, he could not vouch for all of the points.

34. The second published by George Allen & Unwin, the others by Lawrence and Wishart.

35. D. Torr, *Tom Mann and His Times,* (London: Lawrence and Wishart, 1956). Several chapters of this volume (one of

a projected two) were completed from her notes, at her request, by Christopher Hill and A.L. Morton. Fragments of what were to be volume two were edited and published by E.P. Thompson as 'Tom Mann and His Times, 1890-1892' in *Our History,* 26-7 (1962). Hill states that she was such 'a perfectionist she would probably never have finished it'.

36. J. Saville et al.. *Democracy and the Labour Movement,* p. 8.
37. D. Torr, *Tom Mann and His Times,* p. 13. Quoted from Newton's 'History for the People' (1854).
38. E. Hobsbawm, 'The Historians' Group', p. 26.
39. Ibid., pp. 31-3.
40. See the articles in the hundredth issue: Christopher Hill, Rodney Hilton, and Eric Hobsbawm, 'Origins and Early Years', and Jacques Le Goff, 'Later History', *Past & Present* (August 1983), pp. 3-13, and 14-28.
41. *Past & Present,* 1 (February 1952), p. i.
42. See John Saville, The XXth Congress and the British Communist Party', in *The Socialist Register 1976,* (London: Merlin Press, 1976), pp. 1-23.
43. E. Hobsbawm, 'The Historians' Group', p. 39-42.
44. On the intellectual origins of the Centre, see Paul Jones, 'Organic Intellectuals and the Generation of English Cultural Studies', *Thesis Eleven,* 5/6 (1982), pp. 83-123.
45. The project provided for the publication of two volumes of papers: J. Clarke, C. Critcher and R. Johnson (eds). *Working Class Culture,* and R. Johnson et al. (eds). *Making Histories: Studies in History-Writing and Politics,* (London; Hutchinson, 1982).
46. Referring to some extent to an 'intellectual generation', 'structure of feeling' comes from the work of Raymond Williams, who is himself included by Johnson in the structure of feeling being referred to. On the concept, see R. Williams, *Marxism and Literature,* pp. 128-35.
47. A. Briggs, *Chartist Studies,* (London: Macmillan, 1959).

48. R. Hoggart, *The Uses of Literacy,* (Harmondsworth: Penguin, 1971). Originally 1957. Hoggart was the founder of the Centre for Contemporary Cultural Studies.

49. R. Williams, *Culture and Society,* (Harmondsworth: Penguin, 1971). Originally 1958.

50. E. Genovese, *The Political Economy of Slavery,* (New York: Vintage Books, 1967). Genovese's work will be discussed briefly in chapter 2 on Dobb and also mentioned in chapter 6 on Thompson.

51. See the lengthy interviews with Raymond Williams by the editors of the *New Left Review* published as *Politics and Letters,* (London: New Left Books, 1979). Also, Williams would call himself a Marxist today.

52. Though they have 'toned down' their insistence on a 'break', scholars at the centre still reject the notion of a British Marxist historical 'theoretical tradition'. See Bill Schwarz, 'The People in History: The Communist Party Historians' Group, 1946-56', in R. Johnson et al.. *Making Histories,* p. 50.

53. See R. Johnson's 'Three Problematics: Elements of a Theory of Working-class Culture', in J. Clarke, C. Critcher, and R. Johnson (eds). *Working Class Culture,* pp. 201-37. The writers at the Centre were not uncritical of structuralism but the project was conducted in its terms and thus the character of the dialogue was pre-determined by structuralism itself.

54. R. Johnson, Thompson, Genovese, and Socialist-Humanist History', *History Workshop,* 6 (Autumn 1978), pp. 79-100.

55. S. Clarke, 'Socialist Humanism and the Critique of Economism', *History Workshop,* 8 (Autumn 1979), pp. 138-56.

56. K. Tribe, 'The Problem of Transition and the Question of Origin', in his *Genealogies of Capitalism,* (London: Macmillan, 1981), p. 2.

57. Thus, I am in basic agreement with the 'position' laid out in

History Workshop by Keith McClelland and Gavin Williams in separate 'Comments' under the general heading 'Towards a Socialist History', 7 (Spring 1979), pp. 101-25. Also, E.P. Thompson has commented that he finds talk of a break 'actively unhelpful' and that from Dobb to himself and the others there is a *'common* tradition of Marxist historiography'. ('The Poverty of Theory', in *The Poverty of Theory,* (London: Merlin Press, 1978), p. 186, fn. 168.) Additionally, see the exchange among Richard Johnson, Stuart Hall, and E.P. Thompson in R. Samuel (ed.). *People's History and Socialist Theory,* pp. 375-408.

58. See Ellen Meiksins Wood's essay on 'The Separation of the Economic and the Political in Capitalism', *New Left Review,* 127 (May-June 1981), pp. 66-95, for an elaboration of 'political Marxism' with particular reference to Brenner's work.

Chapter 2: Maurice Dobb and the Debate on the Transition to Capitalism

1. F. Braudel, *Afterthoughts on Material Civilization and Capitalism,* (Baltimore, Md: The Johns Hopkins University Press, 1977), pp. 45-6.M.

2. Dobb, *Studies in the Development of Capitalism,* (London: Routledge and Kegan Paul, 1946, rev. edition 1963).

3. See Anthony Giddens, *Capitalism and Modem Social Theory,* (Cambridge University Press, 1971), pp. xi-xiii; Don Martindale, *The Nature and Types of Sociological Theory,* (Boston: Houghton Mifflin, 1960), pp. 29-51; and Robert Heilbroner, *The Worldly Philosophers,* (New York: Simon and Schuster, 1972), pp. 16-40.

4. A. Smith, *The Wealth of Nations,* edited by Edwin Canaan (New York: The Modern Library, 1937).

5. See Irving M. Zeitlin, *Ideology and the Development of Sociological Theory,* (Englewood Cliffs, NJ: Prentice-Hall,

1981), pp. 61-74.

6.   See M. Weber, 'Capitalism and Rural Society in Germany' in H.H. Gerth and C.W. Mills (eds). *From Max Weber,* (Oxford: Oxford University Press, 1958), pp. 363-85.

7.   M. Weber, *The Protestant Ethic and the Spirit of Capitalism,* (New York: Charles Scribner's Sons, 1956).

8.   E. Durkheim, *The Division of Labour in Society,* (New York: Macmillan, 1933).

9.   For example, in social history see Peter N. Stearns, *European Society in Upheaval,* (New York: Macmillan, 1975), and for a critical discussion in development studies, see Norman Long, *An Introduction to the Sociology of Rural Development,* (London: Tavistock, 1977), pp. 9-41.

10.   For a brief critique, see Anthony Giddens, *Studies in Social and Political Theory,* (London: Hutchinson, 1977), Introduction, pp. 15-18.

11.   See 'Capitalism' in R. Williams, *Keywords: A Vocabulary of Culture and Society,* (New York: Oxford University Press, 1976), pp. 42-4.

12.   These autobiographical notes are taken from 'Random Biographical Notes' which Dobb wrote in 1965 and which appears as the introductory piece to the 'Maurice Dobb Memorial Issue' of the *Cambridge Journal of Economics, 2* (1978), pp. 115-20. Also, see Eric Hobsbawm's introduction, 'Maurice Dobb', in the Festschrift for Dobb: C.H. Feinstein (ed.). *Socialism, Capitalism and Economic Growth,* (Cambridge: Cambridge University Press, 1967), pp. 1-12; this also includes a bibliography of Dobb's works to 1967.

13.   At Cambridge he was a member of the Socialist Society, the Labour Club, and Keynes' Political Economy Club, and he said the writers who most influenced him were, in addition to Marx, 'the Webbs, Labriola, Croce... ... for a time George Sorel, Bertrand Russell, and... ... the Guild Socialists', a sign that the young economist was avoiding

economism.

14. Reprinted in M. Dobb, *On Economic Theory and Socialism,* (London: Routledge and Kegan Paul, 1955), pp. 3-15.

15. *M. Dobb, Capitalist Enterprise and Social Progress,* (London: Routledge, 1925).

16. M. Dobb, *Russian Economic Development Since the Revolution,* (London: Routledge, 1928); and *Soviet Economic Development Since 1917,* (London: Routledge and Kegan Paul, 1948).

17. M. Dobb, *Economic Growth and Underdeveloped Countries,* (London: Lawrence and Wishart, 1963).

18. M. Dobb, *On Marxism Today,* (London: Hogarth Press, 1932).

19. Ibid., pp. 14, 16, and 20.

20. See Stuart Macintyre, *A Proletarian Science: Marxism in Britain, 1917-33,* (Cambridge: Cambridge University Press, 1980), pp. 121, 170.

21. E. Hobsbawm, 'Maurice Dobb', pp. 4-7. For examples of Dobb's arguments on economic theory in this period, see his *Political Economy and Capitalism,* (London: Routledge, 1937, rev. edition 1945).

22. Reprinted in M. Dobb, *Economic Theory and Socialism,* pp. 93-103.

23. Ibid., p. 103.

24. 'Capitalism', in R. Williams, *Keywords,* p. 42.

25. Dobb capitalized capitalism and feudalism. I shall do so only in direct quotes from *Studies.*

26. Based on Dobb's presentation of each definition (or model) I have adapted them in relation to the debate which ensued and their form in current historical and social theory discussions; thus, I have emphasized Weber and Pirenne in the first two cases.

27. W. Sombart, *The Quintessence of Capitalism: A Study of the History and Psychology of Modern Business Man,* (London: T. Fisher and Unwin, 1915), p. 22.

28. See Gordon Marshall, *In Search of the Spirit of Capitalism*, (London: Hutchinson, 1982); Richard Ashcraft, 'Marx and Weber on Liberalism as Bourgeois Ideology', *Comparative Studies in Society and History*, 14 (March 1972), pp. 130-68; A. Giddens, 'Marx, Weber and the Development of Capitalism', *Studies in Social and Political Theory*, pp. 183-207; and David Landes, *The Unbound Prometheus*, (Cambridge: Cambridge University Press, 1969), pp. 21-5.

29. See H.H. Gerth and C.W. Mills, *From Max Weber*, pp. 66-9. Also of interest is Weber's *General Economic History*, (New York: Collier Books, 1961).

30. M. Weber, *The Protestant Ethic*, p. 17.

31. H. Pirenne, *A History of Europe*, (Garden City, NY: Anchor Books, 1958), pp. 196 and 195.

32. K. Marx, *Capital*, (Harmondsworth: Penguin, 1976), Volume I, p. 874.

33. See R. Ashcraft, 'Marx and Weber on Liberalism', pp. 133-4.

34. K. Marx, *Capital*, (Harmondsworth: Penguin; New York; Vintage Books, 1981), Volume III, p. 450.

35. K. Marx, *Capital*, Vol. I, p. 875.

36. Ibid., p. 876. See William Lazonick, 'Karl Marx and Enclosures in England', *Review of Radical Political Economics*, 6 (Summer 1974), pp. 1-32.

37. See Tadeusz Kowalik, 'The Institutional Framework of Dobb's Economics', *Cambridge Journal of Economics*, 2 (June 1978), p. 148.

38. See the introductory essays by Maxine Berg in *Technology and Toil in Nineteenth Century Britain*, (London: CSE Books, 1979); and the work of David Noble, *e.g. America By Design: Science, Technology and the Rise of Corporate Capitalism*, (New York; Alfred Knopf, 1977).

39. For example, G. A. Cohen, *Karl Marx's Theory of History: A Defence*, (Oxford: Oxford University Press, 1978).

40. M. Weber, *General Economic History,* (New York: Collier Books, 1961), p. 261.
41. See K. Marx, *Capital,* Vol. Ill, pp. 440-55 on 'Merchant's Capital'.
42. There is also, according to a new interpretation, another 'decisive moment' in the history of capitalism, termed the 'second Industrial Revolution' of the late nineteenth- and twentieth-century. For elements of this interpretation in the United States, see Harry Braverman, *Labour and Monopoly Capital,* (New York: Monthly Review Press, 1974); David Noble, *America By Design;* and Stuart Ewen, *Captains of Consciousness,* (New York: McGraw-Hill, 1976).
43. Dobb was quoting from K. Marx, *Capital,* Vol. Ill, pp. 452-3.
44. For example, of the changes carried out by the Commonwealth which furthered the development of capitalism, Dobb notes the abolition of feudal tenures, which were never restored *(Studies,* p. 175).
45. The essays which make up the original 'debate' appeared in *Science and Society.* They are: Paul M. Sweezy, 'A Critique' (Spring 1950); Maurice Dobb, 'A Reply' (Spring 1950); H.K. Takahashi, 'A Contribution to the Discussion' (Fall 1952); Maurice Dobb, 'A Further Comment' (Spring 1954); Paul M. Sweezy, 'A Rejoinder' (Spring 1953); Rodney Hilton, 'Comment' (Fall 1953); and Christopher Hill, 'Comment' (Fall 1953). They were collected into *The Transition from Feudalism to Capitalism: A Symposium,* (New York: *Science and Society,* 1954). Later they were published, together with several related pieces, in Rodney Hilton (ed.). *The Transition from Feudalism to Capitalism,* (London: New Left Books, 1976). Page references are to the Hilton collection and will appear in the text as *Transition.*
46. There are a number of good discussions of the debate which also refer to recent contributions, for example, Robert S. DuPlessis, 'From Demesne to World-System: A Critical

Review of the Literature on the Transition from Feudalism to Capitalism', *Radical History Review,* 3 (September 1976), pp. 3-41; and Robert J. Holton, 'Marxist Theories of Social Change and the Transition from Feudalism to Capitalism', *Theory and Society,* 10 (1981), pp. 805-32. Also, see discussion of the 1940s debate of the Communist Historians' Group on the seventeenth century in Keith Tribe, 'The Problem of Transition and the Question of Origin', in his *Genealogies of Capitalism,* (London: Macmillan, 1981), pp. 1-34.

47. Paul Sweezy is the founder and editor of the American Marxist journal. *Monthly Review,* and author of several outstanding works, including *The Theory of Capitalist Development,* (Oxford: Oxford University Press, 1942) and, with Paul Baran, *Monopoly Capital,* (Harmondsworth: Penguin, 1968).

48. Dobb had discussed it in *Studies;* for example, see pp. 39 and 57.

49. Takahashi was Professor of History at the University of Tokyo until his death in 1982.

50. On this process, see Barrington Moore Jr, *Social Origins of Dictatorship and Democracy,* (Harmondsworth: Penguin, 1969). On Barrington Moore, see Dennis Smith, *Barrington Moore and the Uses of History,* (London: Macmillan, 1983).

51. In *Transition.* There are also several other pieces from this period. Of particular interest is an essay by Hilton which appeared in the first issue of *Past & Present* (February 1952), entitled 'Capitalism – What's in a Name?' pp. 145-58.

52. Dobb's essay, 'From Feudalism to Capitalism' (1962), is included in *Transition,* pp. 165-9. Also, see his piece on the transition and the industrial revolution in the volume, M. Dobb, *Papers on Capitalism, Development and Planning,* (London: Routledge and Kegan Paul, 1967).

53. E. Hobsbawm, 'The Crisis of the Seventeenth Century', *Past & Present,* 5 and 6 (1954); reprinted with a variety of

articles on the period from *Past & Present* in Trevor Aston (ed.). *Crisis in Europe: 1560-1660,* (London: Routledge and Kegan Paul, 1965). Two related pieces by Hobsbawm did appear in *Science and Society,* however: 'The Seventeenth Century in the Development of Capitalism', Vol. 24 (1960), pp. 97-112; and 'From Feudalism to Capitalism', Vol. 26 (1962), which is reprinted in the Hilton (ed.), collection.

54. T. Aston (ed.). *Crisis in Europe,* pp. 5 and 19-20.

55. On Latin American development studies with reference to the transition debate, see also Ian Roxborough, *Theories of Underdevelopment,* (London: Macmillan, 1979) and David Goodman and Michael Redclift, *From Peasant to Proletarian: Capitalist Development and Agrarian Transitions,* (Oxford: Basil Blackwell, 1981).

56. See Jacques Lambert, *Latin America: Social Structures and Political Institutions,* (University of California Press, 1967).

57. For Frank's work, see his *Latin America: Underdevelopment or Revolution?,* (New York: Monthly Review Press, 1969) and *Capitalism and Underdevelopment in Latin America,* (Harmondsworth: Penguin, 1971). More recently, he has written *World Accumulation: 1492-1789,* (New York: Monthly Review Press, 1978).

58. E. Laclau, 'Feudalism and Capitalism in Latin America', *New Left Review,* 67 (May-June 1971), pp. 19-38; reprinted in a collection of his essays, entitled *Politics and Ideology in Marxist Theory,* (London: New Left Books, 1977), pp. 15-50.

59. E. Laclau, *Politics and Ideology in Marxist Theory,* pp. 41 and 33.

60. Ibid., pp. 37-9.

61. Harvey J. Kaye, 'The Political Economy of Seigneurialism: An Interpretation of the Development of Rural Spanish America', (Baton Rouge, La: Louisiana State University, 1976). Also, see H. Kaye, 'Barrington Moore's Paths to Modernisation: Are They Applicable to Latin America?'

Bulletin of the Society for Latin American Studies, 28 (April 1978), pp. 24-40.

62. This paraphrasing is a step beyond Pierre Vilar's paraphrasing of Lenin that 'Spanish imperialism was the highest stage of feudalism', in 'The Age of Don Quijote', in Peter Earle (ed.). *Essays in European Economic History: 1500-1800,* (Oxford: Oxford University Press, 1974), pp. 100-12.

63. A similar argument is presented by Robert Brenner in his essay, 'The Origins of Capitalist Development: A Critique of Neo-Smithian Marxism', *New Left Review,* 104, (July-August 1977), especially pp. 82-92, (to be noted later).

64. For an extended discussion, see H. Kaye, 'Totality: Its Application to Historical and Social Analysis by Wallerstein and Genovese', *Historical Reflections/Reflexions Historiques,* 6 (Winter 1979), pp. 405-19.

65. Detailed in I. Wallerstein, *The Modern World-System: Capitalist Agriculture and the Origins of the European World-Economy in the Sixteenth Century,* (New York: Academic Press, 1974) which was the first of four volumes. Volume 2 has now been published, entitled. *The Modern World-System II: Mercantilism and the Consolidation of the European World-Economy, 1600-1750,* (New York: Academic Press, 1980). Also, for a collection of Wallerstein's more theoretical essays, see his *The Capitalist World-Economy,* (Cambridge: Cambridge University Press, 1979). All of this work has generated a scholarly 'industry', as indicated by the volumes of world-system studies published, e.g. four *Political Economy of the World-System Annuals* (Beverly Hills, Ca. and London: Sage Publications).

66. I. Wallerstein, *The Modern World-System* (1974), pp. 3-11. Wallerstein was working in the sociology of development of Africa and found the African 'societies' inadequate, unto themselves, as levels of analysis.

67. I. Wallerstein, 'The Rise and Future Demise of the World

Capitalist System: Concepts for Comparative Analysis', (1974) in *The Capitalist World-Economy,* p.5.

68. Ibid., pp. 6 and 15.

69. I. Wallerstein, *The Modern World-System* (1974), p. 127. And elsewhere, for example see his discussion in 'A World-System Perspective on the Social Sciences', (1976) in *The Capitalist World-Economy,* pp. 155-6.

70. Braudel's most important works are: *The Mediterranean and the Mediterranean World in the Age of Philip II,* (New York: Harper and Row, 1973) and *Capitalism and Material Life, 1400-1800,* (New York: Harper and Row, 1975). For his method and theory, see the collection of his essays *On History,* (Chicago: University of Chicago Press, 1980). Also, see H. Kaye, 'Totality' and, regarding Wallerstein and the *Annates* school of history, see DuPlessis, 'From Demesne to World-System', pp. 21-3. For Braudel on 'capitalism', see, among other works, his *Afterthoughts on Material Civilisation and Capitalism.* Also, John Day, 'Fernand Braudel and the Rise of Capitalism', *Social Research,* 47 (Autumn 1980), pp. 507-18.

71. On its problems as history, see Peter Gourevitch, 'The International System and Regime Formation', *Comparative Politics,* 10 (April 1978), pp. 419-38, and Val F. Hunt, 'The Rise of Feudalism in Eastern Europe: A Critical Appraisal of the Wallerstein 'World-System' Thesis', *Science and Society,* 42 (Spring 1978), pp. 43-61.

72. See the essay by R. Brenner, 'The Origins of Capitalist Development' for a full critique of Wallerstein in relation to Sweezy and Frank; and the review essay by Theda Skocpoi for a sociologist's critique, 'Wallerstein's World Capitalist System: A Theoretical and Historical Critique', *American Journal of Sociology,* 82 (March 1977), pp. 1085-90.

73. 1. Wallerstein, *The Modern World-System* (1974), pp. 157, 355, 356, and 152.

74. Keith Thomas, 'Jumbo History', *New York Review of Books,* 17 April 1975, p. 25. Though Wallerstein has modified his ideas somewhat in *The Modern World-System II,* the basic problems remain. See the reviews by D. Chirot in the *Journal of Social History,* 16 (Spring 1982), pp. 561-5; and Michael Kimmel in *Theory and Society,* 11 (March 1982), pp. 244-51. Also, see C.H. George, 'The Origins of Capitalism: A Marxist Epitome and Critique of Immanuel Wallerstein's Modern World-System', *Marxist Perspectives,* 5 (Summer 1980), pp. 70-100.

75. *E. Genovese, In Red and Black: Marxian Explorations in Southern and Afro-American History,* (New York: Vintage Books, 1972), pp. 385-6, my emphasis. For Wallerstein on Genovese, see his essay which originally appeared in the *American Journal of Sociology* (1976), 'American Slavery and the Capitalist World-Economy', *The Capitalist World-Economy,* pp. 202-1.

76. E. Genovese, *The Political Economy of Slavery,* (New York: Vintage Books, 1967).

77. E. Genovese, *The World the Slaveholders Made,* (New York; Vintage Books, 1971), pp. vi-viii.

78. E. Genovese, *In Red and Black,* p. 33, my emphasis.

79. E. Genovese, *The World the Slaveholders Made,* p. vii.

80. A. Gramsci, *Selections from the Prison Notebooks,* edited and translated by Q. Hoare and G.N. Smith (London: Lawrence and Wishart, 1977), p. 377.

81. E. Genovese, *In Red and Black,* p. 322.

82. E. Genovese, *Roll Jordan, Roll: The World the Slaves Made* (New York: Pantheon, 1974). At the same time, I should state that Genovese's essays of the late 1960s indicate 'base-superstructure' more as metaphor than model.

83. E. Genovese, 'Slavery – The World's Burden', in Harry P. Owens (ed.). *Perspectives and Irony in American Slavery,* (Jackson, Ms: University Press of Mississippi, 1976), pp.

27-50, and, with Elizabeth Fox-Genovese, 'The Slave Economies in Political Perspective', *Journal of American History,* 66 (June 1979), pp. 7-23.

84. P. Anderson, *Passages from Antiquity to Feudalism,* (London: New Left Books, 1974); and *Lineages of the Absolutist State,* (London: New Left Books, 1974). These few paragraphs do not do justice to Anderson's two volumes, which are exciting in their breadth (through time and space). In spite of the problems I have with Anderson's 'structuralist' language, I strongly recommend them.

85. On Anderson's *Passages* and *Lineages,* which were often reviewed along with Wallerstein's *The Modern World-System,* see K. Thomas, 'Jumbo History', and R.J. Holton, 'Marxist Theories of Social Change'; also Michael Hechter, 'Lineages of the Capitalist State', *American Journal of Sociology,* 82 (March 1977), pp. 1057-74, and W.G. Runciman, 'Comparative Sociology or Narrative History: A Note on the Methodology of Perry Anderson', *European Journal of Sociology,* 21 (1980), pp. 162-78.

86. Modes of production never appear in 'pure forms'. 'Social formation' refers to what exists historically. Made up of, possibly, several modes of production, a social formation is dominated by a single mode, characterized by specific social relations of production. See P. Anderson, *Lineages,* pp. 154-5.

87. Ibid., pp. *403M.* This is not the place to take up a critique of structuralism. On 'mode of production' in structuralist thought, see Louis Althusser and Etienne Balibar, *Reading Capital,* (London: New Left Books, 1970) especially Part III (by Balibar), pp. 199-399, and Nicos Poulantzas, *Political Power and Social Classes,* (London: New Left Books, 1974), especially pp. 12-17. Thompson as we shall see later, did confront 'structuralism'.

88. P. Anderson, *Lineages,* p. 11.

89. P. Anderson, *Passages,* pp. 182-209.

90. P. Anderson, *Lineages,* pp. 15, 18.

91. R.J. Holton, 'Marxist Theories of Social Change', pp. 860-1.

92. P. Anderson, *Lineages,* p. 21.

93. J. Merrington, 'Town and Country in the Transition to Capitalism', *New Left Review,* 93 (September-October 1975). Reprinted in R. Hilton (ed.). *Transition,* pp. 170-95.

94. P. Anderson, *Lineages,* p. 21 (in footnote).

95. R. Hilton, 'Towns in English Feudal Society', *Review,* 3 (Summer 1979), p.19.

96. P. Anderson, *Lineages,* pp. 420, 422-6, 137, and 428-9, respectively.

97. Brenner is an American. In addition to the three articles to be discussed, he wrote 'The Civil War Politics of London's Merchant Community', *Past & Present,* 58 (February 1973), pp. 53-107.

98. Guy Bois, 'Against the Neo-Malthusian Orthodoxy', *Past & Present, 79* (May 1978), pp. 60-9.

99. R. Brenner, 'Agrarian Class Structure and Economic Development in Pre-Industrial Europe', *Past & Present,* 70 (February 1976), pp. 30-75.

100. The contributions to the symposium were M.M. Postan and John Hatcher, 'Population and Class Relations in Feudal Society', Patricia Groot and David Parker, 'Agrarian Class Structure and Economic Development', and Heide Wunder, 'Peasant Organisation and Class Conflict in East and West Germany', *Past & Present, 78* (February 1978), pp. 24-55; Emmanuel Le Roy Ladurie, 'A Reply to Professor Brenner', and Guy Bois, 'Against the Neo-Malthusian Orthodoxy', *Past & Present, 79* (May 1978), pp. 55-69; Rodney Hilton, 'A Crisis of Feudalism', and J.P. Cooper, 'In Search of Agrarian Capitalism', *Past & Present,* 80 (August 1980), pp. 20-65; and Arnost Klima, 'Agrarian Class Structure and Economic Development in Pre-Industrial Bohemia', *Past & Present,* 85

(November 1979), pp. 49-67. For Brenner's reply, see 'The Agrarian Roots of European Capitalism', *Past & Present*, 97 (November 1982), pp. 16-113. All will soon be collected in one volume and published by *Past & Present/Cambridge University Press*.

101. See M.M. Postan's 'The Economic Foundations of Medieval Economy' (1950) in the collection of his *Essays on Medieval Agriculture and General Problems of the Medieval Economy*, (Cambridge: Cambridge University Press, 1973), pp. 3-27; and 'Medieval Agrarian Society in its Prime: England', in M.M. Postan (ed.). *The Cambridge Economic History of Europe*, (Cambridge: Cambridge University Press, 1966), Volume 1, pp. 549-632; and Le Roy Ladurie's *The Peasants of Languedoc*, (Champaign, 111.: University of Illinois Press, 1974).

102. R. Brenner, 'Agrarian Class Structure', pp. 30-1. There is also an approach which denies the very existence of class structure, he says, directing us to Douglas C. North and Robert Paul Thomas, *The Rise of the Western World* (Cambridge, Cambridge University Press, 1973).

103. R. Brenner, Agrarian Class Structure.' He notes that classes are not a universal phenomenon, existing 'only where there is a surplus-extraction...relationship as implied here'.

104. Ibid., p. 31. (Brenner himself did not use the term 'theory of class determination' but his approach implies it.)

105. Ibid., p. 60.

106. Ibid., 32, 41, 41-2, 61-75 and 67-78.

107. R. Brenner, 'The Origins of Capitalist Development: A Critique of Neo-Smithian Marxism'.

108. R. Brenner, 'The Origins of Capitalist Development: A Critique of Neo-Smithian Marxism'. R. Brenner, 'Maurice Dobb and the Transition from Feudalism to Capitalism', *Cambridge Journal of Economics*, 2 (June 1978), p.122.

109. E. Hobsbawm, 'The Historians' Group of the Communist

Party', in Maurice Cornforth, *Rebels and Their Causes,* (London: Lawrence and Wishart, 1978), p.23.

110. Richard Johnson, 'Edward Thompson, Eugene Genovese and Socialist-Humanist History', *History Workshop,* 6 (Autumn 1978), pp. 78-100, and Simon Clarke, 'Socialist Humanism and the Critique of Economism', *History Workshop,* 8 (Autumn 1979), pp. 138-56.

111 Jon S. Cohen, The Marxist Contribution to Economic History', *Journal of Economic History,* 38 (March 1978), pp. 29-57.

Chapter 3: Rodney Hilton on Feudalism and the English Peasantry

1. M. Bloch, *Feudal Society,* (Chicago: University of Chicago Press, 1961), p. xix.

2. G. Lefebvre, 'Some Observations', in Rodney Hilton (ed.), *The Transition from Feudalism to Capitalism,* (London: New Left Books, 1976), p. 122.

3. John Merrington, 'Town and Country in the Transition to Capitalism', in R. Hilton (ed.). *Transition,* p. 179.

4. These biographical notes were provided by Professor Hilton in a personal communication of 5 August 1982 and conversations in January 1983. He writes that for the political traditions of the place where he grew up, i.e. Middleton, one should look at Samuel Bamford's *Passages in the Life of a Radical,* and he adds that his 'grandfather lived in a cottage which had a plaque on it saying that this was the place where Bamford was arrested in 1819 after Peterloo.'

5. R. Hilton, 'A Thirteenth-Century Podny about Disputed Villein Services', *The English Historical Review,,* 56 (1941).

6. *R. Hilton, The Economic Development of Some Leicestershire Estates in the Fourteenth and Fifteenth Centuries* (Oxford: Oxford University Press, 1947).

7. For a bibliography of Hilton's writings (as of January 1982), see the compilation by Jean Birrell in T.H. Aston, et al. (eds.). *Social Relations and Ideas: Essays in Honour of R.H. Hilton,* (Cambridge; Cambridge University Press, 1983), pp. 319-22. Also, forthcoming is *Class Conflict and the Crisis of Feudalism: Essays of R.H. Hilton* (London: Hambledon, 1984).

8. J. Berger, *Pig Earth,* (London: Writers and Readers, 1979), pp. 211-12.

9. R. Hilton, *Transition,* p. 30.

10. Ibid.

11. *R. Mousnier, Peasant Uprising in Seventeenth-Century France, Russia and China,* (New York: Harper and Row, 1970), p. 5.

12. R. Hilton, 'The Peasantry as a Class' (Ford Lectures, 1973) in Hilton, *The English Peasantry in the Later Middle Ages* (Oxford: Oxford University Press, 1975), p. 10.

13. Ibid. Hilton quotes from H.H. Gerth and C.W. Mills (eds). *From Max Weber,* (Oxford: Oxford University Press, 1958), pp. 181, 186-7.

14. Bloch, as stated, was a founder of what is known as the *Annales* school of history. Probably the greatest medieval historian of this century, Bloch fought in the French resistance in the Second World War, was caught, tortured and executed by the Germans in 1944. For appreciative comments by two Marxist historians who do not feel the same about later *Annalistes,* see Elizabeth Fox-Genovese and Eugene Genovese, 'The Political Crisis of Social History', *Journal of Social History,* 10 (Winter 1976), pp. 205-9.

15. M. Bloch, *French Rural History,* (Berkeley: University of California Press, 1966).

16. M. Bloch, *Feudal Society,* p. 446.

17. Ibid., pp. 91 and 446.

18. Georg G. Iggers, *New Directions in European Historiography* (Middletown, Ct.: Wesleyan University Press, 1975), pp.

55-6.

19. M. Bloch, *French Rural History,* p. 170.

20. Postan, a British economic historian of East European origin, was Professor of Economic History at Cambridge University (1938-65) and the editor of the *Economic History Review* and *Cambridge Economic History of Europe.*

21. M.M. Postan, *Essays on Medieval Agriculture and General Problems of the Medieval Economy,* (Cambridge: Cambridge University Press, 1973); and *The Medieval Economy and Society,* (Harmondsworth: Penguin, 1975).

22. R. Hilton, *Transition,* p. 28.

23. M.M. Postan, *The Medieval Economy and Society,* p. 31.

24. R. Brenner, 'Agrarian Class Structure and Economic Development in Pre-Industrial Europe', *Past & Present,* 70 (February 1976), pp. 30-75. Postan's co-authored response is in *Past & Present,* 78 (February 1978), pp. 24-37.

25. R. Hilton, *Transition,* p. 30.

26. R. Hilton, *The Decline of Serfdom in Medieval England,* (London: Macmillan, 1969), p. 25.

27. M.M. Postan, *The Medieval Economy and Society,* pp. 172-3.

28. Duby is a Professor at the College de France. His most recent work available in English is *The Three Orders: Feudal Society Imagined,* (Chicago: University of Chicago Press, 1981). For Hilton's comments, see 'Warriors and Peasants', *New Left Review,* 83 (January-February 1973), p. 84.

29. G. Duby, *Rural Economy and Country Life in the Medieval West,* (London: Edward Arnold, 1968).

30. G. Duby, *The Early Growth of the European Economy,* (London: Weidenfeld and Nicolson, 1974).

31. R. Hilton, *Transition,* p. 27. Also, 'Warriors and Peasants', pp. 91. For a critical discussion of technological determinism in medieval historical studies (but not directed at Duby), see R. Hilton and P.H. Sawyer, 'Technical Determinism: The Stirrup and the Plough', *Past & Present,* 24 (1963), pp.

90-100.

32. Particularly by Russian historians. For a survey of such work, see Peter Gatrell, 'Historians and Peasants: Studies of Medieval English Society in a Russian Context', *Past & Present*, 96 (August 1982), pp. 3-21. Additionally, George Homans' *English Villagers of the Thirteenth Century*, (Cambridge, Mass: Harvard University Press, 1941).

33. See R. Hilton, 'The Peasantry as a Class', pp. 4-12.

34. For example, see George M. Foster, 'Peasant Society and the Image of Limited Good', in Jack M. Potter et al. (eds). *Peasant Society: A Reader*, (New York: Little, Brown and Co., 1967), pp. 300-23. For a recent critique of the interpretation of peasant conservatism, see J. Berger, *Pig Earth*, pp. 203-9. Also, Gerrit Huizer, *Peasant Rebellion in Latin America*, (Harmondsworth; Penguin Books, 1973).

35. For example, Henry Landsberger, 'Peasant Unrest: Themes and Variations', in H. Landsberger (ed.). *Rural Protest: Peasant Movements and Social Change*, (London: Macmillan 1973), p. 17.

36. E. Wolf, *Peasant Wars of the Twentieth Century*, (New York: Harper and Row, 1969). Also, see Wolf's monograph, *Peasants*, (Englewood Cliffs, NJ: Prentice-Hall, 1966). And Barrington Moore Jr, *Social Origins of Dictatorship and Democracy: Lord and Peasant in the Making of the Modern World*, (Boston: Beacon Press, 1966).

37. For example, Teodor Shanin, *Peasants and Peasant Societies*, (Harmondsworth: Penguin, 1971); Joel Migdal, *Peasants, Politics and Revolution*, (Princeton, NJ: Princeton University Press, 1974); and Jeffrey M. Paige, *Agrarian Revolution*, (New York: Free Press, 1975).

38. Published together in English translation as A.V. Chayanov, *The Theory of Peasant Economy*, (Homewood, 111.: Irwin Publishing, 1966). On Chayanov's work, see Basile Kerblay, 'Chayanov and the Theory of Peasant Economy as a Specific

Type of Economy', in T. Shanin (ed.). *Peasants and Peasant Societies,* pp. 150-60.

39. B. Kerblay, 'Chayanov and the Theory of Peasant Economy', p. 151.

40. D. Thomer, 'Peasant Economy as a Category in Economic History' (1962) in T. Shanin (ed.). *Peasants and Peasant Societies,* pp. 203-5.

41. R. Hilton, 'The Peasantry as a Class', pp. 6-9.

42. E. Le Roy Ladurie, *Carnival in Romans,* (Harmondsworth: Penguin, 1981), p. 62.

43. K. Marx, *Pre-Capitalist Economic Formations,* (New York: Internatihonal Publishers, 1965), Introduction, pp. 20 and 29-30.

44. K. Marx, *Surveys From Exile: Political Writings Vol. II,* (London: New Left Books, 1974), pp. 238-9.

45. For example, David Mitrany, *Marx Against the Peasant,* (London: Weidenfeld and Nicolson, 1951).

46. See Michael Duggett, 'Marx on Peasants', *Journal of Peasant Studies,* 2 (January 1975), pp. 159-82.

47. F. Engels, *The Peasant War in Germany,* (New York: International Publishers, 1966).

48. E. A. Kosminsky, *Studies in the Agrarian History of England in the Thirteenth Century,* edited by R. Hilton, (Oxford: Basil Blackwell, 1956). Also, see P. Gatrell, 'Historians and Peasants'.

49. R. Hilton, 'The Peasantry as a Class', p. 13. Also, see his 'Medieval Peasants: Any Lessons?' *Journal of Peasant Studies,* 1 (January 1974), pp. 207-19.

50. R. Hilton, 'A Crisis of Feudalism', *Past & Present,* 80 (August 1978), p. 7.

51. R. Hilton, 'Social Structure of Rural Warwickshire in the Middle Ages', Occasional Paper of the Dugdale Society, no. 9 (1950), reprinted in *The English Peasantry in the Later Middle Ages,* pp. 113-38.

52. R. Hilton, *A Medieval Society: The West Midlands at the End of the Thirteenth Century,* (Cambridge: Cambridge University Press, 1983). Originally 1966.

53. R. Hilton, 'A Crisis of Feudalism', p. 9.

54. R. Hilton, *Transition,* p. 114.

55. R. Hilton, 'Warriors and Peasants', p. 93.

56. R. Hilton, 'Capitalism: What's in a Name?', *Past & Present,* 1 (February 1952), reprinted in *Transition,* p. 157.

57. R. Hilton and H. Fagan, *The English Rising of 1381,* (London: Lawrence and Wishart, 1950), pp. 9-10.

58. R. Hilton, *A Medieval Society,* p. 4.

59. R. Hilton, 'Peasant Movements in England Before 1381', *Economic History Review* (1949), reprinted in E.M. Carus-Wilson (ed.). *Essays in Economic History,* (London: Edward Arnold, 1962), pp. 73-90.

60. R. Hilton, *Bond Men Made Free: Medieval Peasant Movements and the English Rising of 1381,* (London: Maurice Temple Smith, 1973; reprinted London: Methuen, 1977).

61. R. Hilton, 'Peasant Society, Peasant Movements, and Feudalism in Medieval Europe', in H. Landsberger (ed.), *Rural Protest: Peasant Movements and Social Change,* pp. 75, and 76-77.

62. R. Hilton, *Bond Men Made Free,* pp. 61, 14-17, and 96.

63. See, e.g. R. Hilton, 'The Village Community', Ch. 6 of A Medieval Society, pp. 149-66; also, his 'The Social Structure of the Village', 'The Peasants' Economy', and 'Conflict and Collaboration', chapters 2-4 of *The English Peasantry in the Later Middle Ages,* pp. 20-75.

64. R. Hilton, *Bond Men Made Free,* pp. 32-5.

65. Ibid., p. 96.

66. R. Hilton, 'A Crisis of Feudalism', p. 14.

67. R. Hilton, *Bond Men Made Free,* pp. 96-109, and 118-19.

68. See Nicholas Abercrombie, Stephen Hill and Bryan S. Turner, *The Dominant Ideology Thesis,* (London: George

Allen & Unwin, 1980), Ch. 3 on Feudalism, pp. 59-94.

69. R. Hilton, 'Medieval Peasants: Any Lessons?' p. 211.

70. R. Hilton, 'The Peasantry as a Class', p. 16.

71. R. Hilton, *A Medieval Society,* p. 154.

72. R. Hilton, *Bond Men Made Free,* p. 114.

73. R. Hilton, 'The Peasantry as a Class', p. 14, my emphasis.

74. R. Hilton, *Bond Men Made Free,* pp. 130-4, and 220.

75. R. Hilton, 'Wat Tyler, John Ball and the English Rising', *New Society,* 30 April 1981, p. 171.

76. R. Hilton, *Bond Men Made Free,* p. 221.

77. Ibid., p. 229.

78. N. Cohn, *The Pursuit of the Millennium: Revolutionary Messianism in Medieval and Reformation Europe and Its Bearing on Modern Totalitarian Movements,* (New York: Harper and Row, 1961 rev. edition), p. 217.

79. R. Hilton, 'Wat Tyler, John Ball, and the English Rising', p. 173.

80. R. Hilton, 'The English Rising of 1381', *Marxism Today,* (June 1981), p. 19.

81. R. Hilton, 'The Rebellion of 1381', in David Rubinstein (ed.). *People for the People,* (London: Ithaca Press, 1973), pp. 22-3.

82. R. Hilton, 'Wat Tyler, John Ball, and the English Rising', p. 173.

83 The urban history pieces published thus far include R. Hilton, 'Towns in English Feudal Society', *Review,* 3 (Summer 1979), pp. 3-20; 'Popular Movements in England at the End of the Fourteenth Century', in *Il tumulto dei ciompi* (Florence, 1981), pp. 223^0; and 'Towns in societies – medieval England', in *Urban History Yearbook,* (Leicester: Leicester University Press, 1982), pp. 7-13.

84. R. Hilton, 'Towns in English Feudal Society', pp. 18-19.

85. R. Hilton, 'Popular Movements in England', pp. 235 and 239. Also, see his recent essay, 'Lords, Burgesses and

Hucksters', in *Past & Present,* 97 (November 1982), pp. 3-15.

86. 'An Interview with Eric Hobsbawm', *Radical History Review,* 19 (Winter 1978-9), pp. 127-8.

87. Elizabeth Fox-Genovese and Eugene Genovese, 'The Political Crisis of Social History', p. 219.

88. R. Hilton, *Transition,* p.27.

89. R. Hilton, 'The Peasantry as a Class', p. 13.

90. R. Hilton, 'The Origins of Robin Hood', *Past & Present,* 14 (November 1958); reprinted in R. Hilton (ed.). *Peasants, Knights, and Heretics: Studies in Medieval English Social History,* (Cambridge: Cambridge University Press, 1976), pp. 221-35. Included in the volume are the responses to Hilton's argument. Also, see Hilton's critical review of a recent study of Robin Hood, 'The Robber as Hero', *Times Literary Supplement,* 11 June 1982, p. 631.

91. Barrington Moore Jr, *Social Origins of Dictatorship and Democracy,* p. 480, my emphasis.

92. Alan Macfarlane, *The Origins of English Individualism,* (Oxford: Basil Blackwell, 1978).

93. For Hilton's own criticism of Macfarlane's book, see his review, 'Individualism and the English Peasantry', *New Left Review,* 120 (March-April 1980), pp. 109-11.

94. Steven Lukes, *Individualism,* (Oxford: Basil Blackwell, 1973), especially pp. 124-58.

95. R. Hilton, 'The English Rising of 1381', p. 19.

96. R. Hilton, *Bond Men Made Free,* p. 235.

Chapter 4: Christopher Hill on the English Revolution

1. L. Febvre, *A New Kind of History and Other Essays,* edited by Peter Burke, (London: Routledge and Kegan Paul, 1973), p. 3.

2. C. Hill, *Society and Puritanism in Pre-Revolutionary England,* (London: Seeker and Warburg, 1964).

3. C. Hill, *Intellectual Origins of the English Revolution*, (Oxford: Oxford University Press, 1965, 1980 corrected edition).

4. C. Hill, *The World Turned Upside Down: Radical Ideas During the English Revolution*, (Harmondsworth: Penguin, 1975).

5. C. Hill, *Milton and the English Revolution*, (Harmondsworth: Penguin, 1979).

6. For a comprehensive bibliography of Hill's work, see M.F. Roberts, 'Christopher Hill: A Select Bibliography, 1938-1977', in Donald Pennington and Keith Thomas (eds), *Puritans and Revolutionaries: Essays in Seventeenth-Century History Presented to Christopher Hill*, (Oxford: Oxford University Press, 1978), pp. 382-402.

7. See R.C. Richardson, *The Debate on the English Revolution*, (London: Methuen, 1977). For a most recent essay on the continuing controversy, see Mary Fulbrook, 'The English Revolution and the Revisionist Revolt', *Social History*, 7 (October 1982), pp. 249-64.

8. For example, C, Hill, The Agrarian Legislation of the Revolution' (1940) in his *Puritanism and Revolution: Studies in Interpretation of the English Revolution of the 17th Century*, (London: Seeker and Warburg, 1958).

9. K.E. Holme, *The Two Commonwealths*, (London: George G. Harrap, 1945). The book was a comparative study of the United Kingdom and the USSR, written as part of the war effort.

10. This, and the notes which follow, unless otherwise indicated, were provided by Christopher Hill in a personal communication of 23 September 1982, and in conversations in January 1983.

11. T.S. Eliot, 'The Metaphysical Poets' (1921) in *Selected Prose of T.S. Eliot*, (New York: Harcourt Brace Jovanovich, 1975), p. 64.

12. R. Samuel, 'British Marxist Historians, 1880-1980: Part I', *New Left Review*, 120 (March-April 1980), pp. 42-55.

13. See S. Rowbotham's biographical statement in the 'Introduction to the American Edition', of her *Hidden From History,* (New York: Vintage Books, 1974), pp. x-xxii.
14. R. Hilton, in D. Pennington and K. Thomas (eds.), *Puritans and Revolutionaries,* p. 7.
15. C. Hill, *Economic Problems of the Church: From Archbishop Whitgift to the Long Parliament,* (Oxford: Oxford University Press, 1956).
16. R.H. Tawney, *Religion and the Rise of Capitalism,* (London: 1926; rev. edition, Harmondsworth: Penguin, 1965, p. 11.
17. See Hill's 'The English Civic War: Interpreted by Marx and Engels', *Science and Society,* 12 (1948), pp. 130-65; and his 'Soviet Interpretations of the English Interregnum', *Economic History Review,* 8 (1938), pp. 159-67; 'Land in the English Revolution', *Science and Society,* 13 (1948-9), pp. 22-49; as well as 'Agrarian Legislation of the Revolution'.
18. So-named because it was developed by S.R. Gardiner (1829-1902) in his multi-volume *History of England, 1603-56.* It was furthered by Charles Firth (1857-1936) in *The Last Years of the Protectorate, 1656-58* (1909). On the historiography of the Revolution, see R.C. Richardson, *The Debate on the English Revolution.* It is the best survey of the subject and presents a good discussion of Hill in that context (pp. 98-112).
19. Tawney wrote not only history but also social criticism, occasionally of book length, e.g. *The Acquisitive Society* (London: 1920) and *Equality* (London: Unwin, 1931). On Tawney, see R. Terrill, *R.H. Tawney and His Times: Socialism as Fellowship,* (London: Andre Deutsch, 1974).
20. R.H. Tawney, *The Agrarian Problem in the Sixteenth Century* (London: 1912); *Religion and the Rise of Capitalism* (London: 1926); and 'The Rise of the Gentry, 1558-1640', *Economic History Review,* (1941), reprinted in E.M. Carus-Wilson (ed.). *Essays in Economic History,* (London: Edward Arnold,

1954), Volume I, pp. 173-214.

21. M. Weber, *The Protestant Ethic and the Spirit of Capitalism* (New York: Charles Scribner's Sons, 1956).

22. The controversy came to involve not only Tawney but also Lawrence Stone and H.R. Trevor-Roper. See R.C. Richardson, *Debate on the English Revolution,* pp. 89-96. Also, for excerpts from the contributions to the debate, see Lawrence Stone (ed.). *Social Change and Revolution in England, 1540-1640,* (London: Longman, 1965).

23. This analysis owed much to the seventeenth-century writer James Harrington, whose work Tawney discusses in 'Harrington's Interpretation of His Age', *Proceedings of the British Academy, TJ* (1942); reprinted in Lucy Sutherland (ed.). *Studies in History, British Academy Lectures,* (Oxford: Oxford University Press, 1966).

24. A.L. Morton, *A People's History of England,* (London: Lawrence and Wishart, 1979 rev. edition). First published in 1938.

25. M. Dobb, *Studies in the Development of Capitalism,* (London: Routledge and Kegan Paul, 1946, 1963 rev. edition).

26. A.L. Morton, *A People's History of England,* p. 229.

27. C. Hill, *The English Revolution, 1640,* (London: Lawrence and Wishart, 1955). The essay was originally published in 1940 as part of a three-essay collection, but was re-issued on its own under the same title. Hereafter referred to as *1640.*

28. Ibid., p. 6.

29. Keith Tribe, 'The Problem of Transition and Question of Origin', in his *Genealogies of Capitalism,* (London: Macmillan, 1980), pp. 1-34.

30. Ibid. For the Historians' Group's 'official position' on this issue, see 'State and Revolution in Tudor and Stuart England', *Communist Review,* (July 1948), pp. 207-14. Also, by Hill, 'The English Revolution and the State', *Modern*

Quarterly, 4 (Spring 1949), pp. 110-28.

31. Kuczynski, a German labour historian, wrote *Labour Conditions Under Industrial Capitalism,* (London: 1942) and *The Rise of the Working Class,* (London: Weidenfeld and Nicolson,1967).

32. As noted previously, Kiernan, retired Professor of Modern History at Edinburgh University, was a leading member of the Historians' Group and author of numerous works. His most recent books are *State and Society in Europe, 1550-1650,* (Oxford: Basil Blackwell, 1980), and *European Empires from Conquest to Collapse, 1815-1960,* (London: Fontana, 1982). Also, see his *Marxism and Imperialism,* (London: Macmillan,1973), and *The Lords of Human Kind,* (London: Weidenfeld and Nicolson, 1969).

33. Hill notes this himself in the new introduction he provided for the revised edition of the work he edited with Edmund Dell, *The Good Old Cause: 1640-1660,* (London: Frank Cass and Co., 1968), pp. 19-21.

34. See the discussion by Hill in 'Historians on the Rise of British Capitalism', *Science and Society,* 14 (1950), especially pp. 307-10.

35. C. Hill, 'Recent Interpretations of the Civil War' (1956), reprinted in *Puritanism and Revolution,* p. 31.

36. K. Marx, *Capital,* (Harmondsworth: Penguin, 1976) Volume I, p. 876.

37. C. Hill, 'A Bourgeois Revolution?' in JGA.G.A. Pocock (ed.). *Three British Revolutions: 1641, 1688, 1776,* (Princeton, NJ: Princeton University Press, 1980), p. 110.

38. C. Hill, *Some Intellectual Consequences of the English Revolution,* (Madison, Wi: University of Wisconsin Press, 1980), p. 34.

39. C. Hill, 'A Bourgeois Revolution?', p. 132.

40. *C. Hill, The Century of Revolution, 1603-1714,* (Edinburgh: Thomas Nelson, 1982 rev. edition), p. 4. Originally 1961.

41. C. Hill, 'A Bourgeois Revolution?', p. 111.

42. C. Hill, *Reformation to Industrial Revolution: A Social and Economic History of Britain, 1530-1780,* (Harmondsworth: Penguin, 1969).

43. Ibid., pp. 47-60, and 70.

44. See some of Hill's articles reprinted in *Puritanism and Revolution* and *Change and Continuity in Seventeenth-Century England,* (London: Weidenfeld and Nicolson, 1975).

45. C. Hill, 'Protestantism and The Rise of Capitalism', in *Change and Continuity,* pp. 81-102.

46. C. Hill, *Economic Problems of the Church,* pp. xi.

47. Ibid., p. xiv. At the same time. Hill's work has not ignored leaders. See his *God's Englishman: Oliver Cromwell and the English Revolution,* (Harmondsworth: Penguin, 1972).

48. C. Hill, *Society and Puritanism.* On 'The Definition of a Puritan', see pp. 13-29; and on 'The Industrious Sort of People', see pp. 124-44.

49. Ibid., pp. 153, 223, 142.

50. C. Hill, *Economic Problems of the Church,* p. x.

51. F.J. Fisher (ed.). *Essays in the Economic and Social History of Tudor and Stuart England,* (Cambridge: Cambridge University Press, 1961).

52. C. Hill, *Change and Continuity,* pp. 83-84, 95, and 99.

53. Based on his Ford Lectures of 1962. Hill's work on this subject was controversial. See the essays in *Past & Present* in 1964 and 1965, published together as a book: C. Webster (ed.). *The Intellectual Revolution of the Seventeenth Century,* (London: Routledge and Kegan Paul, 1974).

54. C. Hill, *Intellectual Origins,* pp. 87, 289.

55. Hill himself has never presented a comprehensive class-struggle analysis of the uprisings and revolts of the Civil War, but his former student, Brian Manning, has, in *The English People and the English Revolution,* (Harmondsworth: Penguin, 1978).

56. See Hill's *The Century of Revolution* and *God's Englishman: Oliver Cromwell and the English Revolution.* His latest statement on this is 'A Bourgeois Revolution?'.

57. Again, for his comprehensive argument, see Hill's *Reformation to Industrial Revolution* and *The Century of Revolution.*

58. See, for example., Hill's 'The English Civil War: Interpreted by Marx and Engels', pp. 152-56, and 'Historians and the Rise of British Capitalism', pp. 319-21.

59. C. Hill, 'Marxism and History', *Science and Society,* 3 (Spring 1948), p. 53.

60. C. Hill, *Intellectual Origins,* p. 3. The paragraph closes: 'This is the very opposite of saying that once we have related the ideas of a Luther to his society, then they can be disregarded. There is a danger that historians, trapped in the Namier method, may too lightly assume that the ideas which swayed men and women in the past can be dismissed as hypocrisy, rationalisations or irrelevancies.'

61. C. Hill, 'Partial Historians and Total History', *Times Literary Supplement,* 24 November 1972, p. 3.

62. Colonel Rainsborough, in C.E. Aylmer (ed.). *The Levellers and the English Revolution,* (London: Thames and Hudson, 1974), p. 100.

63. C. Hill, 'John Bunyan and the English Revolution', *Marxist Perspectives,* 2 (Fall 1979), pp. 8-9.

64. C. Hill, *The Century of Revolution,* p. 264.

65. C. Hill, 'Historians and the Rise of British Capitalism', p. 321.

66. C. Hill, 'The Norman Yoke', in John Saville (ed.). *Democracy and the Labour Movement,* (London: Lawrence and Wishart, 1954); reprinted in *Puritanism and Revolution,* pp. 50-122.

67. C. Hill, *Change and Continuity,* pp. 282-3.

68. C. Hill, 'The Norman Yoke', p. 57.

69. See H.N. Brailsford, *The Levellers and the English Revolution,*

(London: The Cresset Press, 1961), which was edited and prepared for publication by Hill after Brailsford's death. Also, see C.B. Macpherson, *The Political Theory of Possessive Individualism,* (Oxford; Oxford University Press, 1962), especially pp. 107-54; and B. Manning, *The English People and the English Revolution,* pp. 308-40.

70. C. Hill, 'The Norman Yoke', pp. 87-88 for a summary statement on seventeenth-century versions.

71. C. Hill, *Antichrist in Seventeenth-Century England,* (Oxford: Oxford University Press, 1971), p. 101. Originally presented as the Riddell Memorial Lectures at the University of Newcastle upon Tyne in November 1969.

72. C. Hill, *The World Turned Upside Down,* pp. 15 and 14.

73. Winstanley, quoted in Hill's *The World Turned Upside Down,* p. 133.

74. This episode has been told in a novel, David Caute's *Comrade Jacob* (1961), and in film as 'Winstanley' (released in 1976).

75. C. Hill, *The World Turned Upside Down,* pp. 339, and 340. Also, see A.L. Morton, *The World of the Ranters,* (London: Lawrence and Wishart, 1970).

76. C. Hill, *The World Turned Upside Down,* pp. 385-86, and 15.

77. See Hill's essay "Reason' and 'Reasonableness" (1969) in *Change and Continuity,* pp. 103-23.75.

78. C. Hill, 'A Bourgeois Revolution?', p. 133. For another recent statement by Hill, see 'Religion and Democracy in the Puritan Revolution', *Democracy,* 2 (April 1982), pp. 39-45.

79. See Hill's *Some Intellectual Consequences of the English Revolution.* For recent studies by Hill of one of the radical religious sects, see his contributions to Christopher Hill, Barry Reay, and William Lamont, *The World of the Muggletonians,* (London: Temple Smith, 1983).

80. P. Laslett, *The World We Have Lost,* (London: Methuen,

1965). For Hill's review of Laslett's book, see 'A One-Class Society?', in *Change and Continuity*, pp. 205-18.

81. C. Hill, 'A Bourgeois Revolution?', p. 130.

82. See Hill's essays 'The Many-Headed Monster' (1965) in *Change and Continuity*, pp. 181-204, and 'From Lollards to Levellers', in M. Cornforth (ed.). *Rebels and Their Causes*, (London: Lawrence and Wishart, 1978), pp. 49-67.

83. C. Hill, *The World Turned Upside Down*, p. 14.

84. Hill has recently discussed the state of the field in 'Parliament and People in Seventeenth-Century England', *Past & Present*, 92 (August 1981), pp. 100-24.

85. C. Hill, *God's Englishman*, pp. 253, 266.

86. C. Hill, *Milton and the English Revolution*, pp. 5, 107-16.84.

87. On the Muggletonians, see C. Hill, B. Reay and W. Lamont, *The World of the Muggletonians*.

88. C. Hill (ed.), *Winstanley: The Law of Freedom and Other Writings*, (Cambridge: Cambridge University Press, 1983). Originally 1973.

89. C. Hill, *The Religion of Gerrard Winstanley*, (*Past & Present* Supplement no. 5, 1978).

90. C. Hill (ed.), *Winstanley: The Law of Freedom*, Introduction, pp. 9-10.

91. C. Hill, 'Why Bother About the Muggletonians?', in *The World of the Muggletonians*, pp. 11, 13. Also, see the concluding remarks to 'From Lollards to Levellers'.

92. E. Hobsbawm, 'The Historians' Group of the Communist Party', in M. Cornforth (ed.). *Rebels and Their Causes*, pp. 38, 44.

93. C. Hill, *The World Turned Upside Down*, p. 343.90.

Chapter 5: Eric Hobsbawm on Workers, Peasants and World History

1. P. Vilar, 'Marxist History, A History in the Making: Toward a Dialogue with Althusser', *New Left Review*, 80 (July – –

August, 1973), pp. 65-106.

2. 'Editorial Statement', *Marxist Perspectives,* 1 (Spring 1978), p. 9, and James Cronin, 'Creating a Marxist Historiography: The Contribution of Hobsbawm', *Radical History Review, 19* (Winter 1978-9), p. 87-109.

3. For a comprehensive list of Hobsbawm's writings, see the Bibliography by Keith McClelland in Raphael Samuel and Gareth Stedman Jones (eds). *Culture, Ideology and Politics: Essays for Eric Hobsbawm,* (London: Routledge and Kegan Paul, 1983), pp. 332-63. Recent projects of Hobsbawm have been to edit and contribute to *The History of Marxism,* (Brighton: Harvester Press, 1982) Volume One, *Marxism in Marx's Day* and, with Terence Ranger, *The Invention of Tradition,* (Cambridge: Cambridge University Press, 1983).

4. See Tony Coe, 'Hobsbawm and Jazz', in R. Samuel and GS. Jones (eds.). *Culture, Ideology and Politics,* pp. 149-57. Hobsbawm wrote a book on the subject as Francis Newton, *The Jazz Scene* (London: Macgibbon and Kee, 1959).

5. Of interest is Pieter Keunemann, 'Eric Hobsbawm: A Cambridge Profile 1939', in *Granta,* 7 June 1939, reprinted as the final piece in R. Samuel and G.S. Jones (eds). *Culture, Ideology and Politics,* pp. 366-8.

6. See the 'Interview with E.J. Hobsbawm' in *Radical History Review,* 19 (Winter 1978-9), pp. 111-31. Reprinted in MARHO, *Visions of History: Interviews with Radical Historians,* (New York: Pantheon Books, 1983).

7. In E.J. Hobsbawm, *Revolutionaries: Contemporary Essays,* (London: Weidenfeld and Nicolson, 1973), pp. 250-1.

8. 'Interview with E.J. Hobsbawm', p. 116.

9. Ibid., p. 117.

10. J. Cronin, 'Creating a Marxist Historiography', p. 109.

11. E. Hobsbawm, 'The Forward March of Labour Halted?', published, along with critical responses, as *The Forward March of Labour Halted?,* (London: New Left Books, 1981).

12. In this regard, see An Interview by Eric Hobsbawm with George Napolitano of the Italian Communist Party, *The Italian Road to Socialism,* (London: Journeyman Press, 1977).

13. *F. Engels, The Condition of the Working Class in England,*13. *Introduction by Eric Hobsbawm, (London: Panther Books ed., 1969), p. 245.*

14. E. Hobsbawm (ed.)., *Labour's Turning Point, 1880-1900,* (London: Lawrence and Wishart, 1948; Brighton: Harvester Press, 1974 rev. edition).

15. See his 'The Fabians Reconsidered', in E. Hobsbawm, *Labouring Men: Studies in the History of Labour,* (London: Weidenfeld and Nicholson, 1964), pp. 250-71.

16. E. Hobsbawm and G. Rudé, *Captain Swing: A Social History of the Great English Agricultural Uprising of 1830,* (London: Lawrence and Wishart, 1969).

17. On the Webbs as labour historians, see Royden Harrison, 'The Webbs as Historians of Trade Unionism', in Raphael Samuel (ed.). *People's History and Socialist Theory,* (London: Routledge and Kegan Paul, 1981), pp. 322-6; and on the Hammonds and Webbs, see David Sutton, 'Radical Liberalism, Fabianism, and Social History', in R. Johnson et al., (eds). *Making Histories: Studies in History-Writing and Politics,* (London; Hutchinson, 1982), pp. 15-43. Of course, there were also GDH.D.H. and Margaret Cole.

18. R. Harrison, 'The Webbs as Historians of Trade Unionism', p. 322.

19. G. Rudé, 'Introduction', in J. Hammond and B. Hammond, *The Skilled Labourer,* (New York; Harper and Row, 1970), p. vii.

20. Ibid., p. xvii. Rudé is paraphrasing E.P. Thompson's criticism of the Hammonds.

21. E. Hobsbawm, 'Introduction', in J. Hammond and B. Hammond, *The Village Labourer,* (New York: Harper and Row, 1970), p. xiii.

22. E. Hobsbawm, *Labouring Men*, p. vii.

23. See the discussions of the trend to apolitical social history by Elizabeth Fox-Genovese and Eugene Genovese, 'The Political Crisis of Social History: A Marxian Perspective', *Journal of Social History*, 10 (Winter 1976), pp. 205-20; and Tony Judt, 'A Clown in Regal Purple: Social History and the Historian', *History Workshop*, 7 (Spring 1979), pp. 66-94.

24. E. Hobsbawm, 'Labour History and Ideology', *Journal of Social History*, 7 (Summer 1974), pp. 371-81.

25. E. Hobsbawm, 'The Machine Breakers', originally published in 1952, reprinted in *Labouring Men*, pp. 5-17.

26. Ibid., pp. 5-6, 7, 10, 11, 13, and 17.26. E. Hobsbawm, 'Methodism and the Threat of Revolution in Britain', originally published in 1957, reprinted in *Labouring Men*, pp. 23-33.

27. Hobsbawm's pieces on the standard- of- living question were written over the years 1958-63 and are reprinted together in *Labouring Men*, pp. 64-125. For a collection of contributions to the debate, see A.J. Taylor (ed.). *The Standard of Living in Britain in the Industrial Revolution*, (London: Methuen, 1975).

28. E. Hobsbawm, 'Trends in the British Labour Movement since 1850', (1949, revised in 1963) and 'Labour Aristocracy in Nineteenth-century Britain' (1954), both reprinted in *Labouring Men*, pp. 316-43, 272-315, respectively.

29. See E. Hobsbawm, 'Lenin and the 'Aristocracy of Labour'', in *Revolutionaries*, pp. 121-9.

30. See V.I. Lenin, *Imperialism: The Highest Stage of Capitalism*, (New York: International Publishers, 1939), pp. 106-8.

31. J. Field, 'British Historians and the Concept of the Labour Aristocracy', *Radical History Review*, 19 (Winter 1978-9), pp. 61-85.

32. Also, see Gregor McLennan, *Marxism and the Methodologies of History*, (London: New Left Books, 1981), pp. 206-32.

33. J. Foster, *Class Struggle and the Industrial Revolution: Early Industrial Capitalism in Three English Towns,* (London: Weidenfeld and Nicolson, 1974).

34. R. Gray, *The Labour Aristocracy in Victorian Edinburgh,* (Oxford: Oxford University Press, 1976).

35. See R. Gray, 'Bourgeois Hegemony in Victorian Britain', in J. Bloomfield (ed.). *Class, Hegemony and Party,* (London: Lawrence and Wishart, 1977), pp. 73-93.

36. R. Gray, *The Labour Aristocracy in Victorian Edinburgh,* pp. 188, and 190.

37. See the bibliography to R. Gray, *The Aristocracy of Labour in Nineteenth-century Britain, c. 1850-1914,* (London: Macmillan, 1981), pp.69-76. In historical sociology see, for example, GF. Moorhouse, 'The Marxist Theory of the Labour Aristocracy', *Social History, 3* (January 1978), pp. 61-82.

38. For examples of Hobsbawm's recent labour history studies, see his 'Religion and the Rise of Socialism', *Marxist Perspectives,* 1 (Spring 1978), pp. 14-33, and E. Hobsbawm and Joan Wallach Scott, 'Political Shoemakers', *Past & Present,* 89 (November 1980), pp. 86-114.

39. E. Hobsbawm, 'The Forward March of Labour Halted?'

40. E. Hobsbawm, 'Labour History and Ideology', p. 371.

41. J. Reed, *Insurgent Mexico,* (New York: International Publishers, 1974), p. 122. Originally 1914.

42. E. Hobsbawm, 'Peasants and Politics', *Journal of Peasant Studies,* 1 (October 1973), pp. 3-22.

43. E. Hobsbawm, *Primitive Rebels,* (Manchester: Manchester University Press, rev. edition, 1963), new preface 1971.

44. 'Interview with E.J. Hobsbawm', pp. 112-13, 115-16.

45. Letter from Hobsbawm to the author, 13 March 1983.

46. 'Interview with E.J. Hobsbawm', p. 116.

47. E. Hobsbawm, *Primitive Rebels,* pp. 1, 3, and 2.

48. The first phrase, Gwyn Williams, 'The Primitive Rebel

and the Welsh', in his *The Welsh in Their History,* (London: Groom Helm, 1982), p. 3; and the second E. Fox-Genovese, 'The Politics of Social History', p. 198.

49. E. Hobsbawm, *Bandits,* (New York; Pantheon Books, 1981 rev. edition), pp. 17-18, and 23.

50. E. Hobsbawm, *Primitive Rebels,* p. 2. Also, see his 'Prepolitical Movements in Modern Politics', in Alkis Kontos (ed.). *Powers, Possessions and Freedom; Essays in Honour of C.B. Macpherson,* (Toronto, Ont: University of Toronto Press, 1979).

51. E. Hobsbawm, *Bandits,* pp. 138-50. An important example of the first criticism mentioned is found in the book by Anton Blok, *The Mafia of a Sicilian Village, 1860-1960,* (New York: Harper & Row, 1974), especially pp. 99-102.

52. E. Hobsbawm and G. Rudé, *Captain Swing.* George Rudé is the author of *The Crowd in the French Revolution,* (Oxford: Oxford University Press, 1959); *Wilkes and Liberty,* (London: Lawrence and Wishart, 1983 rev. edition); *The Crowd in History,* (London: Lawrence and Wishart, 1981 rev. edition); and *Ideology and Popular Protest,* (London: Lawrence and Wishart, 1980).

53. E. Hobsbawm and G. Rudé, *Captain Swing,* pp. 14, 16, 195, and 16.

54. Ibid., pp. 281-2, 292-6, and 298.

55. E. Hobsbawm, 'A Case of Neo-Feudalism: La convencion, Peru', *Journal of Latin American Studies,* 1 (May 1970), pp. 31-50; 'Peasant Movements in Colombia', *International Journal of Economic and Social History,* 8 (1976), pp. 166-86; and 'Peasant Land Occupations', *Past & Present,* 62 (February 1974), pp. 120-52.

56. E. Hobsbawm, 'Peasants and Rural Migrants in Politics', in Claudio Veliz (ed.). *The Politics of Conformity in Latin America,* (Oxford: Oxford University Press, 1967), pp. 43-65.

The British Marxist Historians

57. E. Hobsbawm, 'Class Consciousness in History', in I. Meszaros (ed.). *Aspects of History and Class Consciousness,* (London: Routledge and Kegan Paul, 1971), pp. 6-7.

58. E. Hobsbawm, 'From Social History to the History of Society', *Daedalus,* 100 (Winter 1971), p. 37; and 'Peasants and Politics', p. 5.

59. E. Hobsbawm, 'Peasants and Politics', p. 11.

60. R. Samuel and G.S. Jones (eds). *Culture, Ideology and Politics,* Preface, p. x.

61. E.Hobsbawm,'KarlMarx'sContributiontoHistoriography', in Robin Blackburn (ed.). *Ideology in Social Science,* (London: Fontana, 1972), pp. 265-83.

62. *New Statesman,* 2 February 1979, pp. 154-5. (G.A. Cohen, *Karl Marx's Theory of History – A Defence,* (Oxford: Oxford University Press, 1978).)

63. For example, see E. Hobsbawm, 'The Contribution of History to Social Science', *International Social Science Journal,* 33 (1981), pp. 624-40.

64. E.Hobsbawm,'KarlMarx'sContributiontoHistoriography', p. 274, fn. 10.

65. E. Hobsbawm, 'Custom, Wages and Work-load in Nineteenth-century Industry', reprinted in *Labouring Men,* pp. 344-70.

66. E. Hobsbawm, 'Where are the British Historians Going?', *Marxist Quarterly,* 2 (January 1955), p. 22; also, 'Progress in History', *Marxism Today,* (February 1962), pp. 44-8.

67. For example, Hobsbawm's 'Introduction' to Karl Marx, *Pre- Capitalist Economic Formations,* (London: Lawrence and Wishart, 1964), pp. 9-65.

68. E. Hobsbawm, 'Economic and Social History Divided', *New Society,* 11 July 1974. My emphasis.

69. E. Hobsbawm, *The Age of Capital, 1848-1875,* (London: Sphere Books, 1977), pp. 291-3. Originally 1975.

70. Joseph Femia, *Gramsci's Political Thought,* (Oxford: Oxford

320

University Press, 1981), pp. 23, 257 fn. 1. 'Hegemony' will also be discussed in the next chapter.

71. For an example of this criticism of Hobsbawm, see the two articles by James Scott, 'Hegemony and the Peasantry', *Politics and Society, 7* (1977), especially pp. 293-5, and 'Revolution in the Revolution: Peasants and Commissars', *Theory and Society, 7* (January-March 1979), pp. 97-134; and James Cronin's essay, 'Creating a Marxist Historiography: The Contribution of Hobsbawm', pp. 98, 105-6, and fns 37 and 39.

72. For example, his contribution to E. Hobsbawm and T. Ranger (eds). *The Invention of Tradition.*

73. C. Hill, 'Introduction', in Trevor Aston (ed.). *Crisis in Europe: 1560-1660* (London: Routledge and Kegan Paul, 1965), p. 2.

74. E. Hobsbawm, 'The Crisis of the Seventeenth-century', *Past & Present,* 5 and 6 (1954); reprinted with a new postscript in T. Aston (ed.). *Crisis in Europe: 1560-1660,* p. 5. Also, see E. Hobsbawm, 'The Seventeenth Century in the Development of Capitalism', *Science and Society,* 24 (Spring 1960), pp. 97-112.

75. E. Hobsbawm, *Industry and Empire,* (Harmondsworth: Penguin, 1969).

76. W.W. Rostow, *The Stages of Economic Growth,* (Cambridge: Cambridge University Press, 1960).

77. E. Hobsbawm, *Industry and Empire,* p. 21.

78. *The Age of Revolution,* (London: Sphere Books, 1977), originally 1962. *The Age of Capital,* (London: Sphere Books, 1975), originally 1975, and *The Age of Empire,* in preparation for possible 1984/85 publication.

79. Peter Stearns, *European Society in Upheaval,* (London: Collier Macmillan, 1975 rev. edition), p. 1. Originally 1967. In economic history, see David Landes, *The Unbound Prometheus,* (Cambridge; Cambridge University Press,

1972), especially pp. 6-40.

80. P. Stearns, European Society in Upheaval, pp. 2-5. Tony Judt's critique of contemporary social history is directed at the modernization historians in particular. See 'A Clown in Regal Purple'.

81. E. Hobsbawm, *The Age of Revolution*, p. 17.

82. E. Hobsbawm, *The Age of Capital*, p. 15.

83. This is the theme of Cronin's essay, 'Creating a Marxist Historiography: The Contribution of Hobsbawm'. He focuses on *The Age of Capital.*

84. E. Hobsbawm, *The Age of Revolution,* pp. 44-7.

85. Ibid., pp. 217-18.

86. Ibid., pp. 254-8.

87. Ibid., p. 310. On this, a good reader to accompany Hobsbawm's Age of Revolution is Meryn Williams (ed.), Revolutions: 1775-1830, (Harmondsworth: Penguin, 1971).

88. E. Hobsbawm, *The Age of Revolution,* pp. 279-80. My emphasis.

89. E. Hobsbawm, *The Age of Capital,* pp. 22-40, and 177-86.

90. Volume One, *Marxism in Marx's Day* is already published (1982).

91. For responses to Hobsbawm's argument by Labour Party socialists, see *New Socialist,* 15 (January/February 1984).

92. E. Hobsbawm, 'Are We on the Edge of a World War?', 19 January 1984, pp. 83-5.

93. 'Interview with E.J. Hobsbawm,', pp. 129-30.

Chapter 6: EP Thompson on the Making of the English Working Class

1. G. Lefebvre, 'Revolutionary Crowds' in J. Kaplow (ed.). *New Perspectives on the French Revolution,* (New York: John Wiley and Sons, 1965), p. 175.

2. E.P. Thompson, *The Making of the English Working Class,* (Harmondsworth: Penguin, 1968 rev. edition with new

postscript; 1980 edition with new preface). Originally 1963.

3. E.P. Thompson, *Whigs and Hunters,* (Harmondsworth: Penguin, 1977 edition with new postscript). Originally 1975.

4. E.P. Thompson, *William Morris: Romantic to Revolutionary,* (New York: Pantheon Books, 1977 rev. edition with new postscript). Originally 1955.

5. E.P. Thompson, *The Poverty of Theory,* (London: Merlin Press, 1978). References are to the fourth impression.

6. E.P. Thompson, *Writing by Candlelight,* (London: Merlin Press, 1980).

7. E.P. Thompson, *Zero Option,* (London: Merlin Press, 1982). In the United States it appeared as *Beyond the Cold War,* (New York: Pantheon Books, 1982).

8. E.P. Thompson and D. Smith, *Protest and Survive,* (Harmondsworth: Penguin, 1980). In the United States a special edition was published, but under the same title, (New York: Monthly Review Press, 1981).

9. For broader studies of Thompson's work, see Perry Anderson. *Arguments Within English Marxism,* (London: New Left Books, 1980), and Bryan Palmer, *The Making of E.P. Thompson,* (Toronto: New Hogtown Press, 1981). Both of these books contain bibliographies of Thompson's writings.

10. For example, see 'Interview with E.P. Thompson', *Radical History Review,* 3 (Fall 1976), p. 25. Of course, the British Marxist tradition that Thompson identifies with is not limited to the specific historians being considered here.

11. Ibid., pp. 10-11. Also, see E.P. Thompson, 'The Nehru Tradition', in *Writing by Candlelight,* pp. 135-49.

12. It is regularly acknowledged that Thompson's older brother, Frank, a war-hero and communist, was most influential in the former's life. See the book Thompson wrote with his mother. *There is a Spirit in Europe: A Memoir*

of Major Frank Thompson (1947).

13. On this experience, see E.P. Thompson, *The Railway – An Adventure in Construction,* (1948). Also, see his comments in 'Interview with E.P. Thompson', pp. 11-12.

14. These biographical notes were culled from a variety of sources, including conversations with E.P. and Dorothy Thompson in January 1983. Examples of Dorothy Thompson's work are: *The Early Chartists,* (London: Macmillan Press, 1971); 'Women and Nineteenth-Century Radical Politics: A Lost Dimension', in Juliet Mitchell and Ann Oakley (eds). *The Rights and Wrongs of Women,* (Harmondsworth: Penguin, 1976), pp. 112-38; and 'Ireland and the Irish in English Radicalism before 1850', in James Epstein and Dorothy Thompson (eds). *The Chartist Experience* (London: Macmillan Press, 1982). She has recently completed *The Chartists* (London: Temple Smith, 1984).

15. 'Interview with E.P. Thompson', pp. 12-13.

16. Foreword to E.P. Thompson, *The Poverty of Theory,* p. i.

17. See John Saville's article, 'The XXth Congress and the British Communist Party', in *The Socialist Register 1976,* (London: Merlin Press, 1976), pp. 1-23; on Thompson's relationship to the *New Left Review,* see fn. 58. Also, on John Saville, see Ralph Miliband, 'John Saville: A Presentation', in D. Martin and D. Rubenstein (eds). *Ideology and the Labour Movement: Essays Presented to John Saville,* (London: Croom Helm, 1979), pp. 15-31.

18. See his editorial remarks in the first issue of *The New Reasoner,* Summer 1957, and the 1977 postscript to E.P. Thompson, *William Morris.*

19. For example, see E.P. Thompson 'The Poverty of Theory', in *The Poverty of Theory,* pp. 189-91.

20. E.P. Thompson, R. Williams, S. Hall (eds). *May Day Manifesto 1968,* (Harmondsworth: Penguin, 1968).

21. See Thompson's articles under the heading 'Warwick University' in *Writing by Candlelight,* pp. 13-38, and his edited volume, *Warwick University Ltd,* (Harmondsworth: Penguin, 1970).

22. B. Palmer, *The Making of E.P. Thompson.* Also, see Fred Inglis, *Radical Earnestness: English Social Theory, 1880-1980,* (Oxford: Martin Robertson, 1982), pp. 193-204.

23. H. Abelove, 'Review Essay of *The Poverty of Theory', History and Theory,* 21 (1982), pp. 132-42.

24. See E.P. Thompson, 'Education and Experience', lecture presented at Leeds University in June, 1967.

25. E.P. Thompson, *The Making,* p. 915.

26. E.P. Thompson, *Whigs and Hunters,* Appendix 2.

27. H. Abelove, 'Review Essay of *The Poverty of Theory',* p. 142. Also, see the comments on Thompson by James Henretta in 'Social History as Lived and Written', *American Historical Review,* 84 (December 1979), pp. 1293-322. For examples of Thompson's own poetry, see 'King of my freedom here', in P. Buhle (ed.). *Free Spirits: Annals of the Insurgent Imagination (I),* (San Francisco: City Lights Books, 1982), p. 29, and Thompson's collection. *The Infant and the Emperor,* (London: Merlin Press, 1983).

28. K. Marx, quoted in Dona Torr, *Tom Mann and His Times,* (London: Lawrence and Wishart, 1956), p. 15.

29. E.P. Thompson, 'Socialist Humanism', *The New Reasoner,* Summer 1957, p. 113.

30. R. Williams, *The Long Revolution,* (Harmondsworth: Penguin, 1965). Originally 1961.

31. Thompson's review essay of R. Williams' *The Long Revolution,* 'Part IT, *New Left Review,* 10 (September-October 1961), p. 38. The essay was published in three parts; part I was in issue no. 9 and an accidentally dropped page appeared in issue no. 11.)

32. See, for example, E.P. Thompson, 'Revolution Again! Or

Shut Your Ears and Run', *New Left Review,* 6 (November – December 1960), esp. pp. 23-9.

33. E.P. Thompson, *The Making,* p. 10. When Thompson accepted the commission to do the book, it was to be a study of the working class from 1790 to 1945, but became, instead, merely a 'first chapter' of such a history – a first chapter of 900 pages. Also, he has said, he only took the assignment at the time because he was broke and needed the money. See 'Interview with E.P. Thompson', p. 15. Hereafter, in this chapter page numbers referring to *The Making* will appear in the text in parentheses.

34. In particular, he referred to Ralf Dahrendorf's book, *Class and Class Conflict in Industrial Society,* (Stanford, Cal: Stanford University Press, 1959).

35. Thompson was referring, in particular, to the work of Neil J. Smelser, *Social Change in the Industrial Revolution,* (Chicago; University of Chicago Press, 1959).

36. J. Kuczynski, *The Rise of the Working Class,* (London: Weidenfeld and Nicolson, 1967).

37. See E.P. Thompson, 'Commitment in Politics', *Universities and Left Review,* 6 (Spring 1959), pp. 50-5.

38. See G. Rudé, *The Crowd in History,* (London: Lawrence and Wishart, 1981 rev. edition).

39. On the London crowd, see C. Rudé, *Wilkes and Liberty,* (London: Lawrence and Wishart, 1983 rev. edition). Thompson, as we shall see, returns to these in his eighteenth-century studies.

40. See K. Marx, *Capital,* (Harmondsworth: Penguin, 1976), Volume I, especially Appendix, pp. 1019-34.

41. Ellen Meiksins Wood, 'The Politics of Theory and the Concept of Class: E.P. Thompson and His Critics', *Studies in Political Economy,* 9 (Fall 1982), pp. 57-8. This essay is extremely good at showing how mistaken are those who would view Thompson's work as 'Culturalism'. Hereafter,

'The Politics of Theory and the Concept of Class'.

42. R. Johnson, 'Thompson, Genovese and Socialist-Humanist History', *History Workshop,* 6 (Autumn 1978), pp. 79-100. Also, for a critique of Thompson by a colleague of Johnson, see Gregor McLellan, 'E.P. Thompson and the discipline of historical context', in R. Johnson et al. (eds), *Making Histories: Studies in History-Writing and Politics,* (London, Hutchinson, 1982), pp. 96-130. Finally, it is worth noting that Thompson wrote a very warm review of *Studies* in the *Cambridge University Socialist Club Bulletin,* 2 (29 November 1946), pp. 2-3.

43. P. Anderson, *Arguments Within English Marxism,* pp. 32-5. Also, Bryan Palmer rightly shows that some of Anderson's criticisms are quite unfair. For example, in order to point out supposed deficiencies in *The Making,* Anderson cites several works written more than a decade after it, whose authors acknowledge Thompson's inspiration and influence. I would add that much of Anderson's critique is presented as if *The Making* were actually deficient, as opposed to what may actually have been intended by Anderson, to show that the work raised a whole series of questions which still need to be worked out in further historical research and studies. (For Palmer's critique of Anderson, see his *The Making of E.P. Thompson,* pp. 8-18.)

44. K. McClelland, 'Some Comments on Richard Johnson, Edward Thompson, Eugene Genovese, and Socialist – Humanist History', *History Workshop,* 7 (Spring 1979), p. 111.

45. E.P. Thompson, *The Making,* Chapter 10, 'Standards and Experiences', pp. 347-84. Thompson now finds the chapter 'inadequate'. On Hobsbawm and the Hammonds, see my discussion in chapter 5.

46. In his 1968 postscript to *The Making* Thompson defends and clarifies his argument further against criticisms, pp.

917-23.

47. Thompson was criticized heavily for this. His response was to insist on the connection ever more strongly. See the 1968 postscript to *The Making,* pp. 923-37.

48. For a discussion of these criticisms, see F.K. Donnelly, 'Ideology and Early English Working-Class History: Edward Thompson and His Critics', *Social History*, 3 (May 1976), pp. 219-38. Also, see Thompson's reply to criticisms in the 1968 postscript to *The Making.*

49. T. Nairn, 'The English Working Class', *New Left Review*, 24 (March-April 1964), pp. 43-57.

50. *P. Anderson, Arguments Within English Marxism*, pp. 43-9.

51. See, for example, Thompson's discussion (in 1960) in 'Revolution Again! Or Shut Your Ears and Run'; and his 1968 postscript to *The Making*, p. 937.

52. G.S. Jones, 'Working-Class Culture and Working-Class Politics in London, 1870-1900: Notes on the Remaking of a Working Class', *Journal of Social History*, 7 (Summer 1974), pp. 460-508. Thompson calls the article 'brilliant' in the 'Interview with E.P. Thompson'.

53. J. Freeth, 'The Colliers' March', taken from Roy Palmer, (ed.), *A Touch of the Times: Songs of Social Change, 1770 to 1914*, (Harmondsworth: Penguin, 1974), pp. 274-5.

54. 'Interview with E.P. Thompson', p. 15.

55. E.P. Thompson, 'The Peculiarities of the English', originally in *The Socialist Register 1965;* reprinted in *The Poverty of Theory*, pp. 245-302.

56. P. Anderson, 'Origins of the Present Crisis', *New Left Review*, 23 (January-February 1964); reprinted in P. Anderson and R. Blackburn (eds). *Towards Socialism*, (London: Fontana Books, 1965), pp. 11-52. Anderson's response to Thompson's essay is 'The Myths of Edward Thompson, or Socialism and Pseudo-Empiricism', *New Left Review*, 35 (1966), pp. 2-42. Also, see Anderson's essay, 'Components

of the National Culture', in A. Cockburn and R. Blackburn, (eds). *Student Power,* (Harmondsworth: Penguin, 1969) pp. 214-84.

57. T. Nairn's interpretations are all in *New Left Review:* 'The British Political Elite', no. 23 (1964), pp. 19-25; 'The English Working Class', no. 24 (1964), pp. 43-57; 'The Anatomy of the Labour Party', nos. 27 and 28 (1964), pp. 38-65 and 33-62. Nairn is also the author of *The Breakup of Britain,* (London: New Left Books, 1977).

58. P. Anderson, 'Origins of the Present Crisis', pp. 12-13.

59. On the intellectual character of the Thompson-Anderson exchange, see Keith Nield, 'A Symptomatic Dispute? Notes on the Relation between Marxian Theory and Historical Practice in Britain', *Social Research,* 47 (Autumn 1980), pp. 479-506.

60. P. Anderson, 'Origins of the Present Crisis', p. 29.

61. E.P. Thompson, 'Peculiarities of the English', pp. 255-7, and 267.

62. Ibid., p. 280. With reference to Thompson's argument that the working class was *'made* in the 1830s', it is worth noting that he urges (on the next two pages) a *sociological* examination of the changes in working-class experience and the labour movement following the collapse of Chartism in the middle of the nineteenth century.

63. Ibid., p. 295.

64. Ibid., p. 289.

65. Ibid., pp. 291, and 294.

66. 'Interview with E.P. Thompson', p. 16.

67. E.P. Thompson, 'Time, Work-Discipline, and Industrial Capitalism', *Past & Present,* 38 (February 1967), pp. 56-97.

68. M. Weber, *The Protestant Ethic and the Spirit of Capitalism,* (New York: Charles Scribner's Sons, 1956), p. 60.

69. E.P. Thompson, *The Making,* e.g. pp. 391-8.

70. E.P. Thompson, 'Time, Work-Discipline and Industrial

Capitalism', p. 80. This should be read in conjunction with Christopher Hill, 'Pottage for Freeborn Englishmen: Attitudes to Wage-Labour', in his *Change and Continuity in Seventeenth-Century England*, (London: Weidenfeld and Nicholson, 1975), pp. 219-38; and Eric Hobsbawm, 'Custom, Wages and Work-Load', in his *Labouring Men*, (London: Weidenfeld and Nicholson, 1964), pp. 316-43.

71. E.P. Thompson, 'The Moral Economy of the English Crowd in the Eighteenth Century', *Past & Present*, 50 (February 1971), pp. 76-136.

72. Douglas Hay, Peter Linebaugh and E.P. Thompson (eds), *Albion's Fatal Tree: Crime and Society in Eighteenth-Century England*, (Harmondsworth: Penguin, 1975), Preface, p. 13. Thompson was one of the editors and a contributor to the volume ('The Crime of Anonymity', pp. 255-344).

73. E.P. Thompson, *Whigs and Hunters*, p. 64.

74. Ibid., pp. 190-91.

75. Ibid., pp. 206-7.

76. Ibid., pp. 197-206.

77. Ibid., pp. 239-40.

78. D. Hay, 'Property, Authority and the Criminal Law', in D. Hay et al. (eds), *Albion's Fatal Tree*, pp. 17-64.

79. E.P. Thompson, *Whigs and Hunters*, p. 258. On a different view, see J.H. Plumb, *The Growth of Political Stability in England*, (Harmondsworth: Penguin, 1969).

80. E.P. Thompson, 'Patrician Society, Plebeian Culture', *Journal of Social History*, 7 (Summer 1974), pp. 382-405; and 'Eighteenth-century English Society: class struggle without class?' *Social History*, 3 (May 1978), pp. 133-65.

81. E. Genovese, *Roll, Jordan, Roll: The World the Slaves Made*, (New York: Pantheon, 1974).

82. E. Genovese, 'A Reply to Criticism', *Radical History Review*, 3 (Winter 1977) p. 98. Though Richard Johnson is mistaken in his criticisms of Thompson and Genovese, he is correct

in calling attention to the similarity between *The Making* and *Roll, Jordan, Roll.* On this issue, I should add that I am *not* in agreement with Alan Dawley's argument in 'E.P. Thompson and the Americans', *Radical History Review,* 19 (Winter 1978-9), pp. 33-60 and, though I am in general agreement with Bryan Palmer's discussion of the Thompson-Genovese relationship, I do differ on some of the specifics. (See H. Kaye, 'Totality: Its Application to Historical and Social Analysis by Wallerstein and Genovese', *Historical Reflections/Reflexions Historiques,* 6 (Winter 1979), pp. 405-20.)

83. E.P. Thompson, 'Patrician Society, Plebeian Culture', pp. 382-9.

84. Ibid., pp. 388, and 389-90.

85. Ibid., pp. 398-402.

86. Ibid., p. 395.

87. E. Hobsbawm, 'Class Consciousness in History', in Istvan Meszaros (ed.). *Aspects of History and Class Consciousness,* (London: Routledge and Kegan Paul, 1971), p. 8.

88. E.P. Thompson, 'Eighteenth-century English Society', pp. 147-8, and 149.

89. Ibid., pp. 149-50. On 'objective determinations' Thompson refers the reader to Robert Brenner's work. (See the discussion in chapter 2 of this book.)

90. E.M. Wood, 'The Politics of Theory and the Concept of Class', p. 50.

91. P. Anderson, *Arguments Within English Marxism,* pp. 42-3; G.A. Cohen, *Karl Marx's Theory of History: A Defence,* (Oxford: Oxford University Press, 1978), pp. 73-7. Also, see Craig Calhoun, *The Question of Class Struggle,* (Oxford: Basil Blackwell, 1982).

92. E.M. Wood, 'The Politics of Theory and the Concept of Class', p. 51.

93. E.P. Thompson, 'Eighteenth-century English Society', p.

150.

94. K. Marx, *Grundrisse,* (Harmondsworth: Penguin, 1973), p. 90.

95. E.P. Thompson, *Whigs and Hunters,* pp. 259-60, 268. Stated in the 'Interview with E.P. Thompson', where he clarifies his criticisms (pp. 7-8).

96. E.P. Thompson, 'The Poverty of Theory', p. 96.

97. Until Thompson's *Customs in Common* is published, see his comments in 'The Grid of Inheritance', in Jack Goody, Joan Thirsk, and E.P. Thompson (eds). *Family and Inheritance: Rural Society in Western Europe, 1200-1800,* (Cambridge: Cambridge University Press, 1976), pp. 328-60.

98. E.P. Thompson, *Whigs and Hunters,* pp. 258-69.

99. 'Interview with E.P. Thompson', p. 8.

100. P. Anderson, *Arguments Within English Marxism,* p. 71. Anderson refers to the arguments of Nicos Poulantzas.

101. E.P. Thompson, 'Eighteenth-century English Society', p. 151. For a similar translation, see K. Marx, *Grundrisse,* pp. 106-7.

102. E.P. Thompson, 'Folklore, Anthropology, and Social History', *Indian Historical Review,* 3 (January 1977), pp. 247-66.

103. Ibid., pp. 261-4, 265, and 265-6.

104. E.M. Wood, 'The Politics of Theory and the Concept of Class', pp. 60-62.

105. Among Althusser's major works are *For Marx,* (London; Allen Lane, 1969) and, with Etienne Balibar, *Reading Capital,* (London: New Left Books, 1970).

106. Page references to 'The Poverty of Theory' will be indicated in the text in parentheses as 'Poverty'.

107. See Keith Nield and John Seed, 'Theoretical poverty or the poverty of theory: British Marxist historiography and the Althusserians', *Economy and Society,* 8 (November 1979), pp. 383-416, which I found most helpful in condensing the

arguments of 'The Poverty of Theory'.

108. B. Hindess and P. Hirst, *Pre-Capitalist Modes of Production,* (London: Routledge and Kegan Paul, 1975).

109. 'Interview with E.J. Hobsbawm', *Radical History Review,* 19 (Winter 1978-9), p. 123.

110. Robert Holton critically argues that Thompson misleads us here by presenting an image of Althusserian thought more true of Hindess and Hirst than Althusser himself. But Thompson does note that while Althusser claims that by 'theoretical practice' one can distinguish 'scientific from ideological knowledge', he never actually explains how. (R. Holton, 'History and Sociology in the Work of E.P. Thompson', *Australian and New Zealand Journal of Sociology,* 17 (March 1981), p. 60; and E.P. Thompson, 'The Poverty of Theory', p. 11.) For other critiques of Althusserian thought, see the collection of essays edited by Simon Clarke, *One-Dimensional Marxism: Althusser and the Politics of Culture,* (London: Allison and Busby, 1980); Alex Callinicos, *Althusser's Marxism,* (London: Pluto Press, 1976); and Alfred Schmidt, *History and Structure: An Essay on Hegelian-Marxist and Structuralist Theories of History,* (Cambridge, Mass: MIT Press, 1981 edition).

111. For a critique of Thompson's propositions, see Alan Warde, 'E.P. Thompson and 'Poor' Theory', *British Journal of Sociology,* 33 (June 1982), pp. 224-37. It should be mentioned that Thompson, though he does not reject the criticisms he made of Althusserianism, has since acknowledged that there are difficulties in his own propositions which could lead to empiricism. See Thompson's 'The Politics of Theory', in Raphael Samuel (ed.). *People's History and Socialist Theory,* (London: Routledge and Kegan Paul, 1981) p. 407. In the same volume, see the essay by Raphael Samuel, 'History and Theory', pp. xl-lvi.

112. Also, see R.W. Connell, 'A Critique of the Althusserian

Approach to Class', *Theory and Society,* 8 (May 1979), pp. 321-45.

113. E.P. Thompson, 'An Open Letter to Leszek Kolakowski', in *The Socialist Register 1973,* (London: Merlin Press, 1973) reprinted in *The Poverty of Theory.*

114. Thompson has been widely criticized for accusing Althusser of Stalinism. Of course, Thompson was motivated in great part by Althusser's membership of the French Communist Party but, as Perry Anderson rightly points out, at least one of Thompson's 'colleagues' in the tradition with which he identifies remained active in the British Communist Party after 1956, that is, Eric Hobsbawm. (P. Anderson, *Arguments Within English Marxism,* pp. 100-30 on 'Stalinism'.)

115. R. Johnson, 'Thompson, Genovese, and Socialist-Humanist History'.

116. See Thompson's essays 'History from Below', *Times Literary Supplement,* 7 April 1966, pp. 279-80; 'Anthropology and the Discipline of Historical Context', *Midland History,* 1 (Spring 1972), pp. 41-55; 'On History, Sociology, and Historical Relevance', *British Journal of Sociology,* 27 (September 1976), pp. 387-402; and 'Folklore, Anthropology, and Social History'.

117. P. Anderson, *Arguments Within English Marxism,* p. 1. It should be noted that Anderson and Thompson have seemed to come together somewhat around the issue of nuclear disarmament. Thompson is now published by *New Left Review* and he has said that, in spite of Anderson's adoption of certain Althusserian concepts, he is not an Althusserian; in fact, Thompson views him as a 'comrade' ('Interview with E.P. Thompson', p. 18).

118. For American examples, see Jim Green, 'Culture, Politics and the Workers' Response to Industrialization in the U.S.', *Radical America,* 16 (January/April 1982), pp. 101-28.

119. These writings are collected together in Thompson's

Writing by Candlelight. On Thompson as the defender of the 'rights' of the British people, see John Silverlight, 'Coming to the Rescue of the Free-Born Briton', *The Observer, 12* April 1981, p. 27.

120. E.P. Thompson, 'The Secret State', in *Writing by Candlelight,* p. 154.

121. See E.P. Thompson, 'Trial by Jury', in *Writing by Candlelight,* pp. 224-36.

122. E.P. Thompson, 'Beyond the Cold War', in *Zero Option,* pp. 153-89.

123. E.P. Thompson, 'The Heavy Dancers of the Air', *New Society,* 11 November 1982, pp. 243-7.

124. Issued in 1980, the *Protest and Survive* pamphlet became the cornerstone of the collection of essays of the same name which Thompson edited with Dan Smith.

125. EP Thompson, 'Notes on Exterminism, the Last Stage of Civilisation', originally in *New Left Review*, 121 (May-June 1980), and reprinted in Zero Option; this also serves for the collection of essays Thompson edited for *New Left Review* entitled Exterminism and Cold War (London: New Left Book, 1982).

126. Ibid. (in *Zero Option),* pp. 43, 35, 64-5, 69, and 78.

127. R. Williams, 'The Politics of Nuclear Disarmament', *New Left Review,* 124 (November-December 1980), pp. 25-42; also reprinted in *Exterminism and Cold War.*

128. M. Dobb, *On Marxism Today,* (London: Hogarth Press, 1932), p. 20. Previously quoted early in chapter 2 on Dobb. (My emphases).

Chapter 7: The Collective Contribution

1. R. Williams, *Keywords: A Vocabulary of Culture and Society,* (New York: Oxford University Press, 1976), p. 120.

2. Gramsci wrote the letter shortly before his death in 1937, still a prisoner of Italian Fascism after more than 10 years.

For Gramsci's prison letters, see the special volume of *New Edinburgh Review* (1974), or the more accessible *Letters from Prison*, translated and introduced by Lynne Lawner, (New York: Harper and Row, 1973).

3.   Barrington Moore Jr, *Social Origins of Dictatorship and Democracy*, (Boston: Beacon Press, 1966), pp. 521-3.

4.   C. Wright Mills, *The Power Elite*, (Oxford: Oxford University Press, 1956); S. Ewen, *Captains of Consciousness*, (New York: McGraw-Hill, 1976); and H. Braverman, *Labor and Monopoly Capital*, (New York: Monthly Review Press, 1974).

5.   R. Miliband, *The State in Capitalist Society*, (London: Quartet Books, 1973).

6.   See Andre Burguiere, The Fate of the History of *Mentalites* in the *Annales', Comparative Studies in Society and History*, 24 Guly 1982), pp. 424-37.

7.   On the *Annales*, see Traian Stoianovich, *French Historical Method: The Annales Paradigm* (Ithaca, NY: Cornell University Press, 1976), with a Foreword by Braudel. Also, see the excellent discussion of the *Annales* Tradition by Georg Iggers, in his *New Directions in European Historiography* (Middletown, Ct.: Wesleyan University Press, 1975), pp. 43-79; and Alastair Davidson, 'Historical Method and the Social Sciences: A Critique of the *Annales* Historiography', *Thesis Eleven*, 2 (1981), pp. 62-78.

8.   Carlo Ginzburg, *The Cheese and the Worms*, (Harmondsworth: Penguin, 1982), p. xxiii.

9.   P. Burke, *Sociology and History*, (London: George Allen and Unwin, 1980), p.75. Also, Lucien Febvre, *A New Kind of History and Other Essays*, (London: Routledge and Kegan Paul, 1973) especially 'History and Psychology', and 'Sensibility and History', pp. 1-26. And Michelle Vovelle, 'Ideologies and Mentalities', in Raphael Samuel and Gareth Stedman Jones (eds). *Culture, Ideology and Politics: Essays for Eric Hobsbawm*, (London: Routledge and Kegan Paul,

1983), pp. 2-11.

10. On 'civilization see L. Febvre, 'Civilization: evolution of a word and group of ideas', in his *A New Kind of History and Other Essays*, pp. 219-57; and F. Braudel, 'The History of Civilizations', in his *On History*, (Chicago: University of Chicago Press, 1980), pp. 177-218.

11. C. Ginzburg, *The Cheese and the Worms*, pp. xxii-xxiv, xiv-xvi. Regarding the latter problem, Ginzburg was referring to Robert Mandrou's work in particular.

12. F. Braudel, *The Mediterranean and the Mediterranean World in the Age of Philip II*, (New York: Harper and Row, 1973).

13. Elizabeth Fox-Genovese and Eugene Genovese, *The Fruits of Merchant Capital*, (Oxford: Oxford University Press, 1983), pp. 187-8. For a full-length discussion of Braudel's achievement, see Samuel Kinser, '*Annaliste* Paradigm: The Geohistorical Structuralism of Fernand Braudel', *American Historical Review*, 86 (February 1981), pp. 63-110; also, Gregor McLennan, 'Braudel and the *Annales* Paradigm', in his *Marxism and the Methodologies of History*, (London: New Left Books, 1981), pp. 129-44.

14. C. Ginzburg, *The Cheese and the Worms*, p. xx.

15. Note the efforts to reintegrate time and space in social thought by Anthony Giddens, *Central Problems in Social Theory*, (London: MacMillan, 1979).

16. See G. McLennan, *Marxism and the Methodologies of History*, pp. 136-144. On the problem of materialism and Marxism, see Sebastiano Timpanaro, *On Materialism*, (London: New Left Books, 1975).

17. See the comments of the Genoveses in *Fruits of Merchant Capital*, pp. 194-6; and Tony Judt, 'A Clown in Regal Purple: Social History and the Historians', *History Workshop 7* (Spring 1979), especially pp. 74-80.

18. R. Samuel, 'People's History', in his edited volume *People's History and Socialist Theory*, (London: Routlege and Kegan

Paul, 1981), p. xvi.

19. E. Le Roy Ladurie, *The Peasants of Languedoc*. Originally 1966. In English, (Champaign, I11: University of Illinois Press, 1974). This work was, of course, the object of Robert Brenner's criticism. See Chapter 2.

20. See Ladurie's two volumes of collected essays where he strongly supports such work: *The Territory of the Historian*, (London: Harvester Press, 1979), and *The Mind and Method of the Historian*, (London: Harvester Press, 1981).

21. E. Le Roy Ladurie, *Montaillou*, (Harmondsworth: Penguin, 1980); and *Carnival in Romans*, (Harmondsworth: Penguin, 1981). Also, on the *Annales* school's reception in Britain, see Peter Burke, 'Reflections on the Historical Revolution in France: The *Annales* School and British Social History', along with E.J Hobsbawm, 'Comments', in *Review, 1* (Winter/Spring, 1978), pp. 147-65.

22. Lefebvre's *Les Paysans du Nord*, written in 1924, is not available in English; but his *The Great Fear of 1789*, written in 1932, is: (London: New Left Books, 1973).

23. A. Soboul, *The Parisian Sans-Culottes and the French Revolution 1793-4*, (Oxford: Oxford University Press, 1974), and *The French Revolution, 1787-1799*, (London: New Left Books, 1974).

24. T. Judt, 'A Clown in Regal Purple', p. 68. As something of a response to Tony Judt and other critics, see the 'Special Issue on Social History', *Theory and Society*, 9 (September 1980), pp. 667-720, which includes contributions by Louise and Charles Tilly and Edward Shorter.

25. E. Fox Genovese, 'Solidarity and Servitude', *Times Literary Supplement*, 25 February 1977. For examples of Gutman's work, see his *Work, Culture and Society in Industrializing America*, (New York: Vintage Books 1977), and *The Black Family in Slavery and Freedom*, (New York: Vintage Books, 1977). For an appreciative but critical discussion

of Gutman's labor history, see David Montogomery, 'Gutman's Nineteenth-Century America', *Labour History*, 19 (Summer 1978), pp. 416-29.

27. R. Hilton, *A Medieval Society*, (Cambridge: Cambridge University Press, 1983). Originally 1966.

28. C. Hill, *Economic Problems of the Church: From Archbishop Whitgift to the Long Parliament*, (Oxford: Oxford University Press, 1956).

29. E. Hobsbawm, *The Age of Capital*, (London: Sphere Books, 1977).

30. E.P. Thompson, *Whigs and Hunters*, (Harmondsworth: Penguin, 1977).

31. E. Hobsbawm, 'Comments', p. 162.

32. Ibid.

33. See Thompson's own comments in the 1968 postscript to *The Making of the English Working Class,* (Harmondsworth: Penguin, 1968 ed.) pp. 916-17; and Hill's in *The World Turned Upside Down,* (Harmondsworth: Penguin, 1975), e.g. p. 364.

34. By 'normative acceptance' I mean the situation in which one not only accepts for lack of an alternative but accepts because one truly believes that the way things are is the way they ought to be. On this, see Michael Mann, 'The Social Cohesion of Liberal Democracy', *American Sociological Review,* 35 (June 1970), pp. 423-39.

35. W. Benjamin, 'Theses in the Philosophy of History', in his *Illuminations,* (New York: Harcourt Brace, 1969), p. 255.

36. A History Workshop Centre for Social History has just been established in Oxford.

37. See the Ruskin History Workshop Students' Collective, 'Worker-Historians in the 1920s', in R. Samuel (ed.). *People's History and Socialist Theory,* pp. 15-20.

38. R. Samuel, 'History Workshop, 1966-80', in R. Samuel (ed.). *People's History and Socialist Theory,* p. 414.

39. Samuel has written many essays and articles. See the journal and 'History Workshop Series' of books (London: Routledge and Kegan Paul) for examples of his work, especially *East End Underworld: Chapters in the Life of Arthur Harding,* (1980).

40. See, among other of her works, S. Rowbotham, *Hidden from History,* (London: Pluto Press, 1973); and *Women, Resistance and Revolution* (Harmondsworth: Penguin, 1972).

41. G.S. Jones, *Outcast London,* (Harmondsworth: Penguin, 1976); and *Languages of Class,* (Cambridge: Cambridge University Press, 1983).

42. See A. Dawley, *Class and Community: The Industrial Revolution in Lynn,* (Cambridge, Mass: Harvard University Press, 1976).

43. *See S. Wilentz, Chants Democratic: New York City and the Rise of the American Working Class (1790-1865),* (New York: Oxford University Press, 1984).

44. See W. Sewell Jr, *Work and Revolution in France,* (Cambridge: Cambridge University Press, 1980).

45. *See S. Stern, Peru's Indian Peoples and the Challenge of Spanish* Conquest, (Madison, Wi: University of Wisconsin Press, 1982).

46. D. Montgomery, *Workers' Control in America,* (Cambridge: Cambridge University Press, 1979).

47. S. Hall, 'Marxism and Culture', p. 9. It should be noted that Hall adds that 'of course, the beneficiaries of those lessons about the capacities to resist are more often found among middle class intellectuals than among the working class itself'.

48. E.P. Thompson, 'The Poverty of Theory', in his *The Poverty of Theory and Other Essays,* (London: Merlin Press, 1978), p. 170.

49. Ibid. Also, on this subject, see R.S. Neale, *Class in English History 1680-1850,* (Oxford: Basil Blackwell, 1981).

50. Rodolfo Stavenhagen, *Social Classes in Agrarian Societies,* (Garden City, NY: Anchor Books, 1975), p. 22. Stavenhagen provides an excellent, short critique of stratification studies (pp. 19-39), though his discussion of the Marxist alternative is uneven.

51. E.P. Thompson, 'Peculiarities of the English', in *The Poverty of Theory and Other Essays,* p. 295. Also quoted in Philip Abrams, *Historical Sociology,* (Somerset: Open Books, 1982), p. xii. Abrams makes 'time' a central issue in his work, as does Anthony Giddens in such writings as *Central Problems in Social Theory.*

52. Ellen Meiksins Wood, 'The Politics of Theory and the Concept of Class: E.P. Thompson and His Critics', *Studies in Political Economy,* 9 (Fall 1982), p. 60.

53. D. Stark, 'Class Struggle and the Transformation of the Labour Process: A Relational Approach', *Theory and Society,* 9 (1980); abridged version reprinted in Anthony Giddens and David Held (eds). *Classes, Power and Conflict,* (London: Macmillan Press, 1982), p. 320. In particular, Stark refers to works by G. Carchedi and Erik Olin Wright.

54. E.P. Thompson, 'Eighteenth-century English Society: class struggle without class?' *Social History,* 3 (May 1978), pp. 133-65.

55. Ibid., pp. 147-8.

56. R. Williams, *Politics and Letters,* (London: New Left Books, 1979), p. 135.

57. E. Hobsbawm, 'The Contribution of History to Social Science', *International Social Science Journal,* 33 (1981), p. 631; Thompson, 'Folklore, Anthropology, and Social History', *Indian Historical Review,* 3 Qanuary 1977), pp. 262 ff.

58. R. Johnson, 'Thompson, Genovese, and Socialist-Humanist History', *History Workshop,* 6 (Autumn 1978), pp. 79-100.

59. R. Williams, *Marxism and Literature,* (Oxford: Oxford

University Press, 1977), p. 87; P. Abrams, *Historical Sociology*, especially pp. bc-xviii, 67-70, 323-6; and A. Giddens, *Central Problems in Social Theory*. For a study which recognizes the affinity between Thompson and Giddens, see Derek Gregory, *Regional Transformation and Industrial Revolution*, (London: Macmillan, 1982), pp. 9-22.

60. Ralph Miliband, *Marxism and Politics*, (Oxford: Oxford University Press, 1977), p. 8.

61. E.P. Thompson, 'The Poverty of Theory', pp. 170, 164.

62. As previously noted in chapter 6, in Thompson's 'Folklore, Anthropology, and Social History', pp. 261-4.

63. See chapter 6, note 70, for references.

64. E.P. Thompson, *The Making of the English Working Class*, (Harmondsworth, Penguin, 1968 ed.) See especially the chapter, 'Exploitation', pp. 207-32.

65. S. Clarke, 'Socialist-Humanism and the Critique of Economism', *History Workshop*, 8 (Autumn 1979), pp. 137-56.

66. E. Wood, 'The Separation of the Economic and the Political in Capitalism', *New Left Review*, 127 (May-June 1981), pp. 77-80.

67. 'Interview with E.P. Thompson', *Radical History Review*, 3 (Fall 1976), p. 25.

68. P. Anderson, *Arguments Within English Marxism*, (London: New Left Books, 1980), p. 55.

69. E.O. Wright, *Class, Crisis and the State*, (London: New Left Books, 1978), p. 89. See (though not clearly directed at Wright) R.W. Connell, 'A Critique of the Althusserian Approach to Class', *Theory and Society*, 8 (May 1979), pp. 321-45.

70. *E. Genovese, In Red and Black: Marxian Explorations in Southern and Afro-American History*, (New York: Vintage Books, 1971), p. 40.

71. W. Sewell Jr, *Work and Revolution in France*, p. 12.

72. E.P. Thompson, 'The Poverty of Theory', pp. 175-6.

73. See the most enjoyable paper by Robin Brooks, 'Showdown at the Paradigm Corral; E.P. Thompson meets the Wing-spread Bunch', (San Jose State University, unpub'lished paper, 1982).

74. For general discussions of the 'common culture' and 'dominant ideology' theses, see Nicholas Abercrombie, Stephen Hill, and Bryan S. Turner, *The Dominant Ideology Thesis,* (London: George Allen & Unwin, 1980), pp. 7-58.

75. S. Lukes, *Individualism,* (Oxford: Basil Blackwell, 1973). Lukes added that, one, he did not claim to have 'proven' his assertion in the study and, two, such an assertion requires consideration not only of 'equality and liberty' but also of 'community'.

76. The most important writings are C.B. Macpherson, *The Political Theory of Possessive Individualism,* (Oxford: Oxford University Press, 1962); *Democratic Theory: Essays in Retrieval,* (Oxford; Oxford University Press, 1973); and *The Life and Times of Liberal Democracy,* (Oxford: Oxford University Press, 1977).

77. C.B. Macpherson, *Democratic Theory,* pp. 32 ff.

78. See, on Macpherson, Ellen Meiksins Wood, 'C.B. Macpherson: Liberalism and the Task of Socialist Theory', *The Socialist Register 1978,* (London: Merlin Press, 1978), pp. 215-40; and the exchange which followed in *The Socialist Register 1979* between Leo Panitch and Ellen Wood. Lukes seems particularly sensitive to the problem, as evidenced by the discussion in his *Power: A Radical View,* (London: Macmillan, 1974), especially pp. 46-50, which includes reference to Gramsci. For Lukes on Macpherson, see 'The Real and Ideal Worlds of Democracy', in Alkis Kontos, *Powers, Possessions, and Freedoms,* (Toronto, Ont.: University of Toronto Press, 1979), pp. 139-52. Also, see D.F B. Tucker, *Marxism and Individualism,* (New York: St Martin's Press,

1980); and Ellen Meiksins Woods, *Mind and Politics: An Approach to the Meaning of Liberal and Socialist Individualism,* (Berkeley, Cal: University of California Press, 1972).

79. As indicated in their writings, and also in conversations with them on this subject. On the one hand, the difference is merely terminological; on the other, I wonder if it indicates a difference between American and British political cultures?

80. R. Williams, *Marxism and Literature,* p. 112.

81. See Victor Kiernan, 'Socialism, The Prophetic Memory', in B. Parekh (ed.). *The Concept of Socialism,* (London: Croom Helm, 1975), pp. 14-37.

82. K. Marx, 'The Communist Manifesto', in *The Revolutions of 1848,* edited by David Fernbach, (Harmondsworth: Penguin, 1973), p. 80.

83. A Professor of History at Yale University, Montgomery left the (American) Communist Party in the 1956-7 period, as did Hilton, Hill and Thompson.

84. 'Interview with David Montgomery', *Radical History Review,* 23 (December 1980), p. 52.

85. D. Montgomery, 'Spontaneity and Organization: Some Comments' in 'A Symposium on Jeremy Brecher's Strike!' in Radical America, 7 (November-December 1973), p. 77. See the discussion of Montgomery and United States labour history by Jim Green, 'Culture, Politics and Workers' Response to Industrialization in the US', *Radical America,* 16 (Jan-Feb/Mar-April 1982), pp. 101-28. Also, on British labour studies, see the discussion by Richard Price, 'Rethinking Labour History: The Importance of Work', in James Cronin and Jonathan Schneer (eds). *Social Conflict and the Political Order in Modern Britain,* (London: Croom Helm, 1981), pp. 179-214.

86. J. Berger, *Ways of Seeing,* (Harmondsworth: Penguin, 1972), p. 33.

87. A. Gramsci, 'Oppressed and Oppressors', in P. Cavalcanti and P. Piccone (eds). *History, Philosophy and Culture in the Young Gramsci,* (St Louis: Telos Press, 1975), p. 158.

88. R. Hilton, *Bond Men Made Free,* (London: Methuen, 1977), p 236.

89. C. Hill, *Change and Continuity in Seventeenth-Century England,* (London: Weidenfeld and Nicolson, 1975), p. 283.

90. 'Interview with E.P. Thompson,' p. 17.

91. 'The Eighteenth Brumaire of Louis Bonaparte', in *Karl Marx: Surveys from Exile,* edited by David Fernbach, (Harmondsworth: Penguin, 1973), p. 149.

92. J. Berger, *Ways of Seeing,* pp. 11, 33.

93. Quoted in E.P. Thompson, *William Morris,* (New York: Pantheon, 1976), p. 723, from May Morris, *William Morris, Artist, Writer, Socialist,* (Oxford: Basil Blackwell, 1936).

94. A. Gramsci, *Selections from the Prison Notebooks,* edited by Q. Hoare and G. N. Smith, (London: Lawrence and Wishart, 1971), pp. 34-5.

Select Bibliography

Maurice Dobb

On Marxism Today, (London: Hogarth Press, 1932).

Political Economy and Capitalism, (London: Routledge, 1937).

Studies in the Development of Capitalism, (London: Routledge and Kegan Paul, 1946, 1963 rev. ed).

On Economic Theory and Socialism, (London: Routledge and Kegan Paul, 1960).

Soviet Economic Development Since 1917, (London: Routledge and Kegan Paul, 1948).

Economic Growth and Underdeveloped Countries, (London: Lawrence and Wishart, 1963).

Papers on Capitalism, Development, and Planning, (London: Routledge and Kegan Paul, 1967).

Rodney Hilton

The Economic Development of Some Leicestershire Estates in the Fourteenth and Fifteenth Centuries, (Oxford: Oxford University Press, 1947).

The English Rising of 1381, with H. Fagan, (London: Lawrence and Wishart, 1950).

A Medieval Society: The West Midlands at the End of the Thirteenth Century, (Cambridge: Cambridge University Press, 1983). Originally 1966.

The Decline of Serfdom in Medieval England, (London: Macmillan, 1969).

Bond Men Made Free: Medieval Peasant Movements and the English Rising of 1381, (London: Methuen, 1977). Originally 1973.

The English Peasantry in the Later Middle Ages, (Oxford: Oxford University Press, 1975). Includes The Peasantry as a Class'.

Class Conflict and the Crisis of Feudalism: Collected Essays of R.H.

Hilton, (London: Hambledon Press, 1984). Includes 'Peasant Movements in England before 1381', 'A Crisis of Feudalism?', 'Capitalism – What's in a Name?', 'Feudalism and the Origins of Capitalism', and 'Towns in English Feudal Society'.
edited works:

Peasants, Knights, and Heretics: Studies in Medieval English Social History, (Cambridge: Cambridge University Press, 1976). Includes 'The Origins of Robin Hood', and 'Freedom and Villeinage in England'.

The Transition from Feudalism to Capitalism, (London: New Left Books, 1976). Includes the Dobb-Sweezy exchange and later contributions to the transition debate.

Christopher Hill

The English Revolution 1640, (London: Lawrence and Wishart, 1940, 1955 rev. edition).

Economic Problems of the Church: From Archbishop Whitgift to the Long Parliament, (Oxford: Oxford University Press, 1956).

Puritanism and Revolution: Studies in Interpretation of the English Revolution of the 17th Century, (London: Seeker and Warburg, 1958). Includes 'The Norman Yoke'.

The Century of Revolution, 1603-1714, (Edinburgh: Thomas Nelson, 1961, 1982 rev. edition).

Society and Puritanism in Pre-Revolutionary England, (London: Seeker and Warburg, 1964).

Intellectual Origins of the English Revolution, (Oxford: Oxford University Press, 1965).

Reformation to Industrial Revolution: A Social and Economic History of Britain, 1530-1780, (Originally 1967; Harmondsworth: Penguin, 1969).

God's Englishman: Oliver Cromwell and the English Revolution, (Originally 1970; rev. edition Harmondsworth: Penguin, 1972).

Antichrist in Seventeenth-Century England, (Oxford: Oxford

University Press, 1971).

The World Turned Upside Down, (Originally 1972; rev. edition Harmondsworth: Penguin, 1975).

Change and Continuity in Seventeenth-Century England, (London: Weidenfeld and Nicolson, 1974). Includes 'Protestantism and the Rise of Capitalism' and 'Pottage for Freeborn Englishmen: Attitudes to Wage Labour'.

Milton and the English Revolution, (London: Faber, 1977).

Some Intellectual Consequences of the English Revolution, (London: Weidenfeld and Nicolson, 1980).

'A Bourgeois Revolution?', in JGA.G.A. Pocock (ed.). *Three British Revolutions: 1641, 1688, 1776,* (Princeton, NJ: Princeton University Press, 1980), pp. 109-39.

The Experience of Defeat: Milton and Some Contemporaries, (London: Faber, 1984).

edited works:

The Good Old Cause: The English Revolution of 1640-60, with Edmund Dell. (Originally 1949; rev. edition London: Frank Cass, 1969).

Winstanley: The Law of Freedom and Other Writings, (Originally 1973: Cambridge: Cambridge University Press, 1983).

Eric Hobsbawm

'The Crisis of the Seventeenth Century' (1954), reprinted in T. Aston, (ed.) *Crisis in Europe, 1560-1660,* (London: Routledge and Kegan Paul, 1965), pp. 5-58.

Primitive Rebels, (Originally 1959; Manchester: Manchester University Press, 1971).

The Age of Revolution, 1789-1848, (London: Sphere Books, 1977). Originally 1962.

Labouring Men, (London: Weidenfeld and Nicolson, 1968). Originally 1964. Includes 'The Machine Breakers', 'Methodism and the Threat of Revolution in Britain', essays on 'The Standard of Living Debate', 'The Labour Aristocracy in Nineteenth-Century Britain', and 'Custom, Wages, and Work-load'.

'Karl Marx's Contribution to Historiography' (1968), reprinted in R. Blackburn (ed.) *Ideology in Social Science,* (London: Fontana, 1972), pp. 265-83.

Captain Swing, with George Rudé, (London: Lawrence and Wishart, 1969).

Industry and Empire, 1750 to the Present Day, (Harmondsworth: Penguin, 1969). Originally 1968.

'From Social History to the History of Society', *Daedalus,* 100 (Winter 1971), pp. 20^5.

'Class Consciousness in History', in I. Meszaros (ed.). *Aspects of History and Class Consciousness,* (London: Routledge and Kegan Paul, 1971), pp. 5-21.

Bandits, (Originally 1969; rev. edition New York: Pantheon Books, 1981).

Revolutionaries: Contemporary Essays, (London: Weidenfeld and Nicolson, 1973).

The Age of Capital, 1848-1875, (Originally 1975; London: Sphere Books, 1977).

The Forward March of Labour Halted?, with other contributors. (London: New Left Books, 1981).

'Marx and History', *New Left Review,* 143 (January/February 1984), pp. 39-50.

edited works:

Labour's Turning Point, 1880-1900, (Originally 1948; rev. edition Brighton: Harvester Press, 1977).

The History of Marxism, (Brighton: Harvester Press, 1982), Volume One, *Marxism in Marx's Day.*

The Invention of Tradition, with Terence Ranger, (Cambridge: Cambridge University Press, 1983).

E.P. Thompson

William Morris: Romantic to Revolutionary, (Originally 1955; rev.

edition New York: Pantheon Books, 1977).

The Making of the English Working Class, (Originally 1963; rev. edition Harmondsworth: Penguin, 1968).

'Time, Work-Discipline, and Industrial Capitalism', *Past & Present,* 38 (February 1967), pp. 56-97.

'The Moral Economy of the English Crowd in the Eighteenth Century', *Past & Present,* 50 (February 1971), pp. 71-136.

'Patrician Society, Plebeian Culture', *Journal of Social History,* 7 (Summer 1974), pp. 382-405.

Whigs and Hunters, (Originally 1975; reprinted with new postscript, Harmondsworth: Penguin, 1977).

The Poverty of Theory and Other Essays, (London: Merlin Press, 1978).

'Eighteenth-century English Society: class struggle without class?', *Social History,* 3 (May 1978), pp. 133-65.

Writing by Candlelight, (London: Merlin Press, 1980).

Protest and Survive, with other contributors, (Harmondsworth: Penguin, 1980).

Exterminism and Cold War, with other contributors, (London: New Left Books, 1982).

Zero Option, (London: Merlin Press, 1982). US title is *Beyond the Cold War.*

The Heavy Dancers, (London: Merlin Press, 1984).

Index

Abelove, Henry, 199

Abrams, Philip, 24, 25, 39, 265

absolutism, absolutist state, 38, 70, 71, 73, 82–5, 87, 133, 135, 145, 148–50, 206–7

agency, 51, 200, 202–3, 235, 237, 242, 245, 254–5, 262, 265, 270

see also experience

agricultural workers, 56, 64, 85–6, 89, 108–9, 177–9

agriculture, 64–5, 71, 85, 90–2, 101, 106, 136, 188, 209

Althusser, Louis, 18, 20, 58, 208-15, 241, 293 n. 114 and n. 117

42, 44, 82, 237–45, 271, 333 n. 110, 334 n.114

see also structuralism, structuralist-Marxism

American Revolution (War for Independence), 277

Anderson, Perry, 25, 73, 74, 82–7, 93–4, 199, 211, 216–20, 231, 234, 238, 259, 269–71, 296 n. 86, 327 n. 43, 334 n.117

on E. P. Thompson, 211, 216, 231, 269–71

on transition question, 82–7

Annales, 6, 79, 99, 232, 253–7, 300 n. 14

anthropology, anthropologists, 104, 174–5, 234, 255, 260

aristocracy, 84–5, 135–6, 143, 148, 219

art, artists, 189

see also poetry, poets

artisans, 117, 119–21, 136, 208, 209, 211, 212

Bacon, Francis, 141–2, 221

Ball, John, 119

bandits, 175–7, 224

see also primitive rebels; crime, social crime

base and superstructure, base-superstructure model, 27–8, 44, 51, 81–3, 93, 143, 156, 159, 162, 181–4, 187, 196, 200–1, 203, 220, 222, 232, 234–6, 238, 251, 264, 265, 268

see also determinism

Benjamin, Walter, 260

Berger, John, 98, 278

Birmingham, University of, 11, 20, 42, 97, 197, 238

Black Act (1723), 223–5

Blake, William, 15, 198–9, 247

Bloch, Marc, 6, 95, 99–103, 254, 300 n. 14

Blok, Anton, 319 n. 51

bourgeoisie (capitalists), 63–

87, 107, 123, 134–5, 143, 162,
170, 181, 187, 204, 219–20,
242, 273–4
see also merchants, merchant
capital
Braudel, Fernand, 6, 46, 79,
121, 192, 254–6
Braverman, Harry, 253, 290 n.
42
Brenner, Robert, 14, 45, 73–4,
82, 87–92, 102, 267–8, 298 n.
102–104
Briggs, Asa, 43
Burke, Peter, 24, 254

Calhoun, Craig, 331 n. 91
Cambridge University, 7, 12,
49, 51, 159–60, 162, 197
Campaign for Nuclear
Disarmament (CND), 43, 195,
198
capitalism, 13, 14, 28–29, 30,
46–93, 95, 97, 107–8, 110,
119–20, 131–7, 140–3, 145,
153, 170–2, 176, 180, 181–8,
192, 210–11, 222–3, 273, 275
see also transition from
feudalism to capitalism
Captain Swing, 168, 177–80
Carr, E. H., 24–5
Centre for Contemporary
Cultural Studies, 11, 238, 281
n. 6, 285 n. 48
see also Birmingham

University
Chartists, Chartism, 173,189,
217, 285 n. 14, 289 n. 62
201, 218, 247, 329 n. 62
Chayanov, A. V., 105
Childe, V. Gordon, 31
Christianity, 118–19, 149–50
see also Church, Catholic;
Church, English; Methodists,
Methodism; Protestant,
Protestantism; Puritans,
Puritanism
Church, Catholic, 140, 150
Church, English, 137–8, 150
civil liberties, *see* rights and
civil liberties
Civil War, English, 129–38,
142, 144–57
see also English Revolution
Clarke, Simon, 45, 267
class and class struggle, 19,
28–31, 51–3, 58–65, 69–74, 77,
79–85, 87–92, 93, 94, 96–100,
104, 106–20, 121–2, 124, 126,
132–8, 141–4, 147–8, 153, 156,
159, 164–7, 169, 175, 180–190,
191–204, 208–9, 216–7, 218–
32, 235, 236–7, 243, 245, 249–
50, 253, 255–6, 257–60, 276–7,
279, 298 n. 102 and 103
class consciousness, 31, 44, 52,
117, 153, 169–70, 172, 180–1,
201–4, 208, 215, 216–17, 229–
31, 264, 271

Down, 150–3

Hilton, Rodney, 14, 29, 30, 32, 40–5, 72–3, 84–5, 95–124, 125, 129, 158, 173, 180, 197, 250, 251, 259, 261, 265, 267, 275, 275, 291 n.51

biography, 33, 40–1, 96–7

on definition of feudalism, 97–101

on definition of peasantry, 100–10

on peasant movements, 111–24

on Rising of 1381, 110–12, 117–19

on transition question, 72–3

Hindess, Barry, 238

Hirst, Paul, 238

Historians' Group (Communist Party), 6–7, 16, 31–42, 128, 147, 156, 162, 184, 197, 261

historical consciousness, 19–24, 30–1, 142, 251, 278–80

historiography, *see* labour historiography and historians

history and theory, 25–6, 29–31, 44, 47–8, 50–1, 58–9, 101, 105–6, 138, 148, 156–7, 166, 186, 200, 202–3, 204, 219, 222, 232–45, 251–62, 264–5, 269, 271–2

history from the bottom up,

history from below, 19, 23, 29, 31, 32, 38, 42, 84, 96, 110 – 1 , 124, 126, 132, 146, 159, 165 – 6 , 175, 251–4, 256, 257–8, 260, 277

History Workshop, 45, 261

Hoggart, Richard, 43

Hobsbawm, Eric, 19, 22, 29–42, 43–4, 72–4, 107, 121, 156, 158–94, 196, 213–15, 224, 229, 239, 246, 250–1, 257, 259, 261, 265, 267, 321 n.71

biography, 159–62

on bandits and primitive rebels, 173–9

on base-superstructure, 181–4

on class and class consciousness, 180–1

on labour aristocracy, 168–71

on labour movement, 166–74, 193

on machine-breaking, 166–8

on transition question, 73–4, 185

on world history, 181–91

Age of Capital, 1848–1875, 186–7, 190–1

Age of Revolution, 1789–1848, 186–9

Captain Swing, 168, 177–8

Primitive Rebels, 172–6

Holme, K. E., 127

87, 89, 106, 256

Levellers, 146–7, 149–52

liberalism, 160, 187, 190, 226

liberty, *see* freedom;
  individualism; rights and
  civil liberties

London, University of, 160

London School of Economics,
  49, 163

Luddism, 164–6, 177–9, 201,
  215

Lukes, Steven, 274–5

Macfarlane, Alan, 122–3

machine-breaking, *see*
  Luddism; Captain Swing

MacIntyre, Alisdair, 200

Macintyre, Stuart, 288 n. 20

Macpherson, C. B., 274–5

Manning, Brian, 311 n. 55

Marcuse, Herbert, 204

Marx, Karl, 27, 46–7, 54–6, 77,
  87–8, 103, 107–8, 143–4, 200,
  203, 210, 234, 243–4, 264,
  276–7, 279
  on feudalism and peasantry,
  107–8
  on historical and social
  analysis, 27
  on transition question, 55–60
  Communist Manifesto, 28,
  243, 244, 276

Marxism, 6–7, 26–8, 29, 31, 38–
  9, 43–5, 50–1, 57, 59, 70, 76,

82–4, 128–30, 147, 156, 181–3,
  197–8, 200–1, 219, 237–8, 242,
  243, 244–5, 246–7, 251, 262,
  264–5, 267–9,
  see also political Marxism;
  structuralist Marxism

Marxism-Leninism, 198
  see also political Marxism

McClelland, Keith, 211–12,
  217, 285–6 n. 57

McLennan, Gregor, 317 n. 32,
  337 n. 13 and n. 16

mentalities, *mentalité*, 253–6,
  273

merchants, merchant capital,
  53–4, 60–3, 65, 86, 117–18,
  135–6, 148–9, 232

Merrington, John, 85

Methodists, Methodism, 33,
  163, 166–8, 197, 205–6, 214,
  222

Middle Ages, medieval
  history, 55, 83, 85–9, 95–124,
  149, 174–5, 267
  see also feudalism

medieval historians, 72, 95–8

middle class ('middle' or
  'industrious sort'), 136, 138–
  9, 141–5, 311 n. 48

Miliband, Ralph, 31, 253

millenarian movements, *see*
  primitive rebels; Southcott,
  Joanna and Southcottians

Mills, C. Wright, 24–5, 212, 253

CULTURE, SOCIETY & POLITICS

Contemporary culture has eliminated the concept and public figure of the intellectual. A cretinous anti-intellectualism presides, cheer-led by hacks in the pay of multinational corporations who reassure their bored readers that there is no need to rouse themselves from their stupor. Zer0 Books knows that another kind of discourse - intellectual without being academic, popular without being populist - is not only possible: it is already flourishing. Zer0 is convinced that in the unthinking, blandly consensual culture in which we live, critical and engaged theoretical reflection is more important than ever before.

If you have enjoyed this book, why not tell other readers by posting a review on your preferred book site.

You may also wish to
subscribe to our Zer0 Books YouTube Channel.

Bestsellers from Zer0 Books include:

Give Them An Argument
Logic for the Left
Ben Burgis
Many serious leftists have learned to distrust talk of logic. This is
a serious mistake.
Paperback: 978-1-78904-210-8 ebook: 978-1-78904-211-5

Poor but Sexy
Culture Clashes in Europe East and West
Agata Pyzik
How the East stayed East and the West stayed West.
Paperback: 978-1-78099-394-2 ebook: 978-1-78099-395-9

An Anthropology of Nothing in Particular
Martin Demant Frederiksen
A journey into the social lives of meaninglessness.
Paperback: 978-1-78535-699-5 ebook: 978-1-78535-700-8

In the Dust of This Planet
Horror of Philosophy vol. 1
Eugene Thacker
In the first of a series of three books on the Horror of Philosophy,
In the Dust of This Planet offers the genre of horror as a way of
thinking about the unthinkable.
Paperback: 978-1-84694-676-9 ebook: 978-1-78099-010-1

The End of Oulipo?
An Attempt to Exhaust a Movement
Lauren Elkin, Veronica Esposito
Paperback: 978-1-78099-655-4 ebook: 978-1-78099-656-1

Capitalist Realism
Is There No Alternative?
Mark Fisher
An analysis of the ways in which capitalism has presented itself
as the only realistic political-economic system.
Paperback: 978-1-84694-317-1 ebook: 978-1-78099-734-6

Rebel Rebel
Chris O'Leary
David Bowie: every single song. Everything you want to know,
everything you didn't know.
Paperback: 978-1-78099-244-0 ebook: 978-1-78099-713-1

Kill All Normies
Angela Nagle
Online culture wars from 4chan and Tumblr to Trump.
Paperback: 978-1-78535-543-1 ebook: 978-1-78535-544-8

Cartographies of the Absolute
Alberto Toscano, Jeff Kinkle
An aesthetics of the economy for the twenty-first century.
Paperback: 978-1-78099-275-4 ebook: 978-1-78279-973-3

Malign Velocities
Accelerationism and Capitalism
Benjamin Noys
Long listed for the Bread and Roses Prize 2015, *Malign Velocities*
argues against the need for speed, tracking acceleration
as the symptom of the ongoing crises of capitalism.
Paperback: 978-1-78279-300-7 ebook: 978-1-78279-299-4

Meat Market
Female Flesh under Capitalism
Laurie Penny
A feminist dissection of women's bodies as the fleshy fulcrum of capitalist cannibalism, whereby women are both consumers and consumed.
Paperback: 978-1-84694-521-2 ebook: 978-1-84694-782-7

Babbling Corpse
Vaporwave and the Commodification of Ghosts
Grafton Tanner
Paperback: 978-1-78279-759-3 ebook: 978-1-78279-760-9

New Work New Culture
Work we want and a culture that strengthens us
Frithjof Bergmann
A serious alternative for mankind and the planet.
Paperback: 978-1-78904-064-7 ebook: 978-1-78904-065-4

Romeo and Juliet in Palestine
Teaching Under Occupation
Tom Sperlinger
Life in the West Bank, the nature of pedagogy and the role of a university under occupation.
Paperback: 978-1-78279-637-4 ebook: 978-1-78279-636-7

Color, Facture, Art and Design
Iona Singh
This materialist definition of fine-art develops guidelines for architecture, design, cultural-studies and ultimately social change.
Paperback: 978-1-78099-629-5 ebook: 978-1-78099-630-1

Sweetening the Pill
or How We Got Hooked on Hormonal Birth Control
Holly Grigg-Spall
Has contraception liberated or oppressed women?
Sweetening the Pill breaks the silence on the dark side of hormonal
contraception.
Paperback: 978-1-78099-607-3 ebook: 978-1-78099-608-0

Why Are We The Good Guys?
Reclaiming Your Mind from the Delusions of Propaganda
David Cromwell
A provocative challenge to the standard ideology that Western
power is a benevolent force in the world.
Paperback: 978-1-78099-365-2 ebook: 978-1-78099-366-9

The Writing on the Wall
On the Decomposition of Capitalism and its Critics
Anselm Jappe, Alastair Hemmens
A new approach to the meaning of social emancipation.
Paperback: 978-1-78535-581-3 ebook: 978-1-78535-582-0

Enjoying It
Candy Crush and Capitalism
Alfie Bown
A study of enjoyment and of the enjoyment of studying. Bown
asks what enjoyment says about us and what we say about
enjoyment, and why.
Paperback: 978-1-78535-155-6 ebook: 978-1-78535-156-3

Ghosts of My Life
Writings on Depression, Hauntology and Lost Futures
Mark Fisher
Paperback: 978-1-78099-226-6 ebook: 978-1-78279-624-4

Neglected or Misunderstood
The Radical Feminism of Shulamith Firestone
Victoria Margree
An interrogation of issues surrounding gender, biology,
sexuality, work and technology, and the ways in which our
imaginations continue to be in thrall to ideologies of maternity
and the nuclear family.
Paperback: 978-1-78535-539-4 ebook: 978-1-78535-540-0

How to Dismantle the NHS in 10 Easy Steps (Second Edition)
Youssef El-Gingihy
The story of how your NHS was sold off and why you will have
to buy private health insurance soon. A new expanded second
edition with chapters on junior doctors' strikes and government
blueprints for US-style healthcare.
Paperback: 978-1-78904-178-1 ebook: 978-1-78904-179-8

Digesting Recipes
The Art of Culinary Notation
Susannah Worth
A recipe is an instruction, the imperative tone of the expert, but
this constraint can offer its own kind of potential. A recipe need
not be a domestic trap but might instead offer escape – something
to fantasise about or aspire to.
Paperback: 978-1-78279-860-6 ebook: 978-1-78279-859-0

Most titles are published in paperback and as an ebook.
Paperbacks are available in traditional bookshops. Both print and
ebook formats are available online.
Follow us at:
https://www.facebook.com/ZeroBooks
https://twitter.com/Zer0Books
https://www.instagram.com/zero.books